FLAVORS OF MEXICO

Other books by Marlena Spieler:

Naturally Good
Hot & Spicy
Sun-Drenched Cuisine
From Pantry to Table

FLAVORS OF MEXICO

FRESH, SIMPLE TWISTS ON CLASSIC REGIONAL DISHES

MARLENA SPIELER

LOWELL HOUSE
LOS ANGELES

CONTEMPORARY BOOKS
CHICAGO

Spieler, Marlena.
    Flavors of Mexico : fresh, simple twists on classic regional dishes /
Marlena Spieler.
        p.   cm.
    Includes bibliographical references (p.   ) and index.
    ISBN 1-56565-003-4
    1. Cookery, Mexican.   I. Title.
  TX716.M4S68   1992
  641.5972—dc20   92-20851
                                                                                      CIP

Requests for such permissions should be addressed to:
Lowell House
2029 Century Park East, Suite 3290
Los Angeles, CA 90067
Publisher: Jack Artenstein
Executive Vice-President: Nick Clemente
Vice-President/Editor-in-Chief: Janice Gallagher
Design: Michele Lanci-Altomare

Manufactured in the United States of America
10 9 8 7 6 5 4 3 2 1

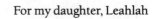

For my daughter, Leahlah

CONTENTS

ACKNOWLEDGMENTS

To: Leah Matisse with love and appreciation.

To: Alan McLaughlan for his good-natured, nearly endless tasting and for his love of cilantro.

To: Janice Gallagher, longtime editor and friend; and Jane Middleton, my British editor, who helped me create the original British publication; Teresa Chris, literary agent, whose enthusiasm for my Mexican feasts resulted in this book; editor Paul Richardson for sending me off to exotic places like Provence, Ireland, or Bulgaria each time I became insufferable on the subject of Mexican food; and Joyce Goldstein, chef-owner of Square One, for her excellent advice.

To friends in tasting: Gretchen Spieler, Paula Levine, Christine Smith, Alex Bratell, Jo McAllister, Robin and Helene Simpson and family, Fred and Mary Barclay, Noah and Dinah Stroe; David Aspin for his tortilla press; Joan and Malcolm Key for their assistance in locating resources.

To: My grandmother, Sophia "Bachi" Dubowsky; parents Caroline and Izzy Smith; and my computer "angels": Estelle and Sy Opper.

PREFACE

I grew up in California, in a neighborhood that bordered on a large Mexican population. I reveled in the cross-cultural richness this provided. At school this meant learning bits of Spanish and teaching English to the new arrivals, delighting in their different lifestyle, holidays and fiestas, way of life. Mexican culture exerted other influences on my childhood as well. Like much of the rest of America's Southwest, California once belonged to Spain/Mexico, and contemporary California lifestyle reflects this. Everyday life is constantly colored by our shared heritage, especially in architecture and food.

Ah, the food. Weekly outings to our local Mexican restaurant, tacos for school lunches, a big cauldron of chilli con carne as a special treat, tamales homemade by our neighbors at fiesta times. It was food that made eating fun, unlike the ordinary three square, meat-and-potato meals. This was spicy food, full of flavors so vibrant I was surprised we children were allowed to eat it. In my young mind it surpassed mere physical nourishment and became something other than, more than, food. No doubt it kindled my interest in food and travel.

Yet the food I grew up eating was but a small regional (Mexican-American) variation of an ancient, complex cuisine. As a teenager I visited Mexico for the first time and thrilled at the sophistication and variety of the country and its cuisine. I emerged from the train in Guadalajara after a train journey of 48 hours and was immediately captivated. Everything was wildly different from what I had come to expect from life: here were tropical aromas in the air, mariachis serenading café patrons, parrots resting on perches lining the path through the park. Schoolgirls walked arm in arm, as did mothers and daughters; it was more like the South of France or the Mediterranean than a short distance from my U.S. home. And the food was scarcely the delicious but not terribly delicate fried minced-meat tacos, sloppy chilli stews, and red chilli enchiladas I had grown up with. First of all, food was everywhere. In the marketplace cafés known as *fondas,* row upon row of *cazuelitas* (earthenware pots) held an endless variety of fragrantly sauced dishes. Food stalls lined the streets, each one with its own special offering. Outdoor restaurants with their umbrella-topped tables emitted the aroma of savory grilled foods. Street vendors offered a rainbow assortment of fruit ices. A bright mosaic of colors and flavors beckoned to me.

I dipped into bowls of pungent salsa, freshly cooked tortillas wrapped around savory bits of meat, seafood cocktails of pristine freshness. I sampled grilled turtle meat slathered with salsa; funny little worms that tasted delicate rather than offensive as I expected worms would; quesadillas filled with cheese or with soft brains; lightly cooked eggs splashed with salsa and scattered with enough chillies to daunt even the most macho.

I remained ever eager, admittedly greedy and unrestrained. I tasted my way avidly through the Republic. There were bad moments, to be sure—the unexpected tuft of fur that peered out of my taco somewhere in a desolate patch of Baja, or the several days of Montezuma's revenge visited on me after a particularly enjoyable bout of marketplace feasting. But mostly I thrived both in body and mind. It was a time of discovery, filled with images of exotic land-scapes and flavored with foods that have colored the way I have lived my adult life.

I have since visited Mexico often, but not nearly enough. I have learned and cooked, yet the more I feel I have mastered the language of Mexico's cui-sines, the more I feel it slip away. The country has a richness of culture and cuisine that one lifetime is far too short for.

In the following book I have tried to share my enthusiasm and joy, as well as a collection of what I hope you will agree are vibrant and exciting dishes. Because the variety of Mexico's regional dishes is far too extensive for even the most dedicated cook to research and catalog, many dishes are not represented here. I offer my apologies for any glaring omissions of the reader's favorites. A number of Mexican specialties can be found in my other books, *Hot & Spicy* (J. P. Tarcher), *Sun-Drenched Cuisine* (J. P. Tarcher), and *From Pantry to Table* (Addison-Aris/Wesley).

I have at times veered from the dictates of culinary convention and fol-lowed the "spirit rather than the letter" of Mexican cooking. While I've been creative, often pairing less-than-likely ingredients or techniques, the essential flavor remains.

For further background flavor, I urge the reader to:

◆ Learn a little Mexican history from such works as
A Short History of Mexico by J. Patrick McHenry (Dolphin Books/
Doubleday, 1962), or seek out a copy of *La historia universal
de las cosas de Nueva Espana,* a work by the 16th-century Spanish monk,
Father Bernadino de Sahagun,
in which he chronicles Indian life pre- and post-conquest.

◆ Read the eloquent writers on Mexican food, most
notably Elisabeth Lambert Ortiz and the detailed collections
of Diana Kennedy, and seek out many of the
smaller, community-based home-style cooking publications.

◆ Devour the work of travel writers such as Kate Simon
and Sybel Bedford, both of whom offer further
glimpses into life in a land of great complexity and richness.

◆ Stroll through the pages of Patricia Quintara's
beautifully photographed books; each
page nearly exudes the tropical scent of Mexico.

INTRODUCTION

Cocina mexicana, the cookery and cuisine of this vast and mysterious land, is one of the world's greatest cuisines, staggering in its complexity and range. Its history speaks of antiquity, with dishes as old as civilization itself. Layers of foreign influence have contributed to its character, but in the end Mexican cooking is distinct from all other cuisines and is as eloquent an expression of the country as are its music, dance, and painting.

Mexican cuisine is tied up not only with the country's religious, cultural, and political history but with the landscape itself. Just being in Mexico makes everything taste different. Take a deep breath; in Mexico the air has as much flavor as does the food.

If you are patient, have endurance, and have luck and time enough, you will visit Mexico, entering by land at a U.S.A-Mexico border crossing. You will need your patience, for the northern reaches of the country are endless expanses of desert, broken up only by tumbleweeds and cacti. At times this austere landscape glides right into the sea, but soon the seacoast grows lush with small villages and tourist resorts juxtaposed against each other. Away from the coast the desert transforms itself into tropical jungle, with moist, verdant smells and exotic wildlife. Then come the mountains, breathtakingly capped with snow and dotted with myriad lakes. The Yucatán is flat and so densely covered with jungle that until the relatively recent motorway was completed, the peninsula was not connected with the rest of Mexico except by air or sea. The Maya were never completely conquered by the Spanish; their self-pride remains undiminished.

As exotically beautiful as is the landscape, even the arid desert, so too are the cities. Even in industrial decay, they shimmer with a vitality and inexplicable complexity.

Mexico City, once known as Tenochtitlán, was the glory of the Aztecs in the 14th and 15th centuries. It was one of the largest cities known to humankind then, as it is today. Contemporary Mexico City is a place of startling contrasts, where well-dressed cosmopolites walk next to sarape-draped campesinos, where automobiles share the roads with donkeys—and sometimes the latter move faster than the cars in the horrendous traffic. Pollution hangs in the air, covering all in its ominous cloak. Modern office blocks share the street with Spanish-colonial mansions and the ruins of Aztec palaces. Indian vendors spread their humble offering on cloths laid out in the street, outside the door of a huge, ultrasleek shopping center.

You can sit in a café and watch young trendsetters swing down the street, looking as glamorous as those in Paris; an old Indian man might try to sell you a snake; a group of schoolgirls giggle down the street in starched white shirts, their black hair in tight plaits down their backs, hugging their books to their chests as they window-shop; black-coated, fur-hatted Chassidim hurry past, lost in discussion and contemplation of life's mysteries. You dip your churro or croissant into your *café de olla* (boiled coffee, Mexican style) and continue to watch the parade of life outside the window.

While none compares in variety or size with Mexico (as the natives call it), there are so many cities, towns, and villages, each with its own distinctive architecture, ethnic makeup, historical influences, and geography. Guadalajara, Mexico's second-largest city, is eminently hospitable; founded in 1539, its architecture reflects that period: beautiful plazas, a city scattered with trees, monuments, fountains. Oaxaca is a rugged mountain city descended from the Zapotecs rather than the Aztecs; nearby Tehuacan is characterized by its matriarchal tribe of very tall, very strong women. San Luis Potosí, the Spanish mining town founded on the site of the Cimichimec Indian town of Tanga-Manga, grew rich as the Spanish discovered great veins of silver that ran beneath the region. The architecture remains beautiful and lavish today. Pátzcuaro is another colonial town, quiet and charming; Tarascan Indian land, with pleasant weather, lush surroundings, and secure peace. Southeast is the Caribbean port city of Veracruz, as raucous and wild as Marseilles, with its European and Afro-Caribbean flavor apparent in everything: the language, the music, the beat of the city. Housefronts form patterns of red, yellow, pale and bright blue, ochre, and umber, against the lush tropical greenery that weaves its way through the city. To the northeast lies the Yucatán Peninsula and its capital, Mérida, a Mayan-descended colonial town with recent Lebanese influence added to the cultural stew.

A BRIEF HISTORY

You can tuck into a plate of enchiladas, or nibble on *antojitos* (tacos, tostadas, and similar dishes), or sit down to a plate of grilled meat and roll up a supper of do-it-yourself tacos. Once you learn a bit about Mexico—the proud Aztec, Toltec, Mayan, Zapotec, and other Indians who have bequeathed their heritage, the Spanish conquest, brief French occupation, and modern North American influence—the more you can taste each layer of influence in the food.

The earliest Mexicans were Stone Age people who lived by hunting and gathering. Sometime after 5200 B.C. signs of agriculture and domestication appeared: corn, beans, squash, and tomatoes were raised; turkeys and dogs were kept for meat. We know that by 3500 B.C. chillies had been discovered as edible. This is essentially the beginning of Mexican cuisine.

By 2400 B.C. pottery was being fashioned, the ancestors of today's rustic *cazuelitas* and *ollas*. By around this time, Mesoamerica (from northern Mexico south through Guatemala) was developing a farming culture. Terraces and irrigation ducts were built; religious institutions were devoted to the earth's fertility. Skillful Indian plant breeders traded seeds and information with other tribes throughout the Americas. (It is estimated that half of the world's varieties of fruits, vegetables, and grains are due to the work of the Indian botanists and farmers.) For the first time, humankind had time to devote to other than scraping together a living, and this leisure encouraged the blossoming of artistic and religious culture. By this time *pipiáns,* stews prepared from ground pumpkin seeds and chillies, had become part of the diet, much as they are today.

From 1200 to 400 B.C. the Olmecs lived in what is today the region of Tabasco, south of Veracruz. They were the first to use a calendar of 365 days. An outstanding characteristic of their culture is their stone sculpture of great deformed creatures and faces, the significance of which has still not been explained. From 300 to 900 A.D. was Mexico's Classic Period, when society was no longer centered in the villages but in the cities. Artistic, cultural, and religious life prospered, as did economic life: a merchant and artisan class arose, landlords took control of the fields, essentially enchaining the farmer. The Maya are at the apex of this culture, which also included the Zapotec, Toltec, and Totonac. The Maya were the first to use the concept of zero in mathematics, and it could be said that they were obsessed with time: their calendars were calculated for centuries and centuries to come.

In general this was a time of great achievement. The Mayan cultural level has been compared with that of the Etruscans. They have left reliefs and frescoes, pyramids, hieroglyphics, figurines, all depicting a joyful and rich life.

Around 800 to 900 A.D. some sort of major disruption occurred; the paintings of the time depict war and large-scale migration. People wandered from their homes and lost faith in their gods; the fabric of society unraveled into loose threads of lost souls.

Then, around the 1300s, the Aztecs settled into the Mexico Valley on Lake Texcoco, with the island of Tenochtitlán their capital. It, along with its surroundings that grew into states and territories, grew rich . . . very rich. Gold, food, clothing, and perfumes were in abundance; events of state or religion entailed elaborate ceremony.

Most of the people lived on a diet of corn, prepared in the same way pozole (hominy soup-stew) is today, often ground into flat cakes, and a variety of beans, augmented with an occasional bit of meat (especially the little hairless dogs they raised as food) or fowl. Everything was seasoned with a wide array of chillies. To forget their troubles, the Indians drank pulque, the fermented sap of the maguey, still drunk today through the more rural, rustic areas of the Republic.

The ruling classes also had luxury foods such as chocolate, in addition to their occasional cannibal feasts of sacrificial victims' arms and legs. Though we have no Aztec recipes and records, some of the early Spanish visitors described the royal feasts: a myriad of dishes (many of which are still eaten in modern-day Mexico, though in a somewhat changed form): sweet tamales, birds cooked with chillies and seeds, turkey with tomatoes, squash seeds and chillies, tamales with beans, birds with dried corn, and a wide variety of tortillas were among the dishes described by Bernadino de Sahagun, the Spanish friar who chronicled the conquest of Mexico. He also described many varieties of chocolate, each with a distinct color, consistency, and fragrance.

The Aztecs were a warlike people, but they developed a culture of great richness and diversity. Tenochtitlán, the island capital, was grander than anything in Europe at the time. A pyramid sat at the center of the city, and before it an enormous open-air market where women sold corn tortillas much as they do today. Canals wove through the city, transporting sleek canoes piled high with fruit, vegetables, and flowers destined for the market.

In 1519 Hernán Cortés landed in what would later be called Veracruz. He made his way to Tenochtitlán and surveyed the riches. Cortés decided he wanted it all.

The Aztec ruler, Montezuma II, offered the Spaniards payments of gold to entice them to leave, but that only whetted their greed. The Spaniards were working on sheer bravado, hardly a match for the huge numbers of fierce Aztecs. History would have been much different if it hadn't been for the legend of Quetzalcoatl. The ancient story told of a high priest and leader of the Toltecs at Tula who stopped human sacrifice and transformed the warlike Toltecs into peaceful farmers and artisans. The old priests, who depended upon human sacrifice for their livelihood, drove Quetzalcoatl away by tricking him into breaking his vows of chastity. As he sailed away into the Caribbean he promised to return in a future age.

When Montezuma saw Cortés arrive from the sea, he thought it was the prediction fulfilled. He probably felt unable to do battle with this godly reincarnation.

So began the conquest, with its horrendous battles and cruel domination. Out of this grew the Mestizo culture of modern-day Mexico. For an even-handed portrayal of the period of conquest (and indeed of the entire history of the land), read McHenry's *A Short History of Mexico.*

The Spaniards may have intended only to reap the riches of this vast empire, but in the end they contributed much to developing the culture of modern-day Mexico.

The Indians were quick to take to some of the crops and domestic animals introduced by the Spaniards. Pigs changed Indian cooking more than any other ingredient: the fat could be used to fry foods, thereby increasing the culinary range. Pre-Columbian Indians lacked milk, butter, cheese, wheat flour, and chickens; the only eggs they had were those they managed to steal from the nests of wild birds. As a mixed-race culture developed, so did a cuisine based on both Indian and Spanish foods.

I always wondered why olives, olive oil, and wine-making never got a foothold in the combination of Indian and Spanish cultures. No doubt the fruits would grow well in much of this region, and they are, after all, much a part of Spanish Mediterranean cuisine. In the early years of conquest, however, the Spaniards wanted no competition in the marketplace from their overseas territory, and they levied fines and imprisonment against anyone tending olives or wine grapes in Mexico. (Current-day Baja California does produce some quite decent wines, and olives/olive oil are used, if not prominently, in Mexican cookery.)

Spain ruled Mexico until 1821, realizing as early as the 1550s that the Indians were more easily subdued by the quietly determined monks than by the erratic and volatile conquistadors. Hence much of Mexico is a complex combination of Indian culture and religion overlaid with Christianity. By the time independence came, many if not most of the Indians had been converted to Christianity. Political upheaval never abated, and governments rose and fell with alarming rapidity until French intervention in the 1860s. While the country was in a state of civil war, a faction of the Mexican upper class offered the Archduke Maximilian of Habsburg the crown of Mexico, with the support of Napoleon III. It was a short rule (1864–67), with good intentions but without much success; Maximilian was executed (as most former rulers were). The French occupation left an imprint on Mexico's cuisine, including good crusty rolls and creamy pastries.

The Mexican Revolution in the first two decades of the 20th century, spearheaded by such populist leaders as Pancho Villa and Emiliano Zapata, attempted to give the ordinary people a voice in their government. Reforms were enacted and a spirit of surging ahead for the good of the country prevailed, inspiring the present-day presidents of Mexico.

Contemporary Mexican life reflects its great and tumultuous history in all facets: art, architecture, religious observances, lifestyle, culture, and cuisine.

MEXICAN MARKETPLACES

Fruits and vegetables are arranged with breathtaking artistry. It seems as if the act of arranging the produce is the vendor's true purpose; selling the fruits and vegetables seems incidental, almost a compromise of the purity of the arrangement. A silent Indian girl, no older than a child herself, plump brown baby tied to her with a colorful rebozo, takes your money and solemnly wraps your purchase.

A middle-aged vendor flashes her lively smile, revealing a wealth of gold in her teeth. "Buy it!" she exclaims when you pick up one of the melons piled in front of her. "It is sweet!" She cuts it open to offer you a taste. The sweet fragrance of its orange-pink flesh is suddenly set loose and quickly attracts a collection of intimidating insects.

Wander past the piles of produce to the food stalls, with their steaming vats of myterious-looking concoctions: stewed meats redolent of chillies, vegetables stewing in savory sauces, earthenware pots filled with simmering frijoles.

In the *fonda* (informal restaurant—every marketplace has at least one) inside the market, a huge wooden ceiling fan circles listlessly. The smoky smells from the charcoal grills waft through the air offering the enticing promise of shreds of delicious scorched meat wrapped in fragrant, fresh tortillas.

The tortillas are so fresh and tender that a 5-minute-old one is too old to bother with. They are sold by the kilo; you grab a stack and walk a few steps over to the *carnitas* stand (there always seems to be one next to a tortilla stand): Order *surtido,* a little bit of everything. "What is it?" you might ask. Don't; just enjoy the succulence, the meltingly tender meat and crisp piece of crackling *(chicharrón)* you may be lucky enough to have your *carnitas* served on, a sort of an edible plate. Roll a few pieces up in a tortilla, spoon on the salsa—there will no doubt be a bowl or two of salsa, pickled chillies, and/or cactus on hand. Head to the nearest bar—again, it will probably be no farther away than a few steps—and order a cooling beer to accompany your taco.

Marketplace food is often Mexican food at its best. (It can be Mexican food at its scariest, as well. An old saying has it that the best-smelling meat dishes in Mexico are often the chanciest since huge quantities of onions, garlic, and spices are used to camouflage the less than wholesome quality of the meat.)

In Mexico, eating is an occasion, even if it is only a warm tortilla grabbed from a marketplace stall and smeared with a bit of chilli paste, rolled around a little chopped onion. Food (and often the lack of it) is intertwined with life. Much of the Indian food-related attitudes and religious beliefs persist despite centuries of religious conversion, and the act of eating can have a symbolic importance that goes far beyond mere sustenance.

EATING IN MEXICO: VIEWS, VISTAS, AND VIGNETTES

It is not only the food that is so extraordinary. Mexico offers amazing settings in which to eat.

You can dine on a terrace overlooking mountainside or sea; at tiny tables next to a sparkling blue swimming pool; in colonial-era posadas (inns); or in a structure that is little more than an adobe hut. You might enjoy lunch served in a junglelike tangle of greenery that is the restaurant's or your host's garden, or visit a restaurant that specializes in grilled foods and sit protected from the dizzying sun by large umbrellas while your meat or seafood sizzles on the open barbecue. On a warm evening you might sit in a lush garden under the open sky, surrounded by strings of tiny twinkling white lights, while you scoop up your savory platters of food with tender tortillas and down glasses of cold *cerveza*. Mariachis might wander by, stop at your table and caress you with a song.

Visit a park on Sunday and you end up picnicking. Inevitably you'll find vendors with their fragrant, enticing wares. All around you are families with young children, couples courting, all with their parcels of food prepared especially for this outing.

Take a second-class bus that winds through the hillsides on its way to the coast. An old man in the seat in front of you turns around and tries to sell you a snake; or maybe it's just the skin. You stop at a village and a flock of brown-fleshed women descend upon you, bearing huge platters of enchiladas. You buy a couple (*dos, por favor*), and in that hot, dirty bus in the dusty, poverty-burnished village you eat the best enchiladas of your life: unstuffed, they taste of corn and chillies and ancient ways.

On the train, an early morning stop brings on an old man selling jars of strawberry jam and another selling loaves of bread. You buy one of each and happily eat bites of bread smeared with a sweet spread that tastes intensely of strawberries as the landscape of Mexico flows past the windows of the speeding train.

Food is everywhere, and always there are views: views of a green-gray river snaking its way through the bottom of a mountain gorge; views of mountain-rimmed lakes; cactus-studded desert that falls directly to the blue, blue sea; views of the central squares, of the marketplaces, of the kitchens and the sturdy brown women patting out tortillas.

REGIONS

Mexico is not one huge homogeneous nation. It is like a confederation of many small countries, harking back to its pre-Hispanic days when the land was inhabited by many Indian nations in addition to the Aztecs. After the conquest the situation changed somewhat, but rough terrain that made travel difficult helped retain the individuality of the various communities. To this day there are tribes that have never given in to the European, speaking only their native language, adhering to their own customs, dress, and cuisine. Even in regions where a population of mixed Spanish and Indians has evolved, many of the local pre-conquest customs survive. The result is a land with as many variations as possible, yet all held together with loose strings of culture, economics, and religion.

The north, an arid land that borders the United States, was inhabited in the pre-conquest era by aggressive, primitive Indians whom the Aztecs called

Chichimecs (sons of the dog). The arrival of the Spaniards brought cattle to a land that was perfect for grazing. Cowboys—Indian, Spanish, mestizo—moved north to tend the animals. They brought wheat, which thrived in the dry land where corn would not. Thus, wheat and beef are featured prominently in the cuisine of this area, which extends across the border into the U.S. Southwest, especially Arizona and Texas. (New Mexico has its own special culinary history that reflects the blue corn, rainbow of colored beans, and simple regional foods such as greens and chillies.)

The tortillas in this region are apt to be of wheat flour rather than corn, the chilli stews made from beef rather than pork. Texas's chilli con carne comes from this region.

With the abundance of cattle, it's no surprise that the north should have a fondness for cheese. Chihuahua, the northernmost state of Mexico, bordering Texas, prepares a dish of soft, creamy refried beans topped with cheese and baked into a soft, melty bit of pleasure. In the neighboring state of Sonora, one regional dish is a thick potato soup covered with a layer of hot melted cheese. *Queso fundido* is perhaps the simplest dish of all: a large chunk of cheese placed on an open fire or in a hot oven and grilled to crusty, melty bliss, into which soft flour tortillas are dipped. It can be topped with all manner of extras—chillies, shrimp, chorizo—but the cheese is what it is all about.

Beef and cheese make fewer appearances in the rest of Mexico, where goat, lamb, pork, turkey and chicken are easier to raise. In the central areas cabrito (kid) is coated in a chilli paste, stuffed with an elaborate spicy meat filling, and roasted to a crisp-skinned tender perfection.

The central region, with its distinctly colonial style and customs, its gentle and lush landscape, offers a cuisine with equally strong Spanish influence and pre-Columbian heritage. Such Mediterranean-originated dishes as puchero (a boiled dinner or stew), *fiambre Potosino,* (assorted cold, sliced meats splashed with a spicy vinaigrette), and *churros* (long, fluted fritters) share the table with New World foods such as prickly pears and a variety of other cacti, bean soups (specialty of the Tarascan Indians), and a wide variety of tortilla dishes.

The southern part of the country, especially the east and west coasts, offers exotic, tropical flavors not found in the rest of Mexico. Fruit plays more of a role, as does fish. Bananas grow everywhere in dizzying array: small sweet ones for nibbling, large green ones for cooking, nonsweet ones for savory dishes, and on and on. Even the leaves are used, particularly in the Yucatán and in Oaxaca, where they wrap everything from tamales to chicken, fish to pork, imparting their subtle flavor while they seal in the juices. Avocados come in an equally wide profusion—from tiny smooth-skinned ones no bigger than a man's thumb, with creamy mild flesh, to those the size of melons, tasting light and sweet; thick black-skinned avocados, with a heavy, deliciously oily flesh, needing just a squeeze of lemon and half a chopped chilli to transform them into a sparkling guacamole. The green fruit appears anywhere: in soups, stews, tacos, salsas, salads.

The state of Oaxaca offers a cuisine that remains stubbornly and deliciously Indian: red, yellow, green, and black moles (spicy sauces containing chocolate) harken back to pre-conquest days. *Chalupines* (crickets) are a delicacy gathered from the cornfields; edible flowers are also favored, especially the delicate yellow squash blossoms.

No doubt the most distinctive regional cuisine of Mexico remains that of Yucatán; its vast area of jungles and swamps became reachable by air or sea only recently. The heritage of much of the region is Mayan rather than Aztec, and its glorious civilization predated the Aztecs by a long time. Spanish is often considered a foreign language here, as many people still speak one of the many remaining Mayan languages.

Achiote is a favored seasoning in this mysterious land. The small, rock-hard red seeds have a slight citrus quality and combine well with the fruit juices widely used in Yucatecan cooking. Another hallmark of this cuisine is its range of *recados,* seasoning pastes. You will see them in the market piled into great fragrant rainbowlike heaps, made of pumpkin seeds, chillies, roasted garlic, and spices, labeled *para bistek* (for beefsteak), *para pibil* (for roasting, preferably in the pibil style of being first wrapped in fragrant leaves) and so on.

MEALS AND MEALTIMES IN MEXICO

From desert to tropical jungle, seaside to mountain, city to countryside, mealtimes vary greatly. Throughout the country there are traditionally five daily meals, though few would eat all of them on any given day, and many in the larger cities have taken to the American pattern of three meals a day, with the largest in the evening.

Breakfast, *desayuno,* is early, as the nation rises with the dawn to get a head start on the heat of the coming day: mugs of *café de olla* or *café con leche* (coffee with milk) or hot chocolate, sweet rolls or *churros* in the city, rustic sweet tamales in the country. A second breakfast, *almuerzo,* is eaten around 11 A.M. or noon. It consists of robust egg dishes, tortillas, perhaps some savory meat, and is accompanied by *café con leche* or cooling juices or fruit and milk drinks.

Lunch, *comida corrida,* the traditional main meal of the day, is served around 2 P.M. In the Mediterranean-European tradition, it consists of a leisurely procession of courses. A siesta of several hours follows. The meal almost always begins with soup, progressing to a *sopa seca* (pasta, rice, or tortillas in broth), a main plate of meat or fish, one or two of vegetables, and perhaps a plate of simple beans. Lovely fresh tortillas, loosely wrapped in a clean cloth, appear in an endless parade. Finally comes dessert: a fresh or cooked fruit dish, or perhaps a custard, and then coffee.

Around 7 or 8 P.M. is *merienda* (afternoon snack or tea)—coffee or hot chocolate again, or perhaps a mug of atole (a cornmeal beverage). Tamales or a sweet or savory pastry might accompany the drinks.

Cena (supper) might be eaten around 9 or 10 P.M. It could be a main course, or a one-pot soup or stew, or leftovers from lunch; it might be tostadas, tacos, or tortas (hearty sandwiches). If it's a celebration, it will be a heavy meal, lasting well into the night. Generally, however, *cena* is light, and it is often skipped altogether.

SPECIAL INGREDIENTS AND COOKING TECHNIQUES

INGREDIENTS

Achiote: (also called *annatto*): Brick-red and stone-hard, these tiny seeds impart a red-yellow color and an elusive, almost citrus-saffron flavor. They must be soaked overnight to be usable. For directions, as well as a recipe for the basic Yucatecan achiote seasoning paste, refer to Pollo Pibil recipe. Since the seeds need to be soaked and ground, they are often sold ready to use in little squares, with or without additional seasonings. Favored also in Puerto Rico, achiote seeds are used outside of Latin America as coloring agents. The small, hard seeds last nearly forever.

Avocado leaves: (*hojas de aquacate*): The leaves of the avocado tree, cousins of the bay laurel, are used often in Mexican cookery. They have an herby flavor with hints of anise and bay. Unfortunately, houseplants don't have the same qualities—you need a large, outdoor-grown tree for the characteristic flavor and fragrance. Usually, avocado leaves are toasted, then ground with other ingredients into a spicy paste; sometimes they are used whole, to line a steamer or wrap food (especially a whole chicken, Veracruz style). Bay leaves, with or without a sprinkling of anise, make the best substitute.

Avocados or alligator pears: Mexico raises a wide variety of avocados, from huge melon-sized bright green specimens to tiny thumb-sized ones. The favored is Haas, medium-sized with dark green to nearly black, thick, pebbly skin. The flesh of these avocados is creamy and rich, lending itself gracefully to the flavors of chillies, tomatoes, onions, and other seasonings. An avocado is ripe when the pointed end gives just a tiny bit when pressed; soft spots on the rest of the fruit indicate spoilage, not ripeness. Once an avocado ripens, refrigerate it and it will keep for about 10 days.

Banana leaves (*hojas de plátanos*): Large, fragrant fronds of the banana palm, favored throughout the tropical areas of Mexico (the southern, Yucatán, and Gulf coastal regions) for wrapping chicken, pork, tamales, and so on. You can find banana leaves in Asian or Indian grocery stores, or frozen in Chinese shops. Pass them over a flame to make them pliable before using.

Cactus (nopale): The paddles of the prickly pear-bearing cactus, nopales are favored throughout Mexico. Find them fresh in any Latin or Caribbean neighborhood store, or in jars imported from Mexico (usually excellent and much easier to deal with).

To clean and cook: Most likely the large prickly spines will have been removed. Trim the large outer edge of the paddle, including the end where it was cut from the plant. Scrape or slice off the sharp bits where the spines were. Cut the flesh into strips, or dice and toss into a pot of boiling salted water to which you've added half a chopped onion, a handful of chopped cilantro, and a fresh jalapeño. Cook 15 to 20 minutes. Drain, rinse, and toss with a little salt. Store in the refrigerator.

Occasionally nopales are roasted whole over a charcoal fire, then diced or sliced and used as desired. Sometimes they are cooked whole, then stuffed with cheese and grilled or fried.

Chayote: The sweet squashlike fruit that looks somewhat like a smooth avocado and tastes like a zucchini that has been grown on another planet where everything tastes more delicious. Chayote are eaten throughout Latin America and the Caribbean—fried, baked, stuffed, simmered, and so on. Unopened, they keep about a month.

Cheese (*queso*): Before the conquest, Mexico had no tradition of cheese. Since then cheese has come to be sprinkled onto a wide variety of *antojitos,* frijoles, and soups, served with fruit desserts, and so on. Most Mexican cheese is farmhouse and regional; often it is fresh and crumbly; sometimes it is aged for grating.

Mexican and Mexican-style cheeses are often found in America's Southwest, especially in California, and occasionally elsewhere. An interesting story concerns California's Monterey Jack cheese. In the mid-1800s a Monterey coastal ranch owner, named (of course) Jack, noticed that the Mexican workers on his cattle ranch were putting surplus milk to use by making a springy, fresh cheese. He found it so delicious, he asked if they would not sell it and put his name to it. The rest, as they say, is history.

In Mexico, crumbly fresh cheese is known as *queso fresco* or *queso ranchero,* though most Mexican cheeses bear the name of the farmhouse factory or region where they were made. Fresh pecorino, or feta cheese soaked in water for an hour or two to rid it of its extra salt, make good substitutes to use wherever one would use *queso fresco.* Mild, milky fresh goat's cheese can be good in Mexican food as well.

For melting, choose Jack, mozzarella, a sharp mature white cheddar, or a medium asiago. Combinations of shredded cheeses with a bit of a sharper cheese added make a delicious melted mixture. Fresh mozzarella is stringily delicious in many dishes that call for a meltable milk cheese, especially an Oaxaco-type one.

Chicharrones: Airy, crisp, and nearly addictive pork cracklings. They get their distinctive texture from a double frying technique similar to that used in French cooking for *pommes soufflé* and the like. The skins of freshly killed pigs are first dried in the sun for a day, then plunged into a great cauldron of bubbling hot oil and removed. They're allowed to cool, then the process is repeated; in the second frying the skins puff up dramatically, much like the French potato dish. Because of the demands of the process, home preparation is not practical.

In Mexico *chicharrones* are sold loose in nearly every marketplace in the country: great slabs of golden honeycombed crispness, ready for breaking off and nibbling on, electrified with squirts of lime and sprinkles of fierce cayenne pepper. Like chips, they are delicious dipped into guacamole or salsa. *Chicharrones* are also delicious broken into bits and stirred into a mild *salsa verde*: wrap the mixture into tortillas for *chicharrón* tacos.

Actually, they may be at their best just nibbled guiltily.

Chillies: Perhaps Mexico's greatest gift to the culinary, along with corn, tomatoes, potatoes, and chocolate. To catalog the endless variety of chillies in this small space would be an impossible task. For further information on chillies, I refer you to another of my books, *Hot & Spicy* (J. P. Tarcher in the U.S.; Grafton Publishing in the U.K.).

Chillies, also known as *Capsicum frutescens,* are amazingly rich sources of vitamins A and C. Fresh chillies are second only to beef liver in vitamin A, and in vitamin C they fall only slightly behind acerola and rose hips.

The outstanding characteristic of the chilli, its culinary fire, is due to the active ingredient, 8-methyl-N-vanillin-6-neneamide, or more simply, capsaicin. One can measure the heat of chillies using a technique of distilling, diluting, then measuring the heat level of the capsaicin. The method is called the Scoville method and the measurements arrived at are called Scoville Units. Many cookbook writers go into elaborate discussion on the subject, but I don't see the point: it's not difficult to figure out that a chilli is too hot. It becomes immediately apparent.

Then you are left to soothe the tender flesh. Do not reach for water! It may cool the burning sensation for a moment, but the pain will return quickly and unmercifully. Better to try to absorb the volatile oils that carry the capsaicin by spooning down a bit of soft bland rice, corn or flour tortillas, or bread; yogurt is soothing, so is anything icy, especially tequila or vodka-laced drinks, since the alcohol adds to the pain-killer effect. Texans swear by salt, but I can't recommend consuming a large amount of salt.

There are approximately 200 varieties of chillies, ranging from richly mild to searingly hot, from tiny berries no larger than peppercorns, to great chillies larger than a man's fist. In between are a cornucopia of shapes and sizes, colors and flavors, in addition to degrees of heat. For practical purposes, the two main groupings of chillies are fresh and dried.

FRESH CHILLIES

Fresh chillies are most commonly sold green, sometimes ripe yellow or red. They may be sliced and tossed into a dish as is, with their fiery fresh flavor, or they may be roasted and peeled, their inflammatory seeds and veins removed, leaving only rich vegetable flavor and a small amount of heat. The fresh chillies most often called for in this book are described below.

Anaheim: Long, light green mild chillies, about 4 to 6 inches in length and only an inch or so wide at the top. Anaheims have light peppery flavor and are usually quite mild in heat. Bland, but good cooked in stews, chillies, soups, sauces.

Güero: Pale yellow or yellow green, these waxy chillies are 4 to 5 inches long and an inch or so wide at the top. They are also known as Hungarian yellow peppers or sometimes banana peppers. In the Yucatán they are called *xcatic;* in the Veracruz region they may be called *chile largo.* Sometimes a smaller, shorter yellow chilli is available. Güero chillies are lightly flavored, delicate rather than meaty, and range from mild to medium-hot.

Jalapeño: The most ubiquitous of chillies, medium-hot with a nice vegetable flavor. About 2½ inches long and ¾ inch wide at the top, they come in a wide variety, each with subtle flavor differences. Easily the most all-purpose of the chillies, but like most small chillies, they are at their best raw, especially firing up fresh and bracing salsas.

Poblano: Dark green, almost heart-shaped, these large chillies are 3 to 4½ inches long and 3 inches or so wide at the top, narrowing to a point. They are distinctly pepper flavored with a meaty flesh perfect for stuffing. Though poblanos can be rather picante, they tend toward mildness. Best to taste— carefully—first.

Serrano: Narrower in width and slightly shorter, the serrano tends to be hotter than the jalapeño, with a strong green-leafy flavor. Serranos, like jalapeños, are at their best sliced raw and used as a garnish or salsa.

Habanero: Know as Scotch bonnet in Great Britain and the West Indies, it is not commonly available in the U.S. but may be found in some Indian, West Indian, or Latin American shops. I've seen it occasionally in San Francisco's Latin American "Mission" neighborhood. Shaped like a spinning top or tam-o'-shanter cap, it ranges in color from red to yellow, orange, and greenish-yellow, and from very hot to very, very hot. If Habanero is not available, use a fresh cayenne chile instead.

Many green chillies, especially the large ones, need to be roasted for some recipes. To roast: over an open flame or under a hot grill, or in a hot, ungreased frying pan, heat the chillies until they char, turning them so that they char and blacken somewhat evenly. On the stove-top open flame, they may catch fire; don't be concerned, but blow the flames out as too much burning will eat into the flesh of the peppers in addition to the skin. Once blackened, place the hot, charred chillies in a bowl or plastic bag and seal tightly. Let sit for 15 to 30 minutes, then remove the skin. The longer you leave them to sit and sweat, the easier it will be to do this, and the milder they become; this is useful if you have a particularly hot batch of chillies, such as poblano, which you want to be fairly mild.

DRIED CHILLIES

Ancho (dried poblano): *Ancho* means broad, and this is a wide, flat chilli, 3 to 4 inches long and 2 to 3 inches wide. It is brownish in color, with rich, deep flavor that hints of chocolate, prunes, earthiness.

Árbol: Bright orange red in color, the árbol is narrow (½ inch wide) and about 3 inches long. It is brittle and thin-skinned, with a sharp heat.

Cascabel: Round, about 2 inches in diameter, with a rattling sound when shaken. Cascabel chillies are similar in flavor to the guajillo, with a distinctive red color that tints all that stews with it.

Chipotle (smoked and dried jalapeño): Usually sold canned in a spicy adobo marinade, sometimes chipotle is available dried. Sometimes called *moros*.

Guajillo: Long and narrow, shaped much like a New Mexico/California chilli, but lighter red in color, this smooth-skinned chilli delivers a slightly sharper bite. One variety of guajillo, *pulla,* is slightly smaller and hotter still.

Mulatto: Much like an ancho in appearance, with a taste somewhere between that of the ancho and negro or pasilla: rich, complex, full, but not too sweet.

Negro or pasilla: Dark brown-reddish-black in color, with wrinkled skin like an ancho, but with deeper flavor, slightly more intense heat, and absence of sweetness.

New Mexico/California chilli: A smooth-skinned, long (6 to 8 inches), narrow (about 2 inches at its widest) chilli with a color that ranges from burgundy to a brighter brick red. It has a simple, uncomplicated flavor like paprika or sweet pepper, and a slight tanginess. In Mexico such chillies are very bland, but some found in the U.S. can veer toward picante. Also known as *chile colorado* in Sonora, *chilaca* in Monterrey, *chimayo* in New Mexico, *chilacate* in Guadalajara, as well as other names.

There are several ways to use dried chillies. Mild ones may be steeped; toasted, then steeped; whirled into a sauce and strained or the tender flesh scraped from the tough skin; they may be cut into thin strips and fried, or-toasted until nutty in aroma, then ground into a fine powder. Each recipe specifies the techniques that work best for that particular dish.

To make a basic mild chilli sauce, the chillies must be steeped and rehydrated, then pureed and strained to eliminate undigestible gritty bits. You can do this by tearing up the chillies and discarding stems and seeds, then pouring hot water or broth over them and letting them sit and rehydrate. To add a subtle depth of flavor, toast the chillies lightly in an ungreased frying pan or over an open flame, only until they give off a toasted perfume but do not color, then pour the hot water or broth over them.

When chillies are softened, after at least 30 minutes (up to overnight), remove them from the soaking liquid. Save the liquid for the sauce; any leftovers may be used in soups, stews, or braises. Whirl the rehydrated chillies in a blender, along with enough of their soaking liquid to make a sauce, then press through a sieve to strain away the tough bits.

For a smoother, more refined and undiluted chilli paste, take the softened chillies and remove the stems and seeds. Using a paring knife, scrape the flesh away from the tough, papery skin of each chilli. Discard the skin and use the concentrated chilli flesh as desired.

Another way to use mild chillies is as a garnish, cut into very thin strips and fried to a crisp. Cut with scissors, and quickly fry in hot oil, taking care not to burn them. Drain on absorbent paper. Sprinkle onto steamed rice, grilled meats, salads, chewy breads, pasta.

CHILLI POWDER

Mild chilli powder is sold in most supermarkets, a mixture based on chillies such as pasilla and ancho, with other spices and flavoring additives. Pure chilli powder, however, gives a straightforward, strong chilli flavor that you can balance with other spices.

To prepare your own, lightly toast the chillies on an ungreased baking sheet or in a heavy ungreased frying pan; you can do this either in the oven or on top of the stove. Keep the varieties of chillies separate, so that you have one jar of ancho, (or other black, wrinkly skinned chillies) or pasilla (or smooth, red-skinned chillies). Toast in an oven at 400°F, or over medium heat, cooking just long enough for the chillies to grow fragrant and a bit brittle; if toasted too long they will darken and develop a burnt flavor.

Cool, then remove stems and seeds and break the chillies into little pieces. Whirl in a food processor or in a coffee grinder (one that you have cleaned well or use only for grinding spices).

PICKLED CHILLIES

Chipotle: The smoked jalapeño chilli, usualy sold either in a brine or in tins in adobo. It has both smoke and fire in its inimitable aroma and taste and breathtaking heat. A tiny bit of chipotle goes a long way in creating the flavor of Mexico. When you open the tin, remove contents to a glass container and keep in the refrigerator for up to a month. (I tend to keep them in a cup rather than a jar; I'm not sure why—perhaps to provide easy access.) The smaller morita chillies have a similar flavor and may be used interchangeably with chipotles.

Jalapeños en escabeche or serranos en escabeche: Available in jars, these are chillies that have been pickled in vinegar. Sometimes bits of carrots, onion, and cauliflower are added; a spoonful of this mixture, chopped, makes a delicious addition to cheese quesadillas.

Cilantro: Fresh, pungent green leaves grown from the coriander seed. Available in Mexican, Indian, or Chinese shops, and often in supermarkets. You can grow your own easily by sowing a small plot at two-week intervals (it grows quickly, then dies just as quickly). However, sometimes the seeds purchased as spices are too old to germinate.

Corn husks: The outer covering of corn, used to wrap tamales and other edible parcels. Available in Latin American groceries, corn husks need to be soaked in warm water to cover for a least 30 minutes before using. If the leaves have not been separated, cut them apart with a pair of scissors before using. I have tried drying my own husks, pulling them off of corn on the cob, but once dried they are awfully small and not very efficient for even the smallest of tamales. While most corn husks are Mexican, with large separated husks, occasionally one finds African corn husks. These are still attached at the base, with smaller leaves. Instead of using the leaves individually, use the whole husk parcel, placing the filling in the center.

Epazote: A pungent herb, also called pazote, it is known in North America as wormseed or wormweed. In northern Mexico it is used dried, as a medicinal tea to soothe shaky nerves or as vermifuge; in the south it is used and used and used, sometimes in salsas, but especially in bean dishes of all sorts. Its strong, almost unpleasant taste rounds out the beans and gives them a delicious depth of flavor.

Hominy: Kernels of corn that have been treated with slaked lime until they pump up, shed their skins, and develop a distinctive, earthy flavor and fragrance. Hominy is often sold whole in cans. Dried hominy, however, has a much greater depth of flavor.

Huitlacoche: A pearly gray fungus that grows on ears of corn, swelling and deforming them, yielding deliciously inky insides. To paraphrase what has been said of the oyster, whoever was the first to taste *huitlacoche* was brave indeed. It is not readily available, even in Mexico, and like all wild fungi is seasonal. Tinned *huitlacoche* is available, but it's a pale imitation of itself.

Jícama: A large root vegetable somewhat resembling a water chestnut. Remove its brown skin and its white flesh is sweetish and applelike in both texture and flavor. Eaten raw, as a snack, sprinkled with lime juice and cayenne pepper, or used with fruits in salads.

Masa harina: Finely ground corn flour made from dry corn that is boiled with slaked lime until the kernels swell and shed their skins. In Mexico, one can often find fresh masa, the lime-slaked corn ground on the metate, the dough fragrant with corn and the faint whiff of the stone it was ground on.

Masa harina is used for tortillas, tamales, *masa antojitos,* and sometimes as a thickener for sauces, such as chilli Colorado. Quaker Oats makes an excellent corn-scented white masa. Store in a cool, dark place in a well-sealed container.

Plantains (*plátanos machos*): Large, starchy bananas used for cooking rather than for eating raw. Available in Caribbean markets and many supermarkets, plantains are used ripened and sweetened in Mexican cooking.

Prickly Pear: The sharp-thorned sweet fruit of the nopale cactus. Also called tuna, or atún, they have a sweet-tart exotic flavor. Available in Latin American markets and specialty greengrocers.

Seville, or bitter, oranges: Sour with a sharp, sharp citrus flavor, these are a hallmark of the Yucatán and other cuisines of the south. Seville oranges are sometimes available in markets for making marmalade; if not, orange juice combined with grapefruit juice and lemon or lime juice, along with a bit of grated grapefruit peel. The recipes in this book assume that Seville oranges are not available, and use other combinations of citrus juice. If you have access to Seville oranges, enjoy them at their simplest: squeezed over grilled meats, into spicy soups, atop rich rice and bean dishes, or in a salsa-scented vinaigrette.

Shrimp, dried (*camarones secas*): Tiny dried shrimp, sometimes sold crushed into a powder. In addition to Latin American specialty shops, they are sold in

Chinese or Southeast Asian markets. Choose ones as pink in color as possible—pale color denotes an old, faded mixture. Dried shrimp are served in a variety of ways: steep with hot water, season with garlic and mild chillies and you have a simple broth. Add a bit to garlic-buttered white rice for a Lenten specialty, or make into crisp fried patties.

Squash blossoms (*flores de calabaza*): Mexican cooks adore squash blossoms as much as do Italians. Their flowery beauty is as appealing as their delicate flavor. In Mexico squash blossoms are most commonly used in soup, but try tossing them into Arroz con Elote in place of the corn.

To clean, remove the stem and stalk, and cut the flowers with scissors (a knife will crush the tender petals).

Tamarinds: Tamarind pods are curved, slightly rough textured, and appear much as huge, rather dried-out beans in a pod. The inside pulp is soft, and should easily separate from the shell; discard the hard seeds.

Pressed tamarind pulp or liquid tamarind is often available in Asian or Latin American food shops. Follow directions on package.

Tomatillos: A small green tomato that is covered with a papery brown husk. Remove the husk and underneath the skin is slightly sticky, the tomatillo itself firm to the touch, unlike a ripe (red, yellow, or green) eating tomato. Tomatillos add a distinctive, tart, and bright flavor to dishes.

Tomatillos are available in Mexican food shops canned, and often fresh. They should be cooked, though it has become fashionable recently in California to prepare salsas and relishes with uncooked tomatillos (I don't think this suits the fruit to its best advantage). To cook: Husk, rinse briefly, place in saucepan, cover with water, and bring to a boil. Simmer over low-medium heat until tomatillos change color from a bright to a lighter, slightly browner green.

UTENSILS AND COOKWARE

Clay: Mexican cuisine would not look or taste the same without the gaily colored clay cooking utensils, bowls, and pitchers. Cooking in clay imparts a certain inimitable essence to the food, with no metallic tinge to interfere with the flavors of the ingredients.

If cooking with clay, be sure that your pieces can withstand the heat of cooking (ask when you purchase them). Next, you must season the pots, much as a wok needs to be seasoned. Rub the outside of the pots with a cut clove of garlic and fill the inside with soapy water as close to the brim as possible. Place the pot on the heat, bring to a boil, and boil until the water has almost evaporated. Remove from heat and let the pot stand for at least 20 minutes. This seals the clay. Smaller pieces can be boiled in a large pot of soapy water for about an hour rather than placed on their own on top of the stove.

Molcajete and tejolote: A mortar and pestle made from near-black, porous volcanic stone. They have a primitive, exotic appearance. Spices ground in a molcajete rather than a food processor are more finely textured, sauces blended in a molcajete have more intense flavor. If you do find a *molcajete* and *tejolote,* they will need to be tempered before using. First put a little rice or other grain into the mortar along with a little salt. Grind and grind, then empty the *molcajete* and repeat, continuing the process several times until the ground grain and salt is pure in color and free of grit, bits of rock, or dirt.

The metate is one of the oldest kitchen utensils known to Mesoamerica. It is similar to the *molcajete,* but larger and rectangular in shape, supported by three legs, with a rolling pin-shaped stone to roll back and forth. The metate is used to grin *nixtamil,* corn for masa. Like the *molcajete,* the metate needs to be tempered before using.

TECHNIQUES

Mexico's brilliantly varied layering of flavors is achieved by several techniques. A dish might consist of simply tomatoes, chillies, and onions, but if you roast any of the ingredients the sauce will be dramatically transformed. Toss the garlic onto a comal (stone griddle) and cook until charred and sweetly soft; roast the chillies on top of the flame until they blister and blacken; let the skin of the tomato char and shrivel over a flame, so that the once-watery flesh inside concentrates its flavors. This smoky quality adds a new dimension to even the simplest of dishes.

Chillies: To prepare chillies, see the Ingredients listings earlier in this chapter.

Garlic: Place the unpeeled cloves of garlic on a hot, ungreased, heavy frying pan. Cook over medium heat, turning every so often, until the garlic appears charred in places and the cloves are slightly soft to the touch. Garlic may also be done a whole head at a time; each way gives a different flavor. When cool enough to handle, squeeze the soft flesh from the papery skin.

Onion: Toast as for garlic. While whole onions are usually preferred, occasionally I like to use halved onions for the more pronounced grilled flavor. When cool enough to handle, peel and chop or use as desired.

Tomatoes: Tomatoes are often roasted for Mexican sauces, soups, and stewy dishes. Sometimes I roast tomatoes by impaling them whole on forks, then holding them in an open flame until they char and sputter. A less dramatic method is to broil them: Place as many tomatoes as desired under a hot broiler and broil until evenly browned, about 15 minutes. Turn occasionally for even cooking. Place the tomatoes in a blender and whirl, skins, seeds, and all.

Another technique that gives Mexican food a certain distinction is the fact that sauce ingredients—mixtures of raw and/or roasted onions, garlic, chillies, tomatoes, and spices—may first be ground, then poured into a bit of hot oil in a frying pan, "frying the sauce," if you will. This intensifies flavors and thickens the savory mixture. Add broth, meat, rice, whatever; the fried sauce is your base.

SALSAS, RECADOS, Y ADORNOS

....

SALSAS, SAUCES, CONDIMENTS, SPICY SEASONINGS, AND GARNISHES

Raw chillies, chopped and combined with a few equally fresh and assertive flavors, enliven nearly anything they touch. Sauces such as these, known as salsas, give distinction to the simple foods of the Mexican table. A bowl of salsa transforms even the simplest meal into a distinctly Mexican one. Eggs and rice, grilled fish, meat kabobs, simple broth, fricasseed chicken . . . these dishes and many more welcome a splash of zesty sauces and relishes.

Salsas can be extremely simple or more elaborate. Some simple examples are chillies simmmered with spices, fruits, and herbs; a mixture of pickled chillies whirled into a fiery and tangy condiment; fresh tomato sauce seasoned with a sprinkling of chillies and cilantro; crumbled dried hot chillies combined with vinegar.

A practical note: Unless otherwise specified, fresh salsa will last up to 3-4 days in the refrigerator. Be forwarned, however, that it begins losing its fresh flavor and heat from the moment it is prepared. Freeze fresh salsa in ice cube trays, then plop the cubes into plastic bags and seal well. It keeps up to six months in the freezer and each cube may be used individually. While it may lose some of its punch when defrosted, it is still much better than anything found in the stores. You can always add a little more chilli, cilantro, or onion to freshen it up.

SALSA CRUDA
RAW TABLE SALSA OF CHILLIES AND TOMATOES

This is a typical simple Salsa Cruda, a variation of a food that dates back to antiquity.

1 clove garlic, chopped (optional)
1 small to medium onion, chopped
3 jalapeños or serranos, chopped
5 ripe tomatoes, peeled, seeded, and chopped

2 tablespoons chopped cilantro
Salt to taste

Combine all ingredients and serve. (Note: For a saucy consistency, puree in blender or food processor. For a chunky consistency, chop by hand and stir to blend.) ***Makes 1 to 1¹/₂ cups***

SALSA DE CHILES Y AJO
GARLIC AND CHILLI SALSA

This reeks deliciously of garlic. When I have some of this fragrant salsa on hand I use it rather generously. One trick I enjoy is heating a spoonful of oil in a pan, then adding a spoonful or two of this salsa and cooking it into a near-paste consistency, then adding simple stock. It makes the basis for soup that tastes much more complex than it has any right to.

6 cloves garlic, chopped
4 to 5 jalapeños, chopped
4 ripe tomatoes, seeded, peeled, and chopped
1 teaspoon cumin

¹/₂ cup chopped cilantro (or parsley, or combination of the two)
Dash of vinegar or lemon juice
Salt to taste

In a blender or processor, whirl the garlic and chillies into a pastelike consistency. Add remaining ingredients and whirl until the greenish mixture is the consistency you desire; whether chunky or smooth. ***Makes ³/₄ to 1 cup***

····················· **VARIATION** ·····················

NOPALE SALSA

Prepare the above salsa. After blending, add ½ cup diced cooked and drained nopales. (Do not puree the nopales.)

SALSA CON LIMON Y CILANTRO
CHILLI SALSA WITH LIME AND CILANTRO

Tart and lime-tangy, nearly green from fresh cilantro, this zesty condiment is excellent with fresh seafood or roasted meats. The salsa is at its fresh best when served within several hours of preparation.

4 cloves garlic, finely chopped
3 serranos (or to taste), finely chopped
2 to 3 ripe tomatoes, diced or chopped

1 cup finely chopped cilantro
Juice of 1 to 1½ limes
Salt to taste

Combine all ingredients and serve. ***Makes 1⅓ to 1½ cups***

SALSA PICANTE VERDE
GREEN HOT SAUCE

Unlike other green salsas, this one is based not on the tart green tomatillo, but on jalapeños and lots of fresh cilantro. A generous amount of vinegar makes it deliciously sour and puckery; as with most condiments of this sort, the amount of chillies can vary according to the variety of pepper and the eater's palate.

2 cloves garlic, finely chopped
2 jalapeños, chopped
½ cup coarsely chopped cilantro, rather tightly packed
¼ cup cider vinegar or white wine vinegar

Juice of ½ lemon or lime
¼ teaspoon cumin
Pinch turmeric
Salt to taste

Combine all ingredients in food processor, blender, or mortar and pestle, pureeing or grinding until it becomes a smooth sauce. This is best eaten the day it is made; the acid "cooks" the cilantro, soon destroying its bright green color. ***Makes about ¹/₂ cup***

....

SALSA DE CHILE GÜERO
SMOOTH-TEXTURED SALSA OF COOKED HOT CHILLIES AND TOMATOES, SONORA STYLE

This salsa is usually prepared with the güero chilli, a yellow or yellow-green variety that is milder than a jalapeño in both heat and flavor. Jalapeños also work just fine, since the thing that sets this salsa apart from others is that the chillies are first boiled, in the manner favored in northwestern Mexico, then pureed with the other ingredients. Traditionally, the blending is done in a *molcajete,* the ancient stone mortar and pestle still much used in Mexico. This sauce contains no onion, just a whiff of garlic.

The salsa can be quite hot—it all depends upon your chillies. You can use all güeros, all jalapeños, or some of each. I find this salsa at its best when it stings just enough to make things interesting.

3 to 4 medium-sized, medium-hot fresh green chillies, such as jalapeño or güero, or a mixture of the two
1 to 2 cloves garlic, chopped
²/₃ cup diced tomatoes (canned are fine; include a bit of the juice)

Juice of ¹/₂ lemon
¹/₄ to ¹/₂ teaspoon crumbled oregano leaves
¹/₄ cup water
Salt to taste

....

❶ Place chillies in saucepan and cover with water. Bring to boil and simmer, covered, about 10 minutes. Let sit until cool enough to handle.

❷ Remove stems of chillies and as much of the tough skin as possible, but leave the seeds. Place chillies in blender or food processor along with garlic and whirl until smooth, adding only enough of the tomatoes to make a sauce-like mixture. When smooth, gradually add remaining tomatoes, lemon juice, oregano, ¹/₄ cup water, and salt, and process until salsa is once again smooth.

❸ Taste for seasoning and serve as desired. ***Makes 1 cup***

....

SALSA CAMPECHE
ORANGE AND BANANA SALSA WITH MILD DRY RED CHILLIES, YUCATAN STYLE

In the lush Yucatán, tropical fruits grow with abandon, showing up in the savory dishes of the area nearly as often as in the sweet ones. In this salsa, diced banana and orange juice combine with the sweet red pepper flavor of the mild dried chilli.

Serve with grilled seafood tacos, or with Pollo de Plaza or Pollo Pibil.

1 cup orange juice
3 New Mexico/California dried mild chillies (or any smooth-skinned mildish chile; guajillos make a lovely, if more picanté, salsa).

½ onion, finely chopped
1 clove garlic, chopped
½ underripe banana, diced
Salt to taste

❶ Heat orange juice to just boiling. Place chillies in a bowl and pour hot juice over it. Cover and let cool to room temperature.

❷ Cut each chile open lengthwise, then scrape the flesh away from the tough skin. Place scraped flesh in a bowl with enough of the orange juice to make a thin paste.

❸ To the chilli-orange juice mixture, add onion, garlic, and banana. Let sit for at least an hour before serving to let the flavors meld. Add salt to taste. *Makes 2 cups*

SALSA VERDE DE TOMATILLO
GREEN TOMATILLO SALSA

Salsa verde is ubiquitous in Mexico; a small bowl of the tart and tangy, often quite hot salsa accompanies whatever else is on the menu. Based on the tomatillo verde, or husk tomato (*Physalis edulis*), its distinctive flavor adds verve to simmered chicken, fish or egg dishes, corn-based dishes such as *chilaquiles* or enchiladas, tacos, and tamales. Salsa verde is particularly good added to gazpacho, creating an exciting bowl of fire and ice.

Salsa verde makes a contrast both in color and flavor when it is served in addition to red tomato or chilli-based sauces. Often a combination of red salsa, green salsa, and a dollop of sour cream will garnish a dish, representing the three colors of Mexico's flag.

1 lb. fresh tomatillos, quartered, or 1 large (16-oz.) can

2 to 3 jalapeños or serranos, chopped (seed if desired)

1 small onion, chopped

1 clove garlic, chopped

2 tablespoons (or to taste) chopped cilantro

Salt to taste

Cumin to taste (optional)

❶ If using fresh tomatillos, place in a saucepan and just cover with water. Bring to boil, then reduce heat and simmer until tomatillos are soft but not mushy, about 10 minutes. If using canned tomatillos, simply open the can and drain gently, taking care not to lose the tomatillo flesh.

❷ Place the cooked tomatillos in a blender or food processor along with the other ingredients and whirl until smooth. Chill and serve at cool room temperature. *Makes 2 cups*

·· **VARIATIONS** ··

COOKED SALSA VERDE

For a subtly different flavor, simmer the prepared salsa 5 to 10 minutes, or long enough to smooth out the sharp edges of raw onion and garlic. This salsa is particularly good spooned onto creamy mild cheese such as mozzarella, then grilled until melty and sublime. Eat with soft corn tortillas.

MOLE VERDE

This is a mild salsa rather than picante. Simmer meats or fish in it, spoon it over poached eggs or into soups. Mole Verde is delicious as a sauce for cheese enchiladas, topped with cooling sour cream.

Prepare Salsa Verde de Tomatillo but decrease the amount of chillies by at least half, or to taste, and thin the salsa with enough stock to make a cooking liquid for simmering pork, chicken, or fish.

TOMATILLO-CHIPOTLE SALSA

Reduce the amount of chillies to one, and for every ½ cup Salsa, add ½ teaspoon chipotle marinade (or to taste). The balance of smoky chipotle and tart tomatillo is intriguing.

SALSA VERDE DE CHILE ARBOL

Omit fresh green chillies altogether. Instead, crumble several árbol or other small hot dried chillies, lightly fry in a little oil, then whirl in blender with the tomatillos and seasonings. The heat level may be tingly or torrid, depending upon the amount of chillies you choose.

SALSA DE NARANJA
TROPICAL ORANGE SALSA

This salsa has the distinctive flavor and heat of the habanero, the Caribbean's torrid contribution to the chilli front. The habanero is not particularly fleshy or juicy; its fiery heat is dry and somewhat herby. Use fresh cayenne or serrano if habanero is unavailable.

1 small to medium onion, chopped
1 clove garlic, chopped
2 tablespoons olive oil
1½ cups chopped tomatoes (canned are fine)
1 habanero chilli, chopped (or 2–3 serranos, or 1–2 cayenne chilli)

¼ cup orange juice plus rind grated from ¼ orange (or use Seville orange juice)
Pinch oregano leaves or, if available, several sprigs fresh epazote, chopped
Salt to taste

❶ Sauté onion and garlic in olive oil until just translucent, then add tomatoes and chilli. Cook until tomatoes have softened and sauce is somewhat thickened.

❷ Add orange juice, bring mixture to a boil, and cook until thick and saucy.

❸ Remove from heat and add orange rind, oregano or epazote, and salt. Serve at room temperature. *Makes 2 cups*

VARIATION

A shot of cumin adds an earthy, dusky quality to the tart citrus flavors.

SALSA DE CHILE PASILLA
PASILLA SALSA

This salsa is rich with mild dark chilli flavors and gets a tang from the addition of tomatillos and lime. It makes a delicious spread for warm corn tortillas wrapped around shredded pork or duck, black beans, a dip for crisp fried tortilla strips, or accompaniment for grilled fish. Spread it on crusty bread or *naan* (Indian tandoor-baked bread) and top with shredded meat, lettuce, and beans for a savory torta-style sandwich.

4 dried pasilla chillies, or 2 pasilla
and 2 ancho chillies
4 tomatillos, cooked
1 clove garlic, chopped
1 small onion, chopped

¹/₄ to ¹/₂ jalapeño, chopped, or more to
taste
Juice of ¹/₄ lime
Salt to taste

. . . .

❶ Lightly toast the dried chillies over an open flame, then place in a bowl and cover with hot (just under boiling) water. Place a plate over bowl and let the chillies sit and plump at least 30 minutes, preferably an hour. (You want the chillies to soften so completely that you can scrape the flesh from the tough skin.)

❷ Remove the stems from the chillies and carefully scrape the flesh from the skin using a blunt knife. Discard the skins and place the flesh in a blender or food processor along with tomatillos, garlic, onion, and jalapeño.

❸ Whirl until salsa-like in consistency, adding a bit of the soaking liquid if needed. Season with lime juice and salt. *Makes about 1¹/₂ cups*

. . . .

SALSA DE JALAPEÑOS EN ESCABECHE
SALSA OF PICKLED JALAPEÑOS

The simple pureeing of a handful of pickled chillies results in a terrific salsa with a pickley, picante tang. It is, however, as fiery as pure undiluted pickled chillies, so a small dab is the recommended portion. I particularly like it on starchy bland foods such as *molletes* (hot bean and cheese sandwiches on crusty French rolls).

15 jalapeños *en escabeche* (or to
taste), sliced
Liquid from the can or bottle, enough
to make a salsa consistency when
you puree the chillies

. . . .

Place the sliced chillies and a bit of the brining liquid in a blender. Whirl until it forms a salsa consistency. Serve—carefully—as desired. *Makes 1¹/₂ cups*

. . . .

SALSA DE JALAPEÑOS EN ESCABECHE Y JITOMATE
SALSA OF PICKLED CHILLIES, TOMATOES, AND ONIONS

A nose-tingling, invigorating salsa. Feel free to vary the amount of jalapeños: using seven chillies results in an intense salsa, four is a bit calmer, two still gives enough heat for interest but leaves your mouth relatively unmolested. I tend to use about four. Of course, the strength depends on the heat of the chillies.

Since this salsa is so tangy and sharp, I particularly like it with a richly spiced but mild dish such as tacos made of chicken or turkey and Mole Poblano.

2 to 7 jalapeños *en escabeche*, to taste
½ onion, chopped
1 clove garlic, chopped

1 medium-sized ripe tomato, diced
Several generous pinches crumbled dried oregano
Salt to taste

Slice jalapeños and place in blender or mortar and pestle. Whirl (or pound) into a chunky puree. Add onion, garlic, and tomato. Process until it reaches desired consistency. Season with oregano and salt. ***Makes about ½ cup***

SALSA DE CHILE CHIPOTLE Y JITOMATE
CHIPOTLE CHILLI AND TOMATO SALSA

The word *chipotle* is Nahuatl for smoked chilli, since the chipotle is the smoked dried jalapeño.

Tomatoey and smoky hot, this is a smooth and lively salsa welcome on nearly any taco, tostada, rustic bean burrito or torta, or spooned onto enchiladas. Try it on a sandwich of roast pork on crusty rolls, or alongside a dish of mild peppers, tomatoes and braised beef.

½ onion, chopped
½ cup tomatoes, roasted, peeled, and seeded (or use canned, including juice)
Pinch crumbled dried oregano

3 canned chipotle chillies, coarsely chopped
Juice of ¼ lime
Salt to taste

In a blender, whirl onion and tomatoes to a chunky salsa consistency. Add oregano, chipotles, and lime juice and whirl until relatively smooth. Season with salt. ***Makes 1 cup***

....

SALSA DE CHILES CHIPOTLES
SWEET AND HOT SMOOTH SALSA OF CHIPOTLE CHILLIES

This salsa is smooth, hot, and slightly sweet, delicious dabbed onto soft tacos garnished with shredded cabbage, or sprinkled onto *carnitas* or grilled meat or fish. For a hotter and smokier salsa, increase the amount of chillies; for a milder salsa, use fewer chillies.

3 chipotle chillies, chopped
2 tablespoons adobo marinade from the chillies
1 cup tomato sauce or diced tomatoes and their juice

2 tablespoons vinegar
½ cup boiling water
2 to 3 tablespoons dark brown sugar

....

❶ In blender or food processor, whirl chillies and marinade, then add tomato sauce. When smooth, add vinegar, water, and brown sugar, blending until smooth. Thin down with more water if needed; sauce should be rather thin. This lasts longer than most salsas: about a week well-sealed in refrigerator; up to six months in freezer, though it loses some of its punch. ***Makes about 2 cups***

....

SALSA DE CHILES AL CARBON
FLAME-ROASTED CHILLI SALSA

Roasted chilli gives a new dimension to salsa. This one is based on mild green peppers as well as chillies, contrasting with a traditional salsa based only on fiery jalapeños. (That one is pure fire—actually, it is quite good, but with the particular pleasure that comes from surviving danger). This one has the flavor minus the pain.

2 poblano or Anaheim chillies
3 jalapeños, or to taste
3 cloves garlic, chopped

Juice of ½ lime, or to taste
1 teaspoon salt
2 teaspoons olive oil

....

❶ Roast the chillies over an open flame or under a very hot broiler until they are scorched and charred. Place them in a paper or plastic bag or tightly covered bowl until they sweat their skins off. Remove skin and dice the flesh.

❷ Finely chop garlic in blender or food processor, then add chillies, lime juice, and salt. Whirl until it forms a saucelike consistency, then stir in olive oil. Taste for seasoning, and add more chillies if needed. ***Makes about 1 cup***

....

SALSA PICANTE A LA YUCATECA
VERY HOT ROASTED CHILLI SALSA, YUCATAN STYLE

This makes a salsa either very hot or tinged with fire, depending on the chilli you use. I've heard it referred to as *salsa de los machos*, "salsa for he-men," in honor of its potency. The habanero, or Scotch bonnet, is the authentic ingredient, but volatile. Serranos, fresh cayenne, or even jalapeños are all acceptable substitutes. I have added mild green sweet pepper for bulk and body.

Removing the seeds and inside membranes from the chillies tones down the heat. You may find yourself wanting more chillies than the recipe calls for, since the heat is almost always unpredictable. Whether you make this with a torrid heat level, or tone it down to near gentility, it is a lovely salsa, with the delicious quality of roasted peppers and the tart accent of lime.

1 green sweet pepper
1 habanero chilli, or more to taste or
3–5 serranos, jalapeños, or fresh
cayenne

¼ cup lime juice
Salt to taste

....

❶ Toast pepper and chilli(es) on an ungreased frying pan to char evenly. Remove and let sit in covered dish or sealed bag to separate skin from flesh.

❷ Scrape peppers with a sharp paring knife to remove the hard, papery skin as well as the seeds, membranes, and stem. Chop the flesh coarsely.

❸ Combine chopped chilli with lime juice and salt. Serve as desired. ***Makes ½ to ¾ cup***

....

SALSA DE CHILES ARBOL
VINEGAR-BASED HOT SALSA WITH ARBOL CHILLIES

This is pure fire, its incendiary pleasure best shaken out in tiny drops. And it is *muy delicioso,* transforming even the simplest, blandest dish with an electric shock of chilli-infused vinegar. This recipe makes a tiny amount, since it is powerful stuff. By all means make a larger batch if desired: it lasts nearly forever.

6 to 10 small hot dried chillies, crumbled
½ cup vinegar
½ teaspoon salt

In blender, whirl chillies together with vinegar and salt until mixture forms a thin sauce. **Makes about ½ cup**

······ VARIATION ······

TANGY-HOT TOMATO ARBOL SALSA
To the above hot sauce, add 1 medium-sized tomato, diced, and a generous pinch of oregano. Whirl until smooth. Unlike the basic recipe, this must be kept refrigerated and lasts only several days.

Salsas para Cocidar/Sauces for Cooking

The Mexican kitchen is rich with unpretentious yet full-flavored cooking sauces: for marinating, simmering, baking, or saucing whatever is on the menu. Many of the sauces found throughout this book, incorporated into other dishes, can be used to sauce whatever you desire; Mole Poblano immediately comes to mind, as does the sauce from Pollo de Plaza.

SALSA RANCHERA
TOMATO AND MILD CHILLI SAUCE WITH GREEN PEPPERS

Salsa Ranchera is a peasanty mixture of onions, peppers, and tomatoes; it may be chunky or smooth and may be found blanketing a sautéed chicken, simmering a handful of prawns, nestled next to a thin grilled steak, or ladled over fried eggs for the classic Huevos Rancheros. It is an informal sauce, one that I usually prepare according to the dictates of my cupboard: as long as there are tomatoes and a few fresh chillies, there are the makings for Salsa Ranchera. Onions, garlic, cilantro, and peppers, a dash of cinnamon or cumin, might add their savor. It is always delicious.

2 small to medium onions, coarsely chopped or sliced lengthwise
2 to 4 cloves garlic, coarsely chopped
1 green pepper, cut into strips
2 to 3 jalapeños (for more heat, use the chillies raw and include the seeds; for less heat, roast and peel chillies first, discarding the seeds)
2 tablespoons bland vegetable oil
1 teaspoon cumin
1/2 teaspoon (or to taste) mild chilli powder such as ancho or New Mexico/California

10 ripe tomatoes, roasted, seeded, and peeled, then diced (or about 2 1/2 to 3 cups diced canned tomatoes, with only enough of the juice to make a good sauce)
Generous pinch crumbled oregano
Salt to taste
2 tablespoons coarsely chopped cilantro (optional)

❶ Lightly sauté onions, garlic, green pepper, and chillies in vegetable oil until onions are softened; sprinkle with cumin and chilli powder and cook a few minutes longer.

❷ Add tomatoes, oregano, and salt. Simmer until saucelike in consistency.

❸ Serve as desired, sprinkled with cilantro if you like. ***Makes about 2 1/2 to 3 cups***

SALSA DE CHILE VERDE
GREEN CHILLI SALSA, SONORA STYLE

Unlike its Mexican counterpart that derives its color from the tomatillo, *salsa verde* in Sonora (and in New Mexico and Arizona) is green from a large quantity of mild chillies. There, the chilli is doted on for its fine vegetable flavor, the heat a welcome incidental. Relatively mild, and based on stock and tomatoes as well as chillies, it is used as a cooking sauce to simmer meat, to layer tortillas, or to roll up in burritos or tacos.

3 to 4 poblano or Anaheim chillies
3 to 4 green peppers
1 ½ cups chicken or other stock
1 medium onion, chopped
3 cloves garlic, chopped
2 tablespoons (or less) vegetable oil

1 tablespoon flour
1 ½ cups chopped or diced tomatoes and juice (canned are fine)
½ teaspoon ground cumin
Salt and pepper to taste

❶ Roast the chillies and peppers over an open flame, then peel (for directions on roasting fresh chillies, see page 15).

❷ Dice the peeled peppers and chillies.

❸ Place the peppers and chillies in a blender and add about ½ cup stock. Whirl to puree into a chunky mixture. Set aside.

❹ Sauté onion and garlic in the oil; when softened, sprinkle in flour and cook a few minutes, then add the reserved pepper puree. Stir well to incorporate the flour. Continue to cook a few minutes.

❺ Add the remaining stock and tomatoes. Simmer for about 10 to 15 minutes or until saucy and flavorful. Season with cumin, salt, and pepper. *Makes about 2½ to 3 cups*

SALSA DE CHILE ROJO
MILD RED CHILLI SAUCE

This absolutely simple puree of mild red chillies is brick red, with the flavor of pure, sweet chilli. It will taste of the essence of whichever chilli you choose. This is the basic red chilli sauce used to simmer meats, poultry, seafood, vegetables, and beans, and to smear onto tortillas instead of butter. Clear meat broths, bowls of simmered hominy, chunks of rugged meats, all are enlivened by spoonfuls of this sauce.

5 large dried New Mexico/California chilli pods, or whichever other chilli you desire
1 cup hot (just under boiling) water or broth

1 to 2 cloves garlic, chopped
Large pinch salt

❶ Remove stems from chillies, then cut open and shake out the seeds.

❷ Lightly toast chillies, either in an ungreased frying pan over medium heat or over an open flame. You want them only to be fragrant, not to darken too much or to burn.

❸ Crumble or tear the chillies, then place in bowl and pour hot water over them. Cover the bowl with a plate and set stand for about an hour or until they soften.

❹ Whirl chillies and their soaking liquid in blender or food processor, along with garlic and salt, blending until smooth.

❺ Press through a strainer or sieve to remove the coarse skin. *Makes about 1 ½ cups*

VARIATION

CLASSIC NORTHERN ENCHILADA SAUCE

Cook 2 tablespoons flour in an equal amount of oil. When cooked through, add the above chilli paste and stir to mix well. Cook to thicken, then thin down with enough stock to reach the consistency desired. Add a squeeze of fresh lime. Use as desired, especially for simple enchiladas.

SALSA ADOBO ❖ TART AND SPICED MILD CHILLI SAUCE

Adobo sauce is a puree of chillies seasoned with sweet spices and tart vinegar. It is often used as a marinade, with meat or fresh frequently cooked in the same sauce after marinating in it.

Prepare the Salsa de Chile Rojo, using 3 New Mexico/California chillies and 2 to 3 ancho chillies, and seasoning the mixture with 3 tablespoons cider vinegar or red wine vinegar, 6 cloves roasted garlic, ¼ teaspoon each of cumin, cinnamon, oregano, thyme, powdered bay leaf (optional), and a pinch of cloves. Add salt and pepper to taste.

For an adobo paste rather than sauce, use only enough of the soaking liquid to make a paste consistency.

....

PIPIAN SAUCE—YUCATAN
....
GREEN SAUCE OF TOASTED AND PUREED PUMPKIN SEEDS

An ancient food, *pipián* sauces based on ground seeds, are eaten all over Mexico, but are especially enjoyed in the Yucatán. When Cortes' men were feted by Montezuma, *pipián* was on the menu.

Classically served with roasted duck or pork, or with any of the myriad egg and tortilla dishes the Yucatán is particularly fond of. Smear some onto a soft corn tortilla and fill with scrambled eggs and browned chopped meat; dip tortillas into the *pipián* and roll around diced hard-cooked egg, then sauce it all with a spicy tomato sauce. Legumbres en Pipián combines the pureed seed sauce with mixed vegetables.

12 oz. (about 2 cups) hulled pumpkin seeds
1 teaspoon vegetable oil
1 teaspoon cumin
1 teaspoon salt
2 roasted and peeled jalapeño chillies

2 cloves garlic, chopped
2 tablespoons fresh cilantro
Juice of ½ lime
Hot but not boiling broth (chicken or vegetable)
Several sprigs epazote, chopped (optional)

....

❶ Lightly fry or toast pumpkin seeds in vegetable oil until golden. Add cumin and salt and continue frying a few minutes more, until fragrant and slightly browned.

❷ Finely chop or grind the seeds in blender or food processor, then puree with remaining ingredients to form the consistency desired. ***Makes about 2¹/₂ cups***

Relishes and Condiments

Chunky mixtures of raw chillies and/or pickled vegetables (*en escabeche*) are often served instead of or in addition to a smooth salsa.

PICO DE GALLO
DICED RAW CHILLI RELISH, SONORA STYLE

Pico de gallo (literally, "rooster's beak") usually refers to a relishlike mixture of diced crisp ingredients. It is said that its whimsical name is derived from the diced bits of crisp vegetables that appear much like chicken feed. In Central Mexico the mixture is usually jícama and orange, more a snack than a relish. In Texas, however, *pico de gallo* usually refers to a salsalike condiment eaten with fajitas, strips of grilled meat rolled up into soft flour tortillas. The relish is spooned onto the fajita before it is rolled up.

4 to 5 ripe tomatoes, diced
5 or 6 green onions, thinly sliced
5 radishes or ¹/₄ cup jícama, chopped coarsely or diced
3 tablespoons coarsely chopped cilantro

2 to 3 jalapeños, diced (for greater heat, increase amount of chillies and include seeds; for less heat, discard seeds and decrease amount of chillies)
Juice of ¹/₂ lime
Salt to taste

Combine all ingredients and serve immediately. ***Makes about 2 cups***

SALSA MEXICANA
CHUNKY CHILLI TABLE RELISH

The consistency of this relish should be decidedly chunky—bits of tomato and onion dotted with flecks of cilantro and breathlessly hot green chilli. It is an invigorating salsa, perhaps the most basic dish of the Mexican kitchen, and can accordingly be varied endlessly: a squeeze of lime and/or orange, a few mashed tomatillos, green onions instead of white onion, and so on.

4 small to medium-sized ripe tomatoes, diced

1 small to medium onion, chopped or diced

3 tablespoons chopped cilantro, or to taste

6 serrano or jalapeño chillies, coarsely chopped

Generous shaking of salt

....

Stir to combine all ingredients. ***Makes about 1 to 1 1/2 cups***

....

AJOS Y CHILES CHIPOTLES
RELISH OF ONIONS, GARLIC,
AND SMOKY CHIPOTLE CHILLIES

This makes a startlingly good condiment, with tangy tart acidic flavors, pungent garlic and onion, and the smoky nuance of chipotles. Serve as an accompaniment to nearly anything—grilled chicken or fish, pureed black beans—or simply wrap up in a warm, fresh corn tortilla along with a chunk of mild cheese such as *queso fresco* or fresh pecorino. I adore a few chunks of the garlic cloves, coarsely chopped, wrapped in soft, warm *naan* or *focaccio* bread for an invigorating cross-cultural snack.

8 cloves garlic

2 onions, peeled and thickly sliced

3 chipotle chillies, whole or diced

5 whole cloves or a pinch ground cloves

1/4 teaspoon thyme leaves

Several grindings coarse black pepper

Salt to taste

Juice of 1 lemon

Cider vinegar

....

❶ Pound the garlic cloves with a heavy object to lightly crush them and remove skin.

❷ Layer onions with garlic and chipotles, then sprinkle with cloves, thyme, black pepper, and salt.

❸ Squeeze lemon juice over mixture, then add vinegar to cover. Store in refrigerator, well covered, for up to two weeks. ***Makes about 2 cups***

CEBOLLAS CON JALAPEÑOS EN ESCABECHE
CHOPPED ONIONS WITH PICKLED CHILLIES

This is a simple one, and a good way of making use of the pickley brine from jalapeños *en escabeche*. Lemon adds a piquant accent to the pungent onions and hot pickled chillies.

1 to 2 onions, finely chopped
Several pickled jalapeños, chopped, plus a few spoonfuls of the brine

Pinch dried oregano
Juice of ½ lemon

Combine all ingredients. Serve as an accompaniment to hearty foods, especially grilled ones, rice dishes, and beans. Sometimes I spoon it onto hot baked potatoes or marinated grilled potato slices.

CEBOLLAS EN ESCABECHE A LA YUCATECA
PICKLED RED ONION SLICES, YUCATAN STYLE

This simple tangy relish is served on Panuchos, tacos, with various roasted and simmered chicken dishes, with seafood, Pollo Pibil, and indeed nearly anything you might eat in the Yucatán.

3 large red onions, thinly sliced
Boiling water to cover
White or cider vinegar (mild, or diluted with a bit of water and a dash of lime or lemon juice), just enough to cover the onions

Large pinch crumbled dried oregano leaves
Salt and pepper to taste

❶ Place onions in a bowl. Pour boiling water over them, then immediately drain in a colander.

❷ Return the drained onions to a bowl. Add remaining ingredients and let chill for at least 30 minutes. ***Makes about 2 cups***

LEGUMBRES EN ESCABECHE
MARINATED MIXED VEGETABLES

In Mexico and the U.S. you can buy jars of mixed vegetables much like Italian *giardiniera* pickles, but made fiery from a generous amount of hot chillies. In fact, *giardiniera* vegetables can easily be given a south-of-the-border flavor by adding a bit of quickly sautéed hot chillies and a big pinch of oregano.

4 carrots, thickly sliced diagonally
(or use a crinkly cut knife)
1 or 2 onions, thinly sliced
About 2 tablespoons vegetable oil
½ cauliflower, cut into florets

1 stalk celery
4 or 5 jalapeños or serranos
½ cup white vinegar
1 teaspoon salt
1 teaspoon crumbled oregano leaves

❶ Quickly sauté carrots and onions in a little of the oil, then set aside in a bowl. Repeat in two or more batches with cauliflower and celery, using the remaining oil.

❷ Sauté chillies, then add vinegar to pan and heat. Pour chilli-vinegar mixture over the mixed vegetables. Season with salt and oregano.

❸ Let cool and store covered in refrigerator. Lasts about a week. Enjoy with all sorts of dishes, especially crisp *tacos de camarones*, shrimp tacos. ***Makes about 2 cups***

VARIATION

ESCABECHE DE COL ❖ LIGHTLY PICKLED CABBAGE
A Mayan version of Legumbres en Escabeche: Decrease the amount of carrots by half and use ½ head of cabbage, thinly sliced, in place of the cauliflower and celery. Serve with grilled meats, chillied black beans, and tortillas.

CAMARONES EN ESCABECHE
SHRIMP OR PRAWNS WITH PICKLED CHILLIES

Nuggets of cooked shrimp or prawns tossed with jalapeños *en escabeche* make a sensational relish, especially for potato tostadas or cheese melted onto a flour tortilla.

At its best when you begin with excellent jalapeños *en escabeche,* the type chock-full of seasonings and flavor. If your chillies are a bit pale, add a pinch of oregano, and other seasonings to taste.

⅓ cup jalapeños *en escabeche,*   **1 ⅓ cups cooked shrimp**
including a few tablespoons of the
brine

....

Combine and serve. Do not expect this seafood-based relish to last as long as other pickled foods do. Keep it refrigerated, and use within several days.

....

Recados/Spice Pastes

Recaudo, in Spanish, is the term for seasonings. In Mexican Spanish, however, it has evolved into *recado,* a term for mixtures of spice pastes.

Throughout Mexico spice pastes are used as the basis for countless sauces, moles, *pipiáns,* and marinades. Sometimes they're sold in foil or paper-wrapped tabletlike chunks, other times in jars. They are at their best when sold loose, looking like great piles of artist's pigments, as they are in the Yucatán where these spice pastes contribute to the subtle and distinctive flavors of the local cuisine.

The array of *recados* in the Mérida marketplace looks like an artist's palette gone amok, with large piles of pure color: yellow, red, black, green. Often they are labeled simply *"recado negro"* (black charred chilli paste) or *"recado rojo"* (red achiote/chilli paste), *pipián* (from pumpkin seeds), or *"para pescado,"* *"para bistek,"* etc. (for fish, beef, etc.). They appear mysterious and smell pungently fetching. The Mayan vendor, with her strong, proud, and inscrutable face, will scrape off a bit for you and wrap it in a cone of paper.

RECADO ESCABECHE
·································
ESCABECHE PASTE OF SPICES AND ROASTED GARLIC

This paste is based on roasted garlic, the haunting aroma of which hangs heavy over the fragrant mounds of spices. The whole unpeeled cloves are cooked on an ungreased pan until they are softened and lightly charred, then their sweet, soft flesh is squeezed out and combined with the other spices as well as a bit of vinegar and flour. An interesting note: like in many of the *recados*, there are no chillies at all in this mixture.

To use, spread the paste as is, or dissolve a bit in a small amount of grapefruit or Seville orange juice until it reaches the consistency desired.

Escabeche paste is especially good in Pollo en Escabeche de Valladolid, or try adding a spoonful or two to sautéed swordfish. Top with Cebollas en Escabeche à la Yucateca.

15 to 20 large cloves garlic, whole and unpeeled
¹/₂ teaspoon ground cumin or ³/₄ teaspoon cumin seeds
1 teaspoon black pepper, coarsely ground
¹/₂ teaspoon ground cloves (about 25 cloves, the little heads of the "nails" only, crushed)

2 teaspoons crumbled oregano leaves, or crushed bay leaves
¹/₂ teaspoon salt
1 tablespoon sherry vinegar, cider vinegar, or bitter (Seville) orange juice
1 level to heaping tablespoon flour

···

❶ On an ungreased heavy flat frying pan, cook the whole unpeeled garlic cloves until they are charred in places and softened through. Remove from heat and let cool.

❷ Lightly toast ground cumin or cumin seeds over medium-low heat until they grow fragrant and darken slightly. Remove from heat and let cool.

❸ In a blender or spice grinder, combine black pepper, cloves, oregano or bay leaves, salt, and reserved cumin. Grind until well combined.

❹ Squeeze the soft flesh of the garlic cloves into the spice mixture and combine into a paste, then add vinegar and flour, mixing well. Place in refrigerator and let ripen at least 2 hours; overnight is even better. ***Makes about ¹/₃ cup***

···

RECADO DE AJO Y SALPIMENTADO
ROAST AND RAW GARLIC–SALT AND PEPPER SPICE PASTE

Pungent, salty, and filled with the aroma of peppercorns, coriander, cinnamon, sweet roasted garlic, and sharp raw garlic, pureed onion and the freshness of parsley. Like the above *recado,* this one has no chillies whatsoever; it gets its body from the large amount of onion and garlic.

Rub this paste onto anything that you would season with salt and pepper, especially meat or poultry to be grilled. I especially like to coat chunks of peeled half-cooked potatoes with a bit of this paste and a drizzle of oil, then roast them until crusty brown. Toss with another dab of the *recado* before serving.

10 whole, unpeeled cloves of roasted or pan-toasted garlic
6 cloves raw garlic, finely chopped
2 teaspoons black pepper
4 cloves, crushed
2 teaspoons crushed oregano leaves

½ teaspoon cinnamon
2 teaspoons coriander
2 teaspoons salt
1 onion, finely chopped
1 teaspoon finely chopped parsley

❶ Squeeze flesh of roasted garlic into blender and puree with raw garlic.

❷ Add black pepper, cloves, oregano, cinnamon, coriander, and salt; puree as smooth as you can get it. Add onion and parsley and whirl into a paste.

❸ Store in refrigerator for 3 to 4 days. ***Makes about ½ cup***

RECADO NEGRO
"BLACK" SEASONING PASTE

Not really black, this paste's deep, dark color comes from charring ancho or negro chillies over an open flame. To ensure that they really blacken, the chillies are first sprinkled with vodka or tequila; as they hit the stove they burst into flame.

Recado Negro is traditionally used to season both the stuffing and turkey of the Yucatecan specialty, *pave relleno en negro.* A spoonful of Recado Negro is good added to strips of sautéed nopales, along with a few leaves of epazote. Try a soft taco or a corn tortilla warmed in a lightly oiled pan and spread with a small amount of Recado Negro, topped with a generous spoon of sour cream and a sprinkle of cilantro. Recado Negro also makes an excellent seasoning paste for *frijoles negros refritos,* refried black beans. Add a spoonful or two to the sautéeing onions before you add the mashed beans.

6 large ancho chillies (for a sweeter flavor), or mulatto or negro chillies (for a drier, more astringent flavor)

Tequila or vodka for sprinkling

2 tablespoons achiote seeds, soaked overnight in ½ cup mixture of orange juice and grapefruit juice (if achiote seeds are not available, substitute 2 teaspoons paprika mixed with the juices)

6 cloves or allspice berries, crushed (or a pinch ground cloves)

½ teaspoon ground cumin

1½ teaspoons black pepper

1 head roasted garlic, cool enough to handle, or 15 or so large unpeeled garlic cloves pan-toasted (as for Recado Escabeche)

1½ teaspoons crumbled oregano leaves

1 teaspoon salt

....

❶ Sprinkle the chillies with tequila or vodka, a few generous drops per chilli.

❷ Char over an open flame; keep your face, clothing, and hair away from the process, as the liquid is flammable and will ignite. I find the safest method is to place the pan on top of the *unlit* gas stove, then turn it on and light it quickly. The chillies will catch fire immediately and need cooking for only a minute or so. Turn off the gas and let the flames burn themselves out. You'll probably have to do this in several batches. Alternately, you could line the sprinkled chillies on a flat baking sheet and grill, letting them catch fire and burn themselves out in the same manner.

❸ Take the charred, blackened chillies and remove stems and seeds. Cut or tear the chillies into small pieces and place in blender or food processor. Whirl until it forms a powder or meal, then add remaining ingredients, pureeing until mixture attains the consistency of a paste.

❹ Store well covered in the refrigerator; should last up to about 5 days. *Makes about ¾ cup*

....

RECADO ROJO ACHIOTE
YUCATECAN RED ACHIOTE PASTE

Since this is most often used to prepare Pollo Pibil, directions are in the Pollo Pibil recipe. Like the other *recados*, it may be added to whatever you choose: smear it onto meats for grilling, use to season rice dishes, or thin it with a bit of Seville orange juice (or orange and grapefruit juice mixed half and half), then mix with chopped onions, roasted red bell peppers, green olives, and chopped cilantro or parsley. Serve over fish.

·············· **VARIATION** ··············

ACHIOTE PASTE WITH LIME AND TURMERIC OR MINT
This Yucatecan spice paste bears the distinctly Moorish or Middle Eastern accent that occasionally marks the food of this region. To the basic achiote paste add a dash of lime juice and a sprinkle of turmeric *or* spoonful of chopped fresh mint, to taste.

RECADO ROJO ENCHILADO
RED CHILLI AND CITRUS SPICE PASTE (FOR GRILLING)

Use this chilli and citrus spice paste for any marinade or wherever a citrus and chilli paste is called for. It adds an extraordinary savor.

3 cloves garlic, finely chopped
1 to 2 red or green jalapeños or serranos, chopped
3 tablespoons New Mexico or guajillo chilli powder
2 tablespoons ancho chilli powder
1 teaspoon cumin seeds
1/2 teaspoon oregano

1/2 teaspoon salt
3 tablespoons olive oil
Juice of 1 orange, plus the grated rind of 1/2 orange
Juice and grated rind of 1/2 lime
1 tablespoon tequila (optional)
1/4 to 1/2 cup chopped cilantro (optional)

Combine all ingredients and mix well. Use to coat meat, fish, or poultry as desired, letting it marinate for 30 minutes to overnight, depending upon the meat/fish chosen. Storage: Lasts up to a week, well covered, in the refrigerator, nearly indefinitely if frozen. ***Makes about 1 cup***

·· **VARIATION** ····································

CHILE PASTE WRAPPED IN CORN HUSKS

For a subtle fragrance and unique presentation, serve the chilli paste wrapped in softened corn husks, tamale style. Spice pastes have been served in the Veracruz region like this since pre-Hispanic times. No need to cook, simply wrap and store until ready to use, for up to 3 days in the refrigerator.

Banana leaves may also be used. Heat to make pliable (see special ingredients) then spoon in the desired amount of chilli paste, and fold into a rectangular, tamale-like parcel.

···

Adornos/Garnishes

Along with salsas, fresh garnishes are the hallmark of Mexican cuisine. A few suggestions to strew over chicken, meats, fish, or vegetarian dishes:

◆ Shredded raw cabbage tossed with vinaigrette and oregano
◆ Sliced red onion, thinly sliced jalapeños or serranos, crumbled oregano
◆ Diced pineapple, shredded white or red cabbage, sliced avocado
◆ Julienned jícama, diced orange, and red radishes
◆ Chopped cilantro, sliced pickled jalapeños, diced onion
◆ Diced tomatoes, onion, avocado, strips of
chipotle chilli (sour cream, optional)
◆ Thinly sliced lettuce, diced radishes, green onions, black or green olives
◆ Sour cream mixed with finely chopped or pureed chillies or cilantro

APERITIVOS, BOCADOS, Y ANTOJITOS

·······································

APPETIZERS, LITTLE BITES, AND STREET FOOD SNACKS

Mexican cuisine, with its bold flavors, tradition of street food, and strong drink, offers a wide variety of savory snacks, or "little bites." They can be almost crudely simple—potato crisps with salsa, shrimp marinated with chillies, fruit peppered with cayenne—but they are always filled with the zest that characterizes life south of the border.

I think about the roads near the pyramid of Chichen Itza, in the Yucatán, where street vendors sell sweet juicy oranges that are powdered with red-hot cayenne pepper. They startle and refresh, perfect in that region where the air can be so hot and oppressive that it feels like a thick, warm, moist blanket.

I think about two-bite *taquitos* in Mexico City, filled with shreds of charcoal-grilled meat, a smear of an extraordinary chilli paste, and a sprinkle of finely chopped onions. In the state of Tabasco, I enjoyed fire-roasted and smoked fish, shredded and doused with pickled chillies. In Veracruz I sampled exquisitely fresh shellfish, piled into glasses and dressed simply with a hit of hot salsa, a splash of lime, a scattering of onions.

Many of the dishes in other chapters are traditionally enjoyed as an appetizer or party snack. Peruse the chapter on tortilla dishes for ideas; most can be prepared in diminutive portions. Also, many of Mexico's best starters are based on fish and seafood: refer to the seafood chapter for Ostiones con Salsa de Lima, Camarones a la Parilla, Camarones "Coctel," in addition to the classic Cebiche or Ceviche.

THREE GUACAMOLES

Guacamole, that unctuous green puree of avocado, is nearly synonymous with the term Mexican food. Since the delicate avocado is so mild and creamy on its own, it begs a contrast of lots of lemon or lime and enough chilli flavor to bring it to life.

Guacamole is served as a dip, surrounded with raw vegetables and/or tortilla chips, or as a sauce for tacos, rich roasted meat dishes, chillied stews, soups, grilled fish, robust sandwiches on crusty rolls, enchiladas, and on and on.

Sometimes in restaurants the waiters will prepare guacamole at the table with great flourish, mashing the avocados with the traditional *molcajete,* adding chopped tomato, onions, chillies, and lemon juice. It's fun to watch this ballet of guacamole-making, though I usually find these pristine concoctions on the boring side and spoon in the salsa as soon as the waiter has made his departure.

Besides the variety of flavorings and seasonings, the consistency of guacamole can vary tremendously. Many mash it into a puree; others retain a chunky texture. I lean toward the latter category, but if the guacamole is to be used for a sauce, a smoother texture is appropriate.

The big debate with guacamole is how to keep it from becoming discolored. The standard answer is to save the stone from the avocado, place it in the bowl of guacamole, then cover the whole thing tightly and store in the refrigerator. I'm not sure this works all that well. If I have to keep guacamole for any length of time I sprinkle the top with lemon juice and press a thin film of plastic directly onto the smooth green mixture. If the top still discolors after this effort, I stir it all together. It is only the top that turns a dull gray, and once it is stirred into the rest of the mixture it all looks fetchingly green once again.

While some might think three types of guacamole a bit excessive, each of the following offers distinct, wildly varying flavors.

GUACAMOLE CON JITOMATES
GUACAMOLE WITH TOMATOES

A classic guacamole, this is perfect as a dip surrounded by vegetables and tortilla chips. Or spoon as a sauce onto crisp cheese- or chicken-stuffed *flautas* (flutelike fried tacos), or perhaps prawn tacos. It is also delicious on a bed of thinly sliced romaine lettuce, for textural contrast.

4 ripe black-skinned avocados
2 cloves garlic, chopped
1 small onion, chopped
4 small or 1 ½ large ripe tomatoes, chopped
Juice of 2 limes or lemons

2 tablespoons chopped cilantro
¼ teaspoon cumin
Pinch mild chilli powder
½ to 1 green chilli, seeded and chopped, or to taste
Salt and Tabasco sauce to taste

❶ Cut avocados in half. Remove pits and scoop out flesh.

❷ Combine avocado flesh with garlic, onion, tomatoes, lime or lemon juice, cilantro, cumin, chilli powder, and green chilli. Mash together.

❸ Season with salt and Tabasco to taste, and add extra chilli if needed. Serve soon. ***Serves about 6 to 8***

PASILLA GUACAMOLE
GUACAMOLE WITH MILD CHILLI PUREE

Pasilla Guacamole is particularly good spooned onto grilled fish such as fresh tuna, or onto chilli-marinated chicken paillards.

2 ripe black-skinned avocados
½ onion, chopped
1 jalapeño or serrano chilli, seeded and chopped
1 rehydrated mild dried chilli such as pasilla or ancho, the flesh scraped from the skin; or 1 tablespoon mild chilli powder

Juice of 1 to 2 limes, to taste
Salt to taste

Cut avocados in half. Scoop out flesh and combine with onion, jalapeño or serrano, pasilla chilli flesh or powder, and lime juice. Salt to taste. Serve soon, and keep well covered in the refrigerator until serving. ***Serves 4 to 6***

TOMATILLO GUACAMOLE
GUACAMOLE WITH TOMATILLO PUREE

The tart taste of tomatillo combines with sensuous and smooth avocado to make this very special guacamole. This is particularly good wherever a more tart flavor is desired: spoon onto crab-stuffed soft tacos, enjoy as a sauce for grilled meat with strips of nopales, spoon into Tacos de Tinga Poblano. If tomatillos are unavailable, substitute a mild green salsa to taste.

10 tomatillos, cooked until tender (canned are fine)

2 small or 1 medium onion, finely chopped

2 tablespoons lemon juice, or to taste

1 fresh green chilli, chopped, or to taste

2 medium-large black avocados, mashed coarsely with a fork

Salt to taste

Lightly mash tomatillos, then combine with onion, lemon, and green chilli. Mix in avocado, then salt to taste. *Serves 4 to 6*

CARNE MOLIDA CRUDA
STEAK TARTARE WITH CHILLIES, CILANTRO, AND LIME

Carne Molida Cruda is Mexico's version of steak tartare, enlivened with a good shot of chillies, cilantro, and lime, served scooped up with crisp tortilla chips to contrast with the rich meat. At one time, *carne cruda* was quite popular in bars and cantinas throughout Mexico City, along with a selection of other savory bites: *chicharrones* in salsa, fried fish roe, sharply flavored dried shrimp broth, and fresh cheese with salsa and *totopos* (crisp fried wedges of tortillas). It is clean-tasting and refreshing on a hot and humid evening, and is predictably delicious enjoyed with shots of tequila and chasers of cool beer.

As with all raw meat dishes, use only supremely fresh meat, and chop it yourself so that any bacteria or parasites hanging around the butcher's grinder won't find their way into your beef and make you ill. Never, never use already ground beef. Besides possible contamination, preground beef is fatty and that fat will give you a waxy, greasy quality to your steak tartare instead of the vital savor of the lean meat.

7 to 8 ounces beef sirloin, trimmed of all visible fat and cut into small cubes.

2 to 3 medium shallots, finely chopped

2 to 3 tablespoons finely chopped cilantro

1 jalapeño or serrano, seeded and chopped (to taste; add another if desired)

Salt to taste

1 egg yolk

Juice of 1 lime

Restaurant-style or homemade tortilla chips

Garnishes: Lime wedges and extra cilantro

❶ Chop the sirloin. This can be done in a food processor using an off-and-on pulsing motion to get minced meat rather than pureed. Hand-chopped meat, however, is best, done as soon as possible before serving. To do this, place the meat on a clean chopping board. With a cleaver or chef's knife in each hand, begin cutting the meat, each hand alternately, using a sort of rocking motion, almost as if you were chopping parsley but with two hands rather than one. Let the weight of the knives do the work for you.

❷ Mix the chopped meat with shallots, cilantro, chillies, salt, egg yolk, and lime juice, mixing as quickly as possible to avoid overhandling.

❸ Mound the seasoned beef onto a plate, then garnish with tortilla chips, lime wedges, and cilantro. Serve immediately, because the lime juice begins to "cook" the meat as soon as it touches it. *Serves 2*

LEGUMBRES MIXTA
COOKED VEGETABLE SALAD IN MUSTARD SAUCE

This mixture of steamed and sautéed vegetables, awash in a deliciously gaudy sauce is, like the above lime-and-chilli-seasoned meat, often served in cantinas or bars, with toothpicks provided for spearing. The puckery, mustardy flavor makes the idea of a second . . . or a third . . . *cerveza* very attractive.

1 medium-sized onion, sliced
lengthwise
2 cloves garlic, peeled and halved
⅓ cup olive or vegetable oil
1 small or ½ medium-sized yellow
sweet pepper, cut into strips
1 tablespoon French style mustard
3 tablespoons white wine vinegar or
sherry vinegar

3 or 4 boiled medium-sized potatoes,
cooled and diced
3 or 4 steamed or boiled medium-
sized carrots, cooled and sliced
2 cups green beans, either cooked al
dente or frozen (no need to defrost)
1 jalapeño *en escabeche,* thinly sliced
Salt and pepper to taste

❶ Sauté onions and garlic in about 1 tablespoon oil until softened and lightly browned. Remove and place in bowl. Quickly sauté yellow pepper strips until crisp-tender and add to onions.

❷ Mix mustard with vinegar, then whisk in remaining oil. Pour this dressing in with the onions, garlic, and peppers.

❸ Add remaining vegetables and toss together well. Add salt and pepper to taste. Serve immediately or let sit and marinate (the green beans are loveliest when freshly dressed; they turn gray as they sit). ***Serves 4 to 6 as part of a selection of appetizers***

BOTANA DE ALBANILES
AVOCADO, SALSA, AND FRESH CHEESE APPETIZER

Tangy and hot fresh salsa, combined with creamy smooth avocado and diced fresh cheese, makes a simply prepared, very satisfying appetizer to be dipped into with the contrasting crunch of *totopos.* Whichever salsa you choose will dictate the flavors of the dish.

1 recipe fairly mild salsa of choice:
Salsa Cruda, Nopale Salsa, Salsa de
Chile Güero, Salsa Verde de
Tomatillo, or Salsa Mexicana
2 small to medium-sized ripe
avocados, peeled and diced

3 to 4 oz. string cheese, Jack or feta
cheese, cut into strips or crumbled
Totopos or crisp restaurant-style
tortilla chips

Combine salsa with avocados. Garnish with cheese and surround with chips. ***Serves 4***

QUESO FUNDITO
MELTED CHEESE

As with all simple dishes, this one of melted cheese and assorted seasonings usually tastes too good to be true. It is eaten throughout Mexico, as well as north of the border into the Southwest, in one guise or another. In the state of Jalisco it is called *queso fundito* or *queso al horno,* and it is served as is, merely garnished with a few fresh or pickled chillies. In Sonora, where meat rules supreme, the melted cheese is called *queso flameado* and is topped with bits of sautéed chorizo sausage and eaten as a prelude to the mixed grill, *carne asada.* In the Yucatán a similar dish is prepared, with the addition of a cinnamon-scented tomato sauce and either minced meat or tiny shrimp.

Melted cheese can be prepared on a barbecue, moving the cheese around the grill to a hotter or cooler place to control the amount of heat and melting of the cheese, then served with warm tortillas and pickled chillies or salsa to taste. Or the cheese can be sliced or grated and baked in a hot oven or broiled.

❶ Choose a rather soft meltable cheese and cut into slices. Place in a baking dish.

❷ Garnish with any of the following:

- ◆ A splash of Salsa Ranchera seasoned with a dash of cinnamon and a handful of shrimp, crab, or cooked prawns
- ◆ 1 or 2 mild chopped fresh green and/or red chillies
- ◆ 8 oz. or so of browned crumbled chorizo sausage
- ◆ Roasted and peeled red or yellow peppers, blanched green beans, diced boiled potatoes, diced seeded tomatoes, and salsa of choice

❸ Grill or broil until cheese is melted and bubbly.

❹ Serve hot, accompanied by warm soft tortillas or crisp tostada wedges.

QUESO AL FORNO
BAKED CHEESE WITH FRESH SALSA

Melted cheese with fresh chilli salsa is one of those simple pairings that can be varied and varied but never improved on. It is a great dish to make when you have a selection of several cheeses languishing in the refrigerator.

Take a combination of shredded cheeses of choice and place a handful in individual ramekins. Top with a spoonful of good homemade salsa. Bake in a hot oven until the cheese is melted and bubbly. Serve sizzling, a stack of warm flour or corn tortillas alongside to roll around bits of the melted cheese.

QUESO OAXAQUEÑO AL FORNO
FRESH WHITE CHEESE BAKED IN GREEN SAUCE

Queso Oaxaca is a fresh milky cheese, produced in a wide variety of shapes, sizes, and degrees of saltiness and freshness. Like fresh mozzarella, it may be made in large two-fist-sized balls or tiny one-bite morsels, or any permutation in between. It is particularly good in this recipe, covered with mild green salsa, then baked just long enough to melt into a mixture of mild cheese creaminess and the sharpness of salsa.

When good *queso Oaxaca* is unavailable—that is, anywhere outside of Oaxaca—use fresh mozzarella or similar cheese. Be sure to serve it right away, piping hot from the oven; melted fresh mozzarella forms the most persistent strings known to humankind and once cool they can be difficult to gnaw your way through.

2 rounds fresh mozzarella (the soft white kind that comes in a brine) or any other soft white fresh cheese that is not too salty

About ¾ cup mild salsa verde (either bottled or prepared with fewer chillies than a sharp table salsa would contain)

6 to 8 corn tortillas, either soft and warm, rolled up into scroll-like rolls, or cut into wedges and fried until golden and crisp

❶ Cut the rounds of cheese into halves and place each half in an individual small baking dish or ramekin. (If you prefer, you can place them all in one baking dish.)

❷ Cover with the salsa and bake in a 400°F oven about 10 minutes, just long enough to melt the cheese to a soft and bubbly stage. Alternatively, you can melt the cheese under a broiler.

❸ Serve immediately, accompanied by tortillas or tortilla chips for dipping.

NACHOS
··
TORTILLA CHIPS TOPPED WITH
MELTED CHEESE AND BEANS

Nachos are basically crisp corn tortilla chips topped with cheese, heated until the cheese melts, then topped with pickled or fresh chillies, salsa, chopped onion, sour cream, and the like. Each diner pulls at the tortilla chips, dipping into the melty mixture of cheese, chillies, and whatever else the cook has decided to add. (I like to use beans, and I prefer to add the tortilla chips to the melted cheese and toppings at the end, rather than baking them together.)

Nachos have crept north from Sonora, Mexico, onto mainstream American menus. You can buy them at baseball games and shopping malls, but I don't recommend it—the tortillas come topped with a disgusting gloppy orange sauce that has pretensions of cheese but little else. Homemade, however, they can be good. Very, very good. With the wide variety of good quality tortilla chips available these days, nachos can be an interesting dish.

1 cup refried pinto beans (see Frijoles Refritos), or Frijoles Negro Enchilados
6 oz. shredded cheese of choice (a combination of jack and a crumbly, white one such as feta is good)

Pinch cumin seeds or ground cumin
Tortilla chips

Toppings:

¼ cup sour cream
Thinly sliced pickled chillies to taste, or good hot salsa
1 tablespoon coarsly chopped cilantro

2 tomatoes, diced
Handful shredded lettuce
Fresh salsa to taste

··

❶ Spread beans in a shallow baking dish, then top with cheese and sprinkle with cumin.

❷ Bake in a 375°F oven about 10 minutes or until cheese is bubbly and browned.

❸ Remove from oven and arrange tortilla chips around the edges. Place the extra chips in a basket for each person to take at will. Top hot bean mixture with topping ingredients, preferably in an esthetically pleasing arrangement.

❹ Serve immediately, surrounded by tortilla or blue corn chips and fresh salsa. ***Serves about 4***

··

RELLENITOS DE PLATANO MACHO
....
PATTIES OF MASHED PLANTAINS FILLED WITH SAVORY MEAT AND/OR BLACK BEANS

Only an echo of banana sweetness lingers in this savory snack. The plantain, or *plátano macho* as it is called in Mexico, is first boiled until tender, then drained and mashed. The mashed plantains are then mixed with eggs and flour and patted into flat cakes, stuffed with a bit of savory chilli-shredded pork and mashed beans, then fried until browned and crisp on the outside.

They're good at this point, but they get better: top them with drifts of cool sour cream, fresh tomato-chilli relish, and shreds of lettuce. Sublime.

2 plantains, on the ripe side
About ¾ cup shredded cooked pork
About ⅓ cup vegetable oil, divided
½ teaspoon mild chili powder
1 clove garlic, chopped
Salt and pepper to taste
1 ¼ cups very tender cooked black beans

⅓ cup chopped or diced tomatoes (canned are fine)
2 eggs
⅓ cup flour, plus extra for flouring hands and forming patties

Tomato-Chilli Relish:

⅓ cup diced tomatoes (canned are fine)
2 green onions, thinly sliced
1 clove garlic, chopped
1 serrano, or to taste

Salt to taste
About ⅓ cup sour cream
Green lettuce, cut into thin strips or shreds

....

❶ Peel plantains and cut into pieces. Place in saucepan with water to cover and bring to boil. Cook about 5 to 8 minutes or until tender, then drain and mash.

❷ Meanwhile, brown the pork in 1 teaspoon vegetable oil, seasoning it with chilli powder, garlic, and salt. Set aside.

❸ Puree beans with ⅓ cup tomatoes. Heat about 1 tablespoon vegetable oil in heavy skillet and add bean puree. Cook until it forms a thick paste. Season with salt and pepper as needed. Set aside.

❹ Mix the mashed plantains with the eggs and ⅓ cup flour, mixing well to form a batter. It will be quite sticky.

❺ Form patties by taking a tablespoon or two of the plaintain mixture into your well-floured hand and placing a bit of both the meat and beans stuffing on top, then topping it with more plantain mixture. Work on a plate that is liberally coated with flour. This is rather messy business but not too difficult. If a bit of the filling seeps out, don't worry.

❻ Heat remaining oil (about 1 tablespoon) in heavy pan, then add patties and brown. Turn them over and pat them down to flatten them slightly. Brown on the second side. Remove from pan.

❼ Mix Tomato-Chilli Relish: Combine ⅓ cup tomatoes, green onions, garlic, chilli, and salt to taste.

❽ Serve the patties spread with a bit of the relish, then a layer of the sour cream, topped with a flurry of shredded lettuce. *Serves 4*

MEMELAS OAXAQUEÑAS CON SALSA DE CILANTRO— OAXACA
FLAT THICK TORTILLAS WITH CILANTRO SALSA

Thick doughy tortillas, called *memelas,* freshly made and spread with a green salsa—this tastes of the essence of Mexico. Serve in quarters, accompanied by shots of tequila, wedges of lime, and chunks of cucumber. The salsa can vary from mildly piquant to fiery, as you like.

1 batch freshly made Memelas

Cilantro Salsa:

4 cloves garlic, chopped
2 to 6 serrano chillies, to taste
1 ½ cups chopped cilantro
2 tablespoons vinegar
1 onion, finely chopped

Salt to taste
Cumin to taste
2 ripe tomatoes, chopped (canned are fine, along with a little of the juice)

❶ Combine garlic and chillies and whirl in blender until finely chopped. (Note: use a blender rather than a food processor for this salsa; a food processor tends to pulverize the onion, and it can easily become bitter. Add cilantro and vinegar and whirl together, then add remaining ingredients. Check for seasoning and adjust.

❷ Spread salsa over quarters of Memelas and serve. ***Serves 4 to 6, more if part of a selection of appetizers***

GUSANOS DE MAGUEY—HIDALGO
MAGUEY WORMS

When you purchase a bottle of the potent alcoholic liquor mescal, you'll find a maguey worm curled up at the bottom. It may be intimidating for the squeamish, but that little worm gives the drink its distinctive flavor.

The maguey worm, a grub that burrows into the maguey plant, has been a celebrated delicacy since pre-conquest times. Tender, delicate, slightly smoky and vaguely saline-tasting, they are doted on in many other ways than in the bottom of an alcoholic bath: wrapped into tortillas and fried into crisp tacos, chopped and used as omelet filling, dipped into chilli salsa. In the state of Hidalgo they are fried until crisp and served in a pile, accompanied by wedges of lime and green salsa. I include this recipe for its curiosity value; if you ever have the oportunity to prepare these worms, you should take advantage of it. Serve as a first course, accompanied by crusty bread or with either soft or crisp-fried tortillas to make tacos with.

2 cups vegetable oil	**Avocado and tomato slices**
1 lb. maguey worms, cleaned	**Wedges of lime**
Salsa Verde de Tomatillo	

❶ Heat oil in a heavy skillet until very hot, then fry worms until crisp. You will probably need to do this in several batches. Remove from hot oil with slotted spoon and dry on absorbent paper.

❷ Serve immediately with Salsa Verde, garnished with avocado, tomatoes, and lime wedges. ***Serves 6***

TORTAS
HOT CRUSTY-ROLL SANDWICHES

Walk around any bustling Mexican town and you'll see signs on the food stalls that line each street: "tortas," they proclaim. (By the way, in vulgar sexist street slang, *"torta"* also refers to a very attractive woman.)

Variations of these hearty sandwiches are to be found throughout the country. Each has a unique flavor depending on what meat and salsa combination the vendor chooses. *Carnitas,* fork-shredded beef—even bits of shredded shark—any savory and hearty meat, fish, or poultry may be stuffed into the street sandwich. It is so satisfying: hot crisp roll, soft buttery beans, crisp and refreshing lettuce shreds wilting from the heat of the other ingredients, all set off with a hit of hot chilli. This is a robust snack—and so messy to eat it is impossible to retain any vestiges of dignity: beans and sour cream soon smudge your face and shreds of lettuce hang from the corners of your mouth.

In the streets of America's Latin neighborhoods you find tortas as well, advertised in bright and garish storefront signs that may make you feel like you are in Central America or Mexico.

Any torta may be scaled down for an appetizer-sized snack known as a *pambacito.* Use tiny rolls and hollow them out slightly, then follow the recipe for any of the following tortas.

TORTAS DEL MERCADO CENTRAL
MARKETPLACE TORTAS

This is the classic torta you'll find in marketplaces and street stalls throughout the Republic and in Mexican-American neighborhoods.

4 crusty rolls such as French rolls or bolillos
Hot lard, butter, or olive oil
Good homemade salsa as desired
About ½ cup hot refried beans (canned are fine)
About 1 ½ cups filling of choice (see below for suggestions)
About ⅔ cup shredded lettuce

1 tomato, diced
1 small to medium onion, chopped
2 tablespoons chopped cilantro
1 avocado, sliced and tossed with lemon or lime juice to prevent discoloring
About ¼ cup sour cream
Sliced jalapeños *en escabeche* to taste

❶ Split the rolls lengthwise. Brush the insides of each roll with the hot lard, butter, or olive oil. Grill under a flame or brown on a hot heavy frying pan.

❷ Spread bottom part of each roll with salsa, then beans; then spoon on desired filling. Top with a handful of lettuce, tomato, onion, cilantro, avocado, dollop of sour cream, and several slices of jalapeños *en escabeche.*

❸ Replace top part of rolls. Pour glasses of chilled lager and sit back and enjoy.
Serves 4

SOME SUGGESTED FILLINGS:

◆ Diced vegetables (potatoes, carrots, green beans, peppers, tomatoes) pan-browned with cumin, chilli powder, cilantro, etc.

◆ Browned chorizo scrambled with eggs

◆ Grilled chorizo, *longaniza,* or other spicy sausage

◆ Shredded boiled or roast chicken

◆ Diced roast pork or duck

◆ Sliced rare roast beef

◆ Thinly sliced ham and cheese (such as Gouda)

◆ Ropa Vieja

◆ Mole Poblano de Guajalote

◆ Chilli-stewed chicken from Pollo de Plaza

◆ Leftover Pato con Naranja y Yerbabuena

◆ Thin and tender rare grilled steak (such as fajitas) with onions and peppers

◆ Melted cheese with grilled onions and nopales

◆ *Carne con nopales y chipotle:* Brown shredded meat with a bit of garlic, then simmer with tomatoes and nopales, and season with a bit of chipotle chilli.

MOLLETES
BEAN-STUFFED MELTED-CHEESE ROLLS

The simplest torta, hunger-staving and basic, a crusty roll stuffed with *frijoles refritos,* topped with cheese, then grilled and eaten with salsa or pickled chillies.

4 large crusty rolls
Several spoonfuls salsa of choice or several pickled jalapeño chillies, thinly sliced

About 1 ½ cups refried beans (homemade or canned)
10 oz. shredded meltable cheese
1 to 2 onions, finely chopped

❶ Split the rolls lengthwise. Hollow out by pulling out about half the insides. (Save crumbs for another use.)

❷ Arrange rolls on baking sheet. Spread with a bit of the salsa, then stuff each roll with refried beans.

❸ Top with more salsa, then with a thick layer of shredded cheese. Grill until cheese is melted and bubbly.

❹ Serve immediately, with more salsa as desired and a sprinkling of chopped onions.

Variation: Add crumbled browned chorizo sausage to the refried beans, or choose any of the variations for Frijoles Refritos. **Serves 4**

TORTAS DE FRIJOLES NEGROS Y PAVO
BLACK BEAN AND TURKEY TORTAS

A black bean–stuffed crusty roll, with the smoky fire of chipotles and mild, tender turkey or chicken makes a sumptuous sandwich. The combination would be good as miniatures, as well, stuffed into tiny rolls or pita breads for appetizers or party fare.

4 crusty rolls
Vegetable oil for brushing onto rolls
About 1 ½ cups heated mashed and seasoned black beans or Frijoles Refritos
Chipotle salsa or thinly sliced chipotles, to taste
12 oz. warm roast turkey or chicken, cut into strips or shredded

1 avocado, peeled, sliced, and splashed with a little lime juice
2 green onions, thinly sliced
1 tablespoon chopped cilantro
About ¼ cup sour cream
Generous handful shredded lettuce

❶ Split the rolls lengthwise and hollow out a bit of the inside. Brush rolls with oil and heat on a hot griddle or frying pan, lightly browning on both sides; or bake in a 400°F oven about 10 minutes or until the rolls are crisped a bit.

❷ Spread mashed beans generously on bottom half of each roll. Season with a bit of chipotle salsa (chillies or marinade), then top with turkey or chicken, sliced avocado, green onions, and cilantro. Spread sour cream on inside top half of roll.

❸ Fill with shredded lettuce, then close up sandwich and serve immediately. Offer salsa or extra chipotles on the side. *Serves 4*

···················· **VEGETARIAN VARIATION** ····················

Omit the turkey or chicken and add a slice or two of sweet tomato to each sandwich.

TORTA DE JAIBA Y AGUACATE
CRAB AND AVOCADO TORTAS

Crisp hot rolls filled with savory mayonnaise—dressed crab, shredded lettuce, and slices of avocado, these are deliciously exuberant. The crab salad melts into the hot roll, the lettuce wilts and becomes tender. It is sloppy to eat, so don't expect to keep your dignity in the process—I've never escaped having globs sneak out the back end of the sandwich as I was working on the front end.

4 chewy, crusty rolls, cut lengthwise but left attached
Butter, softened for spreading
8 to 10 oz. cooked crabmeat
Several spoonfuls each of mayonnaise and sour cream
½ teaspoon mild chilli powder
½ onion, finely chopped

Squeeze of lime or lemon juice
¼ head iceberg lettuce, thinly sliced or shredded
1 to 2 small ripe tomatoes, diced
1 avocado, peeled and sliced
Salt and pepper to taste
Salsa of choice

❶ Pull out some of the soft insides from the rolls (reserve crumbs for another use). Butter the insides of the rolls.

❷ Brown rolls on both sides in a hot heavy skillet or griddle, or bake in a 400°F oven about 10 minutes or until crisped.

❸ Meanwhile, mix the crabmeat with enough mayonnaise and sour cream to bind it together, and season with the chilli powder, onion, and lemon or lime juice.

❹ When rolls are hot and crisped, remove from oven and stuff with crab salad, shredded lettuce, diced tomato, and avocado. Sprinkle with salt and pepper and offer salsa of choice. Serve immediately. *Serves 4*

SEMILLAS TOSTADAS DE CALABAZA
TOASTED CHILLIED PUMPKIN SEEDS

Pale drab green in color with an earthy roasted flavor, pumpkin seeds are widely used in Mexican food—in sauces, tamales, stews, and eaten simply spiced and toasted for a crunchy snack. Soaking the seeds before roasting gives them a particular brittleness. They shatter deliciously between the teeth.

1 ½ cups water.
8 oz. raw pumpkin seeds, hulled
1 teaspoon mild chilli powder

1 teaspoon salt
Several cloves of garlic, finely chopped (optional)

❶ Bring water to a boil, then pour over the seeds. Let soak overnight at room temperature.

❷ Drain and spread seeds evenly over a 10- to 15-inch baking dish.

❸ Bake in a 350°F oven 25 to 35 minutes or until seeds are dry and puffed up. They will pop and sputter as they roast, so don't be concerned about any alarming noises coming from the oven. About two-thirds of the way through the baking, add the seasonings.

❹ Let cool, stirring occasionally. Other seasonings, such as cumin seeds, hot pepper, or soy sauce, make good alternatives to the chilli and garlic. The seeds are also good without any seasoning beyond a little salt. *Makes about 1 ½ cups*

A FEW SIMPLE MEXICAN NIBBLES:
GARBANZOS CON CHILES

Sold in little stalls, nutty cooked chick-peas are doused with hot salsa such as Tabasco, then sprinkled with salt and piled into waxed-paper cones for intrepid nibbling

BOCADILLO DE PAPAS COCIDAS
COOKED POTATO SNACK

Another popular street snack is boiled waxy potatoes, at room temperature, diced bite-sized, then splashed with a vinegar-based chilli sauce such as
Tabasco or a homemade one such as Salsa de Chiles Árbol.

PAPITAS CON CHILES Y LIMA
CHILLI-LIME POTATO CHIPS

In Guadalajara I've eaten freshly made potato chips, tasting crisply of
earthy potatoes, served with a splash of green salsa or a good vinegar-based
hot sauce and wedges of lime. Sweet potato chips are good this way too (so are
parsnips), sprinkled with a dusting of mild chilli and paprika along with the
salt.

ENSALADA CAMARON
SHRIMP APPETIZER SALAD

Cold cooked prawns make a refreshing appetizer dressed in olive oil and
lemon, seasoned with jalapeños *en escabeche,* chopped onion, tomato,
pimiento-stuffed green olives, parsley, and crumbled oregano.

CHALUPINES
DEEP-FRIED GRASSHOPPERS

A crispy nibble from Oaxaca, not for the timid, is deep-fried grasshop-
pers, lightly salted and sprinkled with chilli powder or dipped into salsa.

Masa Antojitos

The term *antojitos* encompasses tacos, tostadas, and all of the snacklike masa-
based goodies that we have come to associate with Mexican food. *Antojitos* literally means "little whims": so appropriate a term, since the corn-based dishes
can be varied endlessly depending upon the tastes of the cook and the va-
garies of the marketplace.

In addition to the tortilla-based *antojitos,* masa is also shaped into a wide variety of little cups, boats, patties, and other forms that can either be fried first and stuffed later or vice versa. They come with often amusing descriptive names such as *gorditas* ("little fat ones"), *cazuelitas* ("little pots"), *chalupas* ("tiny boats from the floating gardens of Xochimilco") and *huaraches* ("sandals"). They may be filled with whatever you fancy; you want a pleasing cacaphony of flavors and textures.

BASIC DOUGH FOR *ANTOJITOS*

Antojitos may be made with the ordinary masa used for tortillas. This *antojito* dough, however, is made from masa lightened a bit with wheat flour and baking soda. It's a little easier to handle and less gummy when prepared.

Masa *antojitos* may be in any of a large variety of shapes and sizes. They may be fried and then filled, or made into little cups, stuffed, then fried all together. They can be baked in a hot oven to crunchiness instead of being fried. Fillings can be nearly endless: refried beans, shredded meats, mashed vegetables, cheeses, shellfish. Most important are the lively garnishes and toppings: a dab of sharp salsa or strip of chilli, tangy diced tomatoes, shreds of crunchy cabbage, lettuce, and/or pungent onion. It should all crackle with the excitement of contrasting flavors and textures.

6 heaping tablespoons masa harina **About 1 cup warm water**
2 heaping tablespoons flour **Lard or vegetable oil for frying**
Pinch baking soda

❶ Mix masa with flour and baking soda, then add enough water to make a firm yet moist dough. You might need more than 1 cup, but do not let the dough get too soupy. If it does, let it sit awhile to dry a bit, then proceed (or add a bit more masa or flour).

❷ Heat oil until hot enough for frying.

❸ Shape the dough as desired.

◆ *Chalupas:* For diamond-shaped boats make pieces of dough 3 inches or so long and 1 ½ inches wide.

◆ *Garnachas, picadas, sopes,* or *sopitas,* the name depending on the region: Pull off a walnut-sized piece of dough, then shape the dough into a pot shape, making the walls and bottom of the little pot as thin as possible without tearing.

◆ *Gorditas:* Shaped like a thickish tortilla, but with a little basin to accommodate the filling. Usually fried crisp, then filled.

◆ *Huaraches:* Shaped like a rounded rectangle (or the soles of huarache sandals), about ⅛ to ¼ inch thick, 3 to 4 inches long, and 2 inches wide.

◆ *Cazuelitas:* Shaped like little pots as for *garnachas;* fill the fried *cazuelitas* with an uncooked filling, then bake together until crisp and melty.

❹ Fry *antojitos*, ladling the hot lard or oil into the center of each dough shape and letting it sizzle away as the bottoms brown in the pan.

❺ Drain on absorbent paper. To keep warm for a short time, place on a flat baking sheet in medium-warm oven.

❻ Fill as desired and serve immediately. **Makes 10 to 12 tiny antojitos or 4 to 6 larger ones**

······························ **VARIATION** ·······························

Instead of frying, masa shapes may be laid out onto a nonstick or lightly oiled pan, then baked in a very hot oven for about 20 minutes, or until golden brown and cooked through and very crunchy.

······························ **VARIATION** ·······························

Sometimes a little mild red chilli powder or mashed black beans are added to the masa mixture.

···

SOPES DE CARNITAS

Top flat, fried masa patties with refried beans, Carnitas en Otro Estilo, a strip of chipotle, and a sprinkling of shredded cabbage.

GARNACHAS DE GUACAMOLE Y QUESO

Fill tiny fried tartlet shapes with guacamole, chopped green onions, and a crumble of feta-type cheese.

CAZUELITAS DE PAPAS Y CALABAZA

Coarsely mash 1 to 2 boiled potatoes and mix with 2 boiled, coarsely chopped zucchini and 3 oz. or so shredded Cheddar or similar cheese. Stuff *cazuelitas* with this mixture, then bake in hot oven until cheese melts. Serve topped with chopped green onions, a dab of sour cream, and a sprinkle of chopped fresh serrano chillies.

CHALUPAS DE POLLO

Fill flat boat-shaped masa tarts with shredded chicken, avocado slices, strip of chipotle or jalapeño *en escabeche,* thinly sliced or diced radishes, dab of sour cream, and thinly sliced onion.

GARNACHAS VERACRUZANAS
MASA *ANTOJITOS* TOPPED WITH *CARNITAS,* POTATOES, AND CHILLIES

Small two-bite affairs: the sort of nibbles that warm nights under the stars and chilled *cerveza* were made for.

1 onion, finely chopped
2 cloves garlic, finely chopped
1 tablespoon brine from jalapeños *en escabeche* or from chipotle chillis
Basic Dough for *Antojitos*, pressed into tiny tartlet shapes as for *garnachas*, and fried until golden

About 1 to 2 cups shredded pork or *carnitas a la casera*, heated through
2 waxy boiled potatoes, cooked and diced
Sour cream

❶ Keep *garnachas* warm in oven.

❷ In blender, whirl onion (a food processor tends to turn onion bitter), garlic, and chilli brine until it forms a salsa-like mixture.

❸ Spoon a bit of this into the bottoms of the tartlet shells, then top with a bit of shredded pork and a sprinkle of diced potatoes.

❹ Garnish with sour cream. *Serves 4 to 6 as an appetizer*

SOPITAS DE CARNE Y QUESO
MASA CUPS WITH SPICY MEAT PATE AND SALTY FRESH CHEESE

These masa snacks are filled with a savory pâté-like mixture of finely ground or pureed meats or poultry, then topped with fresh salsa, a sprightly crumble of feta or other slightly salty cheese, and a shredding of fresh crunchy cabbage. It is sensational.

Basic masa cups, as for *sopes* **or**
sopitas, **fried until golden**
About 1 cup broth-simmered meat or
combination of meats and poultry,
coarsely chopped with a little of the
cooking broth

Salsa Cruda
2 to 3 oz. *queso fresco* **or feta cheese,**
crumbled
½ onion, chopped
About ⅛ head of cabbage, shredded

❶ Prepare the masa cups and keep warm.

❷ Chop the meat/poultry finely; include enough broth to form a rich, meaty paste. Heat in a frying pan to evaporate the excess liquid, concentrating the flavors.

❸ Spread a little of the warmed meat into each masa cup, then top with a spoonful of salsa, a scattering of crumbled cheese, chopped onion, and shredded cabbage. *Serves 4 to 6 as an appetizer*

GARNACHAS DE FRIJOLES NEGROS
GARNACHAS FILLED WITH BLACK BEANS, CHIPOTLE SALSA, AND LIME SOUR CREAM

These *garnachas* are deliciously vegetarian, the rich and fragrant black beans topped with smoky chipotle salsa, a scattering of crumbled feta cheese, and a dollop of lime-flavored sour cream.

Fried masa cups, prepared as above for *garnachas*
½ cup sour cream
Juice of ½ lime
Grated rind from ¼ lime
1 recipe Frijoles Negros Enchilados, mashed and kept warm

About 4 oz. crumbled feta or other milky, crumbly, sharp cheese
Salsa de Chiles Chipotles
5 or 6 shredded lettuce leaves, shredded

....

❶ Keep *garnacha* cups warm in oven.

❷ Mix sour cream with lime juice and lime rind. Set aside.

❸ Spoon a bit of the warm black beans into the masa shells, then sprinkle with crumbled feta.

❹ Garnish with a spoonful of salsa, a dollop of the lime sour cream, and a few shreds of lettuce. Serve immediately.

....

SOPAS Y CALDOS

....

HEARTY SOUPS AND SPICY BROTHS

The main meal in Mexico, the *comida corrida*, always begins with a bowl of soup. The Aztecs and Mayans had no tradition of soup—they ate soupy-stewy dishes, but not as a separate course. It was the Spanish who brought to Mexico the European-Mediterranean tradition of the multi-course meal, beginning with soup.

Such a soup can be exquisitely simple, based on the rich broth that always seems to be bubbling on a back burner, the result of a cuisine with many of its specialties based on simmered meal and fowl. In the true frugality of a peasant kitchen, the flavorful broth might contain any bits of vegetables left over from other dishes: half a carrot, a handful of peas, a few shreds of cabbage, nuggets of potato, turnip, zucchini, bits or red tomato. All yield their flavor to the broth that is ladled into bowls of steaming hot, infused with a hit of hot chilli, sprinkled with a bit of fresh cilantro, a wedge of lime floating on top. Perhaps there will be a few strips of tortillas floating in the soup

There are few dishes so satisfying as that simple robust broth. I will never forget my first bowlful; the Guadalajara café was so humble I expected little, yet sitting at that grim Formica table, I was served a broth of such complexity I was taken aback. Tiny bits of vegetables bobbed about in the bowl, and the wedge of lime that accompanied it was a surprise to my young palate. The result was a lifelong addiction to such simple tart and spicy soups.

It is precisely the poverty of the kitchen that contributes to a richly flavored broth. While rich kitchens can afford to pick and choose, in the frugal kitchen little is thrown out: carcasses of yesterday's chickens find their way into the stockpot, along with a handful of bones, the trimmings from the day's vegetables, a nubbin of sausage, and so forth. All of these good strong flavoring ingredients go into the stockpot instead of the rubbish bin.

Garnishes and variations abound for these simple broths: dumpling-like tortilla balls, a bit of soft rice, diced tomatoes, shredded cabbage, crumbled cheese, earthy beans, strips of crisp tortillas, and so forth. And there is always the *sopa de fideo,* a bubbling broth with a handful of thin, thin pasta that has first been fried to golden before being simmered in the soup.

Mexico boasts an array of surprisingly elegant soups as well, all suave and smooth, wrapped in creaminess rather than spiciness. Then there are the bean soups, whose surprisingly wide range of sophisticated flavors seldom sinks to the mundane; for example, chick-pea puree with mint and lemon, or butter beans with rich mild chilli oil, or a spicy puree of black beans enlivened with limes, oranges, lemons—the tastes of the Mexican tropics.

In a land with over 6,000 miles of beaches, soups of fish and seafood offer an inspiring array, many of which are seldom seen outside their regions. A Mexican fish soup can be as simple as a great cauldron of hot briny broth, bubbling away as each small piece of fish and seafood is added. Served with lime and hot chillies, it is a fragrant and steamy joy, tasting of the sea.

Then there is the unusual category of *sopa seca,* or "dry soup," a grouping that refers to pasta, rice, or tortillas cooked in robust broths. These are served as a separate course; on fiestas and other celebrations, meals will generally include a wet soup (*sopa aguada*) followed by a dry soup (*sopa seca*).

The Mexican kitchen also offers several one-pot-meal soup-stews. *Mole de olla,* from central Mexico is a deep red chilli broth with chunks of turkey; *Caldo de Res* is a beef stew. Pork-based pozole (and the similar, tripe-based menudo) is a classic, hearty peasant dish, filled with bits of meat and spicy chilli, as traditional a welcome in the morning after a *parranda* (night of drinking and carousing) as it is for a comforting and warming supper in a cooling mountain village evening. Such soup-stews are traditionally simmered in a large earthenware pot that subtly flavors the broth as much as does the selection of meats.

Though often overshadowed by the robust, colorful, tortilla-based specialties, Mexican soups are one of the sparkling pleasures and discoveries of the Mexican table.

Un Buen Caldo/Rich Broth: The Basis

Good broth is the basis of Mexico's savory soups. I've heard it said that roasting and frying are cooking methods "for the rich only, because with simmering you get two meals from one piece of meat."

A strongly flavored stock, mixed with a bit of mashed tomatoes, ground mild chillies, pureed garlic and onion, a handful of epazote, thyme, or bay leaves, is the beginning of an endless variety of soups.

Rather than seeking specific recipes for basic stocks—chicken, beef, and so on—simply prepare broth by simmering the meat you have chosen along with whatever flavors the pot: a nice plump chicken (including its feet), carrots, celery, onion, and parsley will give a good, grandmother-style chicken soup. Add a parsnip, several slices of leek, and several cloves of garlic for a slightly different flavor. Beef—chunks of whichever cuts you like (chuck, shortribs, neck, etc.)—may be seasoned with the same ingredients, including perhaps chunks of turnips, rutabagas, a few bay leaves. For a brown stock, oven-roast or pan-sear the beef and vegetables before simmering. I've found that sometimes my stocks lack a good, strong flavor; often it's simply because I don't have the time to simmer them long enough or I use too small a quantity of meat, or because the poultry or meat is a bit pale in flavor. Whatever the reason, I confess to adding several boullion cubes to the bubbling broth to help it along.

Once you have this broth prepared, you must skim off the fat. The easiest way to do this is to refrigerate it. The fat solidifies and can be lifted off.

Next, for sparkling clear broth, you should clarify the stock. For each quart of broth use two egg whites. Beat and add to the cold stock, then place over low heat, beating constantly with a wire whisk until it comes to a simmer. Remove from heat and let stand for 15 minutes or until it begins to cool. Strain through a cheesecloth placed inside a colander.

If you do not want to clarify the broth, ladle the whole thing through a strainer to get rid of the bits of meat, vegetables, and bones. Leave the strained broth to settle, then pour off the clear soup, leaving behind the small amount of sediment.

With your good broth you can enjoy simple soups such as the following.

SOPA DE AGUACATE
AVOCADO SOUP

Float a dollop of guacamole in a bowlful of rich chicken broth.

CALDO DE RES
BEEF AND VEGETABLE SOUP

With 1 quart beef broth, including chunks of the tender simmered beef, simmer 2 cups pureed tomatoes, 1 or 2 diced carrots, 1 sliced onion, 2 diced potatoes, 1 to 2 diced zucchini, 1/4 head of cabbage, coarsely chopped, chunks of corn on the cob, cumin to taste, and a handful of chopped cilantro. Serve with Salsa de Chiles Árbol. *Serves about 6*

SOPA DE FLOR DE CALABAZA
SQUASH FLOWER SOUP

Remove the stems from about 1 cup of squash blossoms, then cut them julienne style. Sauté an onion in a little butter until soft, then add the blossoms. Add 1 quart chicken broth and simmer for about 5 minutes. Serve immediately. This simple basic soup can be varied at will: substitute 1 cup of cream; or flavor the broth with a sprig of epazote. You could also puree the sauteed squash flowers by themselves, or with a cup or so sautéed, then pureed onions and tomatoes for a heartier, less delicate broth.

RICH SPICY BROTH

Whirl an onion, several cloves of garlic, 1 chopped jalapeño, and 2-3 medium sized diced tomatoes in blender, along with a handful of cilantro leaves. (Any leftover cilantro-rich salsa whose heat has begun to pale can be used here.) When mixture is the consistency of a paste, heat a tablespoon of oil in a heavy soup pan and fry the paste until it is reduced and intensified. Add 3 cups to 1 quart of good rich broth and simmer for 15 minutes or so. Serve garnished with lime wedges and strips of crisp tortilla chips (low- or unsalted), ladled over crumbled Jack cheese, or simply add unadorned.

CALDO DE CHILE ROJO
MILD RED CHILLI-SCENTED BROTH

Add several mild dried red chillies such as New Mexico, California, or pasilla as you simmer the rich broth. 1 to 2 chillies per quart of broth should be about right. When the broth is ready and the chillies tender, remove the chillies and either puree and strain them or scrape the flesh from the tough skin. Return the tender mild chilli flesh to the broth and serve as the basis for a variety of simple soups such as the following four.

CALDO CON ARROZ Y AGUACATE ❖ BROTH WITH RICE AND AVOCADO

For each bowlful, ladle the hot broth over a spoonful of leftover Arroz Mexicana and garnish with a slice or two of avocado.

CALDO SENCILLA ❖ SIMPLE MEXICAN-STYLE BROTH

Garnish each bowl of Caldo de Chile Rojo with a few strips of crisp golden-fried tortilla chips, wedges of lime, and sprinkling of cilantro.

POZOLE CON FRIJOLES Y CACAHUETES ❖ POZOLE WITH CREAMY BEAN AND PEANUT BROTH

Add 1 to 2 cups cooked hominy to 1 quart hot Caldo de Chile Rojo, then thicken soup with several tablespoons refried beans and a tablespoon of crunchy peanut butter. Serve topped with a sprinkling of chopped cilantro, a squeeze of lime, and offer a salsa of choice.

CALDO DEL MERCADO ❖ MARKETPLACE SOUP

Prepare Caldo de Chile Rojo using lamb for the broth. Add 4 cloves coarsely chopped garlic, 2 cups pureed cooked green tomatillos, and a teaspoon or two of cumin. Bring to boil, reduce heat, and simmer for 30 minutes. Strain to obtain a clear broth. To this clear and tangy broth add 1 large waxy potato, diced, ¼ cup diced rutabaga, ¼ cup diced turnip, ½ cup diced carrot, ¼ cup green beans, and ¼ cup peas. Simmer another 20 minutes, until vegetables are cooked through. Season with oregano, more cumin to taste, and serve with salsa of choice, wedges of lime or Seville orange, and a bowl of plain steamed rice to spoon into the soup.

....

CALDO TLALPEÑO
BROTH WITH CHIPOTLE SEASONING, CHICK-PEAS, CHICKEN BREASTS, AND AVOCADO

Tlalpan is a small town, a suburb really, south of Mexico City where city-folk flock on Sundays for brunches and picnics. Streets are lined with food stalls and restaurants, a holiday atmosphere prevails with mariachi bands working café to café, table to table.

This soup no doubt evolved at one of the stalls as the cook threw a few bits and pieces into the simmering soup cauldron as he or she went along. The anonymous chef hit on a winning combination, and soon the other stalls followed suit. It has since become a favored soup throughout Mexico and has crossed the border north. It tastes essentially of Mexico, with a brilliance that few dishes can claim: a whiff of smoky-hot chipotle, nutty chick-peas, bits of delicate shredded chicken, and nuggets of creamy, mild avocado.

Caldo Tlalpeno makes a vivacious first course preceding any sort of enchilada, or *chimichanga* (fried burritos), or a meat dish such as Puerco con Piña or Chile Colorado.

1 quart rich broth (a mixture of
chicken and pork, simmered with
whole garlic cloves makes a good,
fragrant broth)
1 cup cooked chick-peas
1 to 2 chipotles, cut into thin strips
3 green onions, thinly sliced

About 14 oz. chicken breasts,
cooked, skinned, and torn into large
shreds
1 avocado (preferably Haas) peeled
and thinly sliced or diced
2 tablespoons chopped cilantro
1 lime cut into wedges
Tortilla chips (optional)

❶ Heat broth with chick-peas, then add chipotle.

❷ Serve hot broth in bowls, spooning a bit of the green onions, chicken breast, avocado, and cilantro into each bowlful and serving each portion with a wedge of lime. Crisp tortilla chips make a good accompaniment, either as a crunchy contrast or to break into the soup as croutons. *Serves 4*

·········· VARIATION ··········

In place of the chick-peas. cooked hominy may be used.

·········· VARIATION ··········

CALDO XOCHITLE—GUADALAJARA

To the broth, add 1 rehydrated dried mild red chilli, scraped from its tough, papery skin, or a whiff of mild chilli powder instead of the chipotle. Season with a generous amount of garlic and a handful of bay leaves. Omit the chick-peas and proceed as above.

SOPA DE HABAS
PUREE OF BUTTER BEANS TOPPED WITH A DRIZZLE OF CHILLI OIL

Habas are large dried fava beans, similar to the ones used throughout the Middle East. In Mexico they are often cooked into a soup for Lent, especially in the central mountain regions. Large lima or butter beans are often used in place of fava beans for similar hearty soups such as this one. The cooked beans are sautéed briefly with a bit of onion and garlic, then simmered a few minutes in a tomato-accented broth.

What makes this soup special, however, is the following: the simple bean soup is pureed, then a mixture of mild chilli and oil is heated for a moment and stirred into the soup at the last minute. It is not terribly hot, but the deep rich flavors of the chillies give it depth and complexity.

A hearty beginning to a meal; follow with Camarones con Nopales y Chipotles and serve with fresh fruit and sorbet splashed with a little fruit liqueur.

2 onions, diced
3 cloves garlic, coarsely chopped
3 tablespoons oil
1 ⅓ to 1 ½ cups cooked butter beans (canned are fine)
½ cup tomato sauce (the type in a box, from Italy, has the finest flavor)

1 quart broth of choice
1 tablespoon mild chilli powder
Chopped fresh cilantro or dried oregano leaves

....

❶ Lightly sauté onion and garlic in half the oil until onion is softened. Add beans and toss with onions

❷ Add tomato sauce and broth to bean-onion mixture. Bring to boil, simmer a few minutes, then remove from heat.

❸ Puree soup in blender or processor, beginning with the beans, gradually adding the liquid.

❹ When soup is pureed, place remaining oil and chilli powder in a pan and heat gently for a moment or two to release the fragrance and gently toast the chilli. Remove from heat.

❺ Serve soup with the chilli-oil swirled into it, and a sprinkling of cilantro or oregano in each bowlful. *Serves 4*

....

CALDO DEL PAPAS
POTATO-TOMATO SOUP—YUCATAN

A heady mixture of sautéed tomatoes and onions, good homemade broth, and bits of diced potatoes, given a good shot of lemon, chilli, and cilantro just before serving. As with all simple soups, homemade broth is the best. Sometimes I stretch the homemade broth with an equal amount of water and bouillon cube and it works well.

Serve on a fine summer afternoon, followed by Pescado Yucateca, or with cool poached bass sauced with guacamole.

1 to 2 onions, thinly sliced
1 tablespoon olive oil
3 cloves garlic, coarsely chopped
10 ripe tomatoes, peeled, seeded, and diced (or 1 cup canned)
2 medium to large potatoes, boiled and cooled, then cut into small bites.

1 quart rich homemade broth (or half broth, half water and bouillon cube)
Salt and pepper to taste
½ teaspoon crumbled oregano
1 jalapeño or serrano, chopped
Lemon wedges
2 tablespoons chopped cilantro

❶ Sauté onions in olive oil until softened, then add garlic. Let cook a few minutes, then add tomatoes and let cook down to a thick saucy mixture.

❷ Add potatoes, broth, and salt and pepper. Bring to boil and cook a few minutes, long enough to combine flavors.

❸ Add oregano and chilli and serve up, each portion sprinkled with chopped cilantro and garnished with wedges of lemon to squeeze in. **Serves 4**

VARIATION

CALDO MICHE
Prepare the above soup as a fish stew-soup. Substitute chunks of white-fleshed fish for half or all of the potatoes and use fish stock for the broth. Traditionally Caldo Miche is prepared with catfish, but any firm, white-fleshed fish fillet, cut into bite-sized pieces, is delicious.

CALDO ESPAÑA
CABBAGE AND CHORIZO SOUP

Chorizo gives this simple peasanty soup its character. The highly seasoned pork sausage comes in a wide variety of sizes, shapes, and flavors, depending on the region. While most Mexican chorizo is a fresh, chillied mixture, in some areas such as Chiapas or the Yucatán you'll find Spanish-type sausages, either chorizo or *longaniza,* more smoky and less fiery then their Mexican counterparts. For this soup choose smoky Spanish-type chorizo if possible, or use a combination of Mexican chorizo and smoky Polish-type sausage.

This is a marvelous soup. I find it a perfect vehicle for using up leftover bits of vegetables that might be languishing in the refrigerator: a handful of chopped spinach, a glass of vegetable juice, a half cup of cooked barley and another of white beans, a cup or so of diced sautéed potatoes.

Serve for a cozy supper, along with a hearty salad of vinaigrette-dressed thinly sliced romaine topped with finely shredded or crumbled cheese, guacamole, sour cream, chopped onion, and radishes accompanied by crusty bread or *bolillo* rolls.

1 head cabbage, cut up coarsely

1 onion, thinly sliced

2 cups diced tomatoes (canned are fine)

1 carrot, diced

2 chorizo sausages, broken into bite-sized pieces

3 to 5 cloves garlic (or more to taste), cut up coarsely

1 quart broth of choice

Garnishes:

¼ cup coarsely chopped cilantro

Lime wedges

1 or 2 fresh chillies, seeded and chopped (optional)

❶ Combine everything except the garnishes. Add any leftover vegetables as well if desired, cut into small pieces.

❷ Bring to the boil, then reduce heat and simmer, covered, until cabbage is cooked through.

❸ If broth is terribly fatty from the chorizo, skim off the surface fat.

❹ Serve hot, each portion garnished with cilantro, lime, and chillies if desired (some chorizo is spicy enough to preclude adding extra chillies). *Serves 4*

POZOLE
HOMINY SOUP-STEW

Pozole (also spelled posole), a one-bowl meal, is hearty, hefty fare. It is beloved food, folk-food as it were—pozole to eat from a street stall, pozole to celebrate a local fiesta, pozole to share with the rest of the village, pozole to make life seem right again. It is earthy and sustaining, yet kept interesting by the variety of things you can do to it and put into it. No two cooks' recipes for pozole are the same.

This comfort food consists of a broth of meats, seasoned with lots of onion and garlic, simmered until rich and flavorful, then served ladled over nuggets of chewy maize or hominy. A selection of condiments is tossed in or arranged for each diner to add individually. Each addition contrasts with the richness of the broth and the soft chewiness of the hominy: tangy lime to squeeze over it all, crunchy bits of *chicharrones*, hot crumbled dried chillies, dried oregano, thinly sliced cabbage, diced avocado, bits of soft white cheese, chopped onion, tortilla chips.

Traditionally a whole pig's head is used; in Mexican meat markets you can find the heads halved down the center so that each half has a little bit of all the goodies, the rather terrifying objects marked *"para posole."* For the squeamish (and I include myself in that category) other cuts of stewing pork give equally good flavor—a combination of trotters (pig's feet) and spareribs, for instance, or stewing pork cut from a leg. A luxe version will include chicken in the broth mixture; this robust potful will supply you not only with pork and chicken for the pozole, you will have lots left over to shred for tacos or *tinga* (highly seasoned shredded meat hash), or to serve with moles.

Pozole can come to the table red from simmering with mild dried chilli; green from fresh green chilli, tomatillos, and pumpkin seeds; or white made with only broth and a bit of dried hot chilli or salsa to taste. To a large extent it is regional, with variations eaten in nearly every region except for Yucatán: white pozole hails from Jalisco, green from the moist mountainsides of Guerrero, red from the lush region of Michoacán.

I've included an elegant version of pozole based on duck. To me duck broth is at once refined and suave, yet gutsy and full of flavor. Removing the skin first makes a nearly fat-free broth and gives you enough skin and fat to fry up as cracklings—a delicious addition to your pozole, or to reserve and nibble or toss into a salad or taco.

POZOLE
WHITE POZOLE

Pozole, the dish, is named after the corn it is based on. Known in America as hominy, pozole is corn kernels that have been cooked with slaked lime to soften and swell them, thereby removing the skins and leaving just the plump, earthy insides. It is the same corn that is ground to form masa or masa harina for tortillas and tamales. It is also used for grits. In Mexico you will find the hominy, or *nixtamil*, in whole kernels. In America these kernels are commonly sold precooked in cans; the grain is popular in Southern cuisine and in parts of the East Coast. If you can find hominy dried rather than canned, use that. It is delicious, with a stronger, earthier, and fuller flavor.

Pozole is not usually a delicate first-course dish, rather, serve it for an informal dinner gathering, a Sunday lunch, or a warming after-sports meal. Homemade chocolate ice cream makes a sweet refreshing finale.

1 to 2 lb. dried hominy, or canned
hominy

2 teaspoons salt (or to taste), plus
extra for the broth

About 1 lb. lean pork stew meat

1 lb. spareribs or fattier pork cut, or
several trotters (pig's feet)

Any extra soup bones

3 bouillon cubes each: beef and
chicken (though not traditional, it
adds greater flavor to the broth; the
dish takes quite a bit of salt
anyway—use the seasoning cubes
for some if not all of the salt)

About 1 gallon of water, divided

2 whole heads of garlic

2 onions

2 bay leaves

½ chicken

Condiments:

1 thinly sliced cabbage

1 onion, chopped

Dried oregano leaves

2 to 3 limes cut into wedges

Red chilli flakes

Strips of crisp fried tortilla, or
chicharrones

❶ You will need three large pots. In the first, place the hominy with water to cover. Let sit overnight to swell; or place on stove, boil 10 minutes, then cover and let sit 1 hour to swell. When swollen, add more water so that kernels are submerged.

❷ Bring to boil, reduce heat, and simmer until tender, adding more water as needed several times as the kernels continue to swell. When tender, add 2 teaspoons salt. Set aside. If using canned hominy, omit this procedure and simply open the can, drain, and proceed.

❸ In the second pot, place the pork, soup bones, beef bouillon cubes, about 3 quarts of water, one head of garlic, one onion, and a bay leaf. Bring to boil, reduce heat, and let simmer until tender, about 4 hours.

❹ In the third pot, place the chicken, the remaining bouillon cubes, remaining water, garlic, onion, and bay leaf. Bring to boil, reduce heat, and simmer until fragrant and rich, about 3 to 4 hours.

❺ When ready to serve, remove meats and chicken from their broths. Shred the meat and keep it separate. Skim the broths of fat. Arrange the garnishes on a platter.

❻ Spoon a generous amount of cooked pozole into each bowl, then ladle in the hot broth, shredded meats, and various garnishes. Offer extra hot sauce if desired. *Serves 10 to 12*

·············· **VARIATIONS** ··············

PATO EN POZOLE ❖ DUCK POZOLE

This dish is a delightful combination of elegant and rustic. Prepare as above, but substitute duck for the meats and chicken. Halve the recipe, using only one pot for simmering broth. Before placing duck in broth to simmer, remove all of its skin. Cut the skin into small bits and prepare cracklings as follows: Place skin in heavy skillet with a half cup or so of water and a sprinkle of salt. Bring to boil, cook away the water, then let the cracklings brown in their own fat until crisp and crunchy. (They will be substantially reduced in quantity.)

Serve as above. As a first course, serve the broth with only a few shreds of the duck and a small portion of the hominy, and reserve any of the leftover duck meat for elegant tacos.

·············· **THREE REGIONAL VARIATIONS** ··············

GUERRERO

Add 1½ to 2 cups cooked pureed tomatillos, 1½ toasted ground pumpkin seeds (or Pipián Sauce), and a bit of chopped fresh green chillies to give a distinctive flavor and color to this regional pozole. Let the mixture simmer in the broth for about 30 minutes, stirring often so that it does not stick on the bottom.

SONORA

In northern Mexico and north into New Mexico, pozole is served with a drizzle of sauce based on a mild chilli powder such as ancho, New Mexico, guajillo, or Californian. To prepare: Warm a tablespoon or two of mild chilli powder of choice in a few teaspoons oil, then combine with enough hot broth to make a thin sauce, then simmer until thickened slightly.

POZOLE ROJO
RED POZOLE—MICHOACAN

The broth of this red-hued pozole gets its color from mild dried chillies added to the stew (such as ancho, guajillo, or New Mexico). Lightly toast about 4 chillies on an ungreased skillet until they change color, then cover them with hot water, place a plate on top to weight them down and keep them under water, and let them soak for at least 30 minutes. Remove from water and drain. Whirl in a blender and sieve, or scrape the flesh from the tough skins. Add this chilli puree to the pozole.

SOPA DE FIDEO Y AJO
TOMATO, VERMICELLI, AND GARLIC SOUP

A garlicky tomato broth, in which float thin vermicelli that have been sautéed before simmering, is a comforting beginning to a meal. It can be sipped as is, or garnished with a grating of dry Parmesan-type cheese or a squeeze of lime, or a lashing of hot salsa.

Sopa de fideo is the classic beginning for a traditional multicourse meal. Tongue in chipotle salsa, or Pescado con Dos Salsas, or a homey spicy pot roast would be good entrees, along with Arroz Verde. For a classic dessert, try Flan de Café; for less effort, macadamia nut ice cream topped with fresh berries and nectarines.

About 3 oz. spaghetti, broken into 2-inch lengths	**1 onion, chopped**
3 tablespoons vegetable oil	**2 cups chopped tomatoes (canned are fine)**
6 to 8 cloves garlic, coarsely chopped	**3 cups chicken broth**
Several sprigs fresh oregano, or a pinch dried oregano	**1 to 2 jalapeños, chopped**
	Lemon wedges (optional)

❶ Lightly brown broken spaghetti in vegetable oil; when strands are golden, add garlic and cook a few moments to release its fragrance.

❷ Add oregano, onion, tomatoes, and broth, then bring to boil. Reduce heat and simmer 10 minutes, or until pasta strands are tender.

❸ Serve immediately, sprinkled with jalapeños and accompanied by lemon wedges for squeezing into the soup. *Serves 4*

VARIATION

CON AJO ❖ WITH MORE GARLIC
For added flavor, chop several cloves of garlic and heat them in a little oil. Spoon garlic into the hot soup just before serving.

SOPA DE GARBANZO
MINT-SCENTED PUREE OF CHICK-PEAS—OAXACA

This smooth and elegant puree contains, like many Mexican dishes, not a whiff of chilli. Such dishes—usually based on vegetable or beans—often come as a surprise to those who have preconceived ideas of Mexican food as anything smothered in chillies and wrapped in a tortilla.

Sopa de Garbanzo, with its aroma of olive oil and fragrance of mint, has the distinct Arabian overtones that pop up mysteriously throughout the foods of this great nation. It's really no mystery, however, since at the time of the Spanish conquest Moorish influence was still fresh in Spain (in Mérida on the Yucatán Peninsula, the Arabian influence is even more strongly felt at times, reflecting the large local Lebanese community.)

The usual garnishes for this soup include crisp browned croutons or fried eggs, but I much prefer wedges of lemon squeezed in: they give it a tart and fresh lift.

Serve as a first course, or for a summer lunch, along with Camarones en Frio.

1 onion, coarsely chopped
2 cloves garlic, chopped
2 tablespoons olive oil
2 cups cooked chick-peas
3 cups chicken broth
1 to 1½ teaspoons dried mint, crumbled, or 2 tablespoons fresh mint, chopped

Black pepper and salt to taste
Lemon wedges
Fresh mint for garnish (optional)

❶ Lightly sauté onion and garlic in olive oil until onion has softened and lightly browned in a few places. Add chick-peas and stir through onion mixture, cooking for a minute or two.

❷ Add broth, bring to boil, and cook for a moment.

❸ Drain chick-peas, reserving broth. Place chick-peas in a blender or food processor (a blender will make a smoother puree). Whirl until smooth. Then with the machine still whirling slowly, gradually pour in the reserved broth. By the time all of the broth has been added, the soup will be elegantly smooth.

❹ Season with mint, pepper (and salt if needed) and serve each portion of soup with a lemon wedge. Garnish with extra mint leaves if desired. *Serves 4*

SOPA DE FRIJOLE NEGRO CON TORTILLAS
BLACK BEAN SOUP WITH THREE CITRUS FRUITS AND FRESH TORTILLAS

Black bean soups are ubiquitous in many regions of Mexico, especially Oaxaca and Yucatán. The rich, almost smoky flavor and hearty quality of the beans lend themselves to a wide variety of seasonings. Classic versions use a meaty broth based on a smoked ham hock or similar baconlike meat; some bits of spicy sausage and chopped peppers.

I like this vegetarian version best, with its strong Yucatecan citrus flavors, a smoothing from sour cream, and the chunks of soft, thick tortillas (or *memelas*) broken into the bowl. It all combines to make a strikingly delicious bowlful.

Follow with *carnitas* a la Casera and a platter of refreshing leafy green salad, some guacamole, and end the meal with fruit sorbet sauced with fresh berries pureed with liqueur and a dash of sugar.

2 teaspoons vegetable oil
2 cloves garlic, chopped
½ teaspoon cumin seeds
Pinch mild chilli powder (optional)
2 cups pureed cooked black beans (canned are fine, or see recipe for Frijoles Negros Enchiladas)
2 cups broth of choice
1 tablespoon finely chopped fresh cilantro

1 jalapeño (to taste), seeded and finely chopped
½ orange
½ lemon
½ lime, cut into wedges
About ¼ cup sour cream
2 green onions, thinly sliced
4 freshly made thick corn tortillas (see recipe for Memelas), cut or broken into bite-sized pieces

❶ Heat oil in saucepan and warm the garlic and cumin seeds in it; when fragrant but not browned, stir in chilli powder and black beans. Cook for a minute.

❷ Pour in broth and add cilantro. Cover and simmer together for 5 to 8 minutes.

❸ Ladle out into 4 bowls; sprinkle jalapeño on top and squeeze orange and lemon juice into each bowl. Then squeeze lime into each bowl, and place a lime wedge on each one (the essential oils from the lime peel add their flavor and perfume, plus the diner can squeeze the lime wedge with a spoon to extract more of the tangy juice).

❹ Stir well, then top each bowlful with a dollop of sour cream, sprinkle with green onions, and garnish with pieces of thick tortilla. *Serves 4*

SOPA DE CALABAZA
RICH BROTH WITH ZUCCHINI AND RICE

This simple soup is a great example of what you can do once you have a pot of rich broth. Here I've used the leftover broth, including the whole simmered garlics, from pozole. If you don't have homemade broth, simmer a head of garlic in a broth made from bouillon cubes and water. It won't have as much depth, but the tender, sweet garlic gives the soup an elusive quality of its own.

Fresh pecorino or a not-too-salty feta can be used in place of the *queso fresco*.

A nice soup to start a feast of chicken or turkey mole.

1 quart broth, preferably homemade (I especially like the broth from Pato en Pozole, including about 15 of the whole garlic cloves that have simmered until sweet and tender, and some of the meat)

1 head of garlic, cloves separated but left whole and unpeeled (omit if using already simmered garlic cloves)

⅓ to ½ cup raw rice

2 zucchini, cut into slices or chunks

3 ripe tomatoes, diced (seed and peel if desired)

½ teaspoon crumbled oregano leaves

Salt and black pepper to taste

About 4 oz. *queso fresco*, crumbled (or use Caerphilly, fresh pecorino, Jack, mozzarella, or a not-too-salty feta)

....

❶ If you are not using leftover broth from pozole, with its collection of cooked garlic cloves, simmer garlic cloves in broth until tender. Remove cloves and let cool.

❷ Squeeze garlic cloves into broth; add rice, then bring to boil and simmer 5 minutes or until rice is nearly tender.

❸ Add zucchini, tomatoes, and oregano. Continue to cook until zucchini and rice are tender. Season with salt and pepper.

❹ Serve in bowls, each portion ladled over a bit of crumbled cheese. *Note*: If you are using leftover broth from pozole, include a bit of the meat in each soup portion: a few shreds of chicken, turkey, duck, beef, or pork. **Serves 4**

....

SOPA DE TORTILLA
VEGETABLE SOUP WITH STRIPS OF CRISP TORTILLA, CHEESE, LIME, AND CHILLIES

Sopa de Tortilla could almost be called *sopa mexicana*, for variations are to be found on nearly every table, the simmering daily broth filled with bits of vegetables, served with crisp strips of tortillas, wedges of lime, and chillies: all ingredients close at hand in the Mexican kitchen.

The rich broth makes a perfect foil for the contrasting flavors and textures. If you don't have a big pot of simmering broth, you can improvise by simmering a few bits and pieces of vegetables along with various meats. The neck of a duck, for instance, the odd chicken wing, a few pieces of meat or bones—throw them into the stockpot along with an onion, several garlic cloves, a chopped carrot, and several bouillon cubes (this will shortcut your soup preparation). For a vegetarian broth use vegetable bouillon cubes, a head of garlic or two, a few strips sweet red pepper, and so on. By adding chicken broth and vegetables to a duck or beef broth, you give the soup layers of flavor and complexity.

Once you have a lovely broth made, the rest of the soup is easy: simmer a few vegetables, fry the tortillas, and ladle it all together. It is brilliantly simple and tastes essentially of the Mexican table; a good soup to serve along with Carne Asada, or a selection of grilled meats, vegetables, and cheese.

Broth:

1 duck neck, 2 chicken feet, 3 chicken or duck wings, a chunk of beef with bone, a pig's foot, or similar piece of meat/poultry

3 tomatoes, chopped

1 clove garlic, coarsely chopped

¼ green pepper, cut into strips

1 teaspoon pure red New Mexico or ancho chilli powder (or other mild chilli powder)

2 cups broth of choice

3 cups water

Place all ingredients in a pot and bring to boil. Simmer for an hour or until broth has a lovely flavor. *Note*: If you already have a good rich stock, simply begin with a quart of it and proceed with the following recipe.

1 or 2 small to medium carrots, julienned or diced
1 zucchini, diced
½ sweet red pepper, cut into strips
¼ cup tomato sauce or juice
2 cups chicken broth or other broth
¼ to ½ jalapeño, chopped
6 corn tortillas, cut into strips

About ⅔ cup vegetable oil
8 oz. white Cheddar cheese, grated coarsely or diced
1 lime cut into wedges
2 tablespoons chopped cilantro
Salsa or chopped fresh chillies to taste

❶ Remove whatever meat or fowl you are using from the broth. Add carrots, zucchini, red pepper strips, tomato sauce or juice, chicken broth, and jalapeño. Bring to boil and simmer for 30 minutes or so, until vegetables are tender and broth richly flavored.

❷ Fry tortilla strips in hot oil until lightly golden browned. Drain on paper towel and set aside.

❸ Place a bit of cheese in the bottom of each bowl. Then ladle in broth and vegetables. Top each portion with a handful of crisp tortilla strips, a wedge of lime for the diner to squeeze in as desired, and a sprinkling of cilantro. Offer salsa or chillies for those who want a bit more heat. *Serves 4*

SOPA ROJA DE ELOTE
CORN, SWEET RED PEPPER, AND TOMATO SOUP

Soups made from sweet corn abound throughout Mexico, often enriched with cream, cheese, onions, and either red or green chilli. Sometimes the soups are mild and smooth, other times fiery. This one is judiciously spicy, with a smoothness that comes from swirling in a bit of cream cheese. The bits of tomatoes and red pepper give the soup a pleasing texture and character.

Serve as a first course, followed by Pescado Frito a la Campeche or any simple fish dish accompanied by a sizzling, exciting salsa.

4 small or 3 medium onions, coarsely chopped
2 tablespoons butter
1 tablespoon mild chilli powder
1 to 1½ teaspoons cumin powder
About 3 cups corn kernels (frozen are fine)
½ cup diced roasted and peeled red peppers

1 quart chicken or vegetable broth
1½ cups diced tomatoes in juice (canned are fine)
¼ cup mild green chillies such as Anaheim or poblanos, diced and peeled
8 oz. cream cheese
2 tablespoons chopped cilantro or green onions

❶ Lightly sauté onions in butter until softened. Add chilli powder, cumin, corn, and red pepper, stirring to meld together the flavors of spices and vegetables.

❷ Add broth, tomatoes, and green chillies. Bring to boil, then remove from heat. Mix cream cheese until smooth, then slowly add a little of the hot soup to the cream cheese, stirring as it is absorbed. Repeat until the cream cheese is a sauce consistency.

❸ Add this cream cheese mixture to the hot soup, and stir well to combine. Heat until tiny bubbles form around the edge of the pot.

❹ Serve immediately, each portion topped with cilantro or green onions. **Serves 4 to 6**

SOPA DE PECHUGA DE POLLO Y ALMENDRAS
CHILLED CILANTRO-FLECKED CHICKEN AND ALMOND BISQUE

This is one of the most deliciously unusual soups I have ever tasted. Thickened with pureed chicken breast and almonds, it has a nutty, meaty quality yet is smooth. Cilantro leaves are pureed with the almonds and chicken, creating green flecks throughout.

Though it is traditionally prepared warm, I like it best at cool room temperature. Follow with Tostadas Compuestas or Tacos de Huachinango con Salsa Verde.

¾ cup blanched almonds
1 medium or 2 small onions, diced
6 cloves garlic, peeled but left whole
4 green onions, thinly sliced
2 tablespoons olive oil

2 small cooked chicken breasts (about 6 oz. total), diced
1 quart rich chicken broth
½ to ¾ cup coarsely chopped cilantro
Salt and pepper to taste

❶ Sauté almonds, onion, garlic, and green onions in the olive oil until almonds are golden brown, the onions are browned or golden in spots, and the garlic is soft.

❷ Place half the diced chicken in a blender with the almond-onion mixture. Puree, adding enough broth to make a smooth puree.

❸ Add the cilantro and blend until mixure is green-flecked.

❹ Remove from blender and add remainder of diced chicken. Season with salt and pepper to taste. Serve cool. **Serves 4**

....

SOPA DE FRIJOLE
TARASCAN PINTO BEAN SOUP WITH CRISP TORTILLAS AND STRIPS OF MILD RED CHILLI—PATZCUARO

Bean soups of all types are eaten throughout the country—thick, chunky soups, delicate, subtle purees, one-pot stews, and so on. They are an ideal way of stretching a small amount of meat to feed many people. Nothing quite satisfies as well as a bowl of hearty bean soup, and bland, meaty beans combine superlatively with the chilli flavors of Mexico.

This one is in the style of the Tarascan Indians, from the region of Pátzcuaro. It begins as a simple bean broth. The broth itself is rather bland. But you don't eat it by itself, you ladle it over chunks of melty cheese, and squirt a shot of tart lemon into the mixture, then top it all with quickly fried shreds of mild red chillies and bits of crispy tortillas. Then the blandness of the beans works as a juggler, tossing the various flavors and textures to form an exciting and delicious bowlful.

Serve small bowls as a first course, followed by Pollo en Mole Verde con Nopales, Arroz con Elote, and Verduras con Crema.

2 small to medium onions, chopped
2 tablespoons olive oil
Large pinch cumin seeds
2 tomatoes, seeded and diced (canned are fine)
Large pinch oregano leaves
2 cups cooked pinto beans (canned are fine)
3 cups broth of choice—vegetable, beef, or chicken

1 large, mild, smooth-skinned red dried chilli
3 corn tortillas, slightly stale
4 to 6 oz. white meltable cheese such as Cheddar, diced
About ½ lemon, cut into wedges
Hot salsa or chilli sauce

....

❶ Lightly brown the onions in half the olive oil, then sprinkle in the cumin seeds and let toast a minute or two with the onions.

❷ Add the tomatoes, oregano, and beans. Coarsely mash about half the beans with a fork, then add broth. Bring to boil, then reduce heat and simmer together for a few minutes, to meld flavors.

❸ Meanwhile, cut the chillies with a scissors into very thin strips, almost shreds. Cut the tortillas into thin strips.

❹ Heat the remaining oil and fry chillies and tortillas together until tortilla strips are golden and chillies darken. Do not let burn.

❺ Apportion diced cheese into 4 bowls. Ladle over it the bean soup, squeeze into it a bit of lemon, then top with the bits of fried chilli and tortilla strips. Serve immediately, accompanied by a hot salsa or hot chilli sauce to taste. *Serves 4*

··

CALDO DE CANGREJO
CRAB SOUP—SOUTHEAST COAST

The Mexican kitchen makes a wide variety of savory seafood soup-stews, the seafood simmered into a briny broth, vegetables tossed in and cooked into a homey sustaining dish.

In the following one I have begun with vegetables cooking in a seafood broth. That is because the crabs most easily available are likely to be already cooked. If you have live crabs, by all means begin your broth by plunging the little unfortunates into a pot of boiling water.

This bracing soup is delicious preceding Arroz Verde con Mariscos, Pollo Pibil, or Papa-dzules. Or, for something a bit less taxing, serve a second course of Arroz Mexicana topped with poached eggs and salsa.

2 cups chopped ripe tomatoes (canned are fine)

4 to 5 cups rich, strongly flavored fish or chicken broth

1 small to medium onion, thinly sliced

1 carrot, peeled and diced

2 to 3 cups shredded cabbage (the addition of a little radicchio or chicory gives a lovely bitter edge)

4 to 6 cloves garlic, coarsely chopped

¹/₄ cup coarsely chopped cilantro

1 tablespoon mild red chilli powder (preferably of New Mexico or similar smooth-skinned red chillies)

Oregano leaves, crumbled, to taste

2 small to medium crabs, broken into manageable pieces

Salt to taste

Wedges of Seville orange or lime for garnish

Salsa of choice

··

❶ Combine tomatoes, broth, onion, carrot, cabbage, garlic, cilantro, and chilli powder, and bring to boil. Reduce heat, cover, and simmer until vegetables have cooked through and soup is flavorful, about 30 minutes.

❷ Add oregano and crab. Simmer over low heat 20 minutes or so, seasoning with salt if needed. Serve in deep soup dishes, each portion garnished with a wedge of Seville orange or lime. Offer salsa on the side. Good with crusty bread or tortillas. *Serves 4 to 6*

TORTILLAS, PLATOS DE TORTILLAS, Y TAMALES

....

TORTILLAS, TORTILLA DISHES, AND TAMALES

The distinctive scent of bland, earthy masa being ground or cooked on the comal (stone griddle) tells you that you are in Mexico. It is a fragrance like no other, ancient and ageless. Indeed, tortillas were the bread of the ancient Aztec, Maya, and other Mexican Indian nations.

Corn, the basis of tortillas, originated as a wild grass in the highlands of Mexico about 60,000 years ago. Just when it was cultivated by Indian agriculturists is unknown, but by around 5000 B.C. corn seems to have been the basis of their diet.

The early ears of corn, to judge from samples discovered in caves, were tiny: perhaps an inch or so long. But as small as they were, they were important in the diet. For some tribes corn gods were more important than sun and moon gods, and life abounded with corn festivals, prayers, dances, and rituals.

Early in the development of the civilization, the native tribes in Mexico developed the process of soaking and boiling grains of corn to yield a dough. Eventually the stone metate, a primitive though effective mortar and pestle, was used for grinding corn into a dough that was then patted and cooked to form nourishing flat breads. The original names for these pancakelike breads were many, depending on the size of the cakes and what type of corn was used: *iztactlaolli* referred to white corn, *yauhtlaolli* to black corn, etc. When the Spaniards arrived they were confused: you could starve to death before sputtering out such long phrases as *tatonqui tlaxcalli tlacuelpacholli* (large white tortilla). To simplify things, the Spaniards called them all tortillas, or "little cakes," the same name that refers to the flat omelet of Spain.

From ancient times, the tortilla has been the basis of the Mexican kitchen. Fresh off the grill, sweetly fragrant, the ever-present stack of tortillas appears, covered in a clean cloth, on the table at every meal in Mexico. Indeed, a stack of soft, fresh and tender tortillas, served with a bowl of spicy salsa, turns even the simplest foods into a Mexican meal.

Tortillas provide the basis for tacos, tostadas, enchiladas, *tostaditos*, and so on. As an edible plate, they may be wrapped around or be piled with nearly any filling: shredded meats, soupy beans, chunks of roasted chicken or fish, a wedge of piquant cheese, scrambled eggs and vegetables, or simply a slice of avocado and smear of hot chilli salsa. Before the conquest, tortillas were the eating utensils as well as the food; in many parts of Mexico today they still are.

Tortillas provide an endless variety of sustaining and delicious dishes in the diet of rich and poor alike. In Mexico and most of America's Southwest, tortillas are cheap and plentiful. You can count on their availability to throw together an impromptu meal, even if little else is available.

Good quality storebought tortillas are an essential ingredient in your Mexican pantry, but it is worthwhile learning to make your own as well, as homemade tortillas have such an earthy, rich flavor. In general, homemade tortillas are thicker than the purchased ones. I like to prepare my own when they are to be eaten by themselves or topped with savory bits as tostadas or stuffed with cheese as for quesadillas. If I want thin tortillas, such as for enchiladas, crisp tacos, or nachos, I use purchased ones.

To reheat storebought tortillas, you may either cook them in a very lightly oiled frying pan, spraying each tortilla first with a tiny amount of water, then quickly tossing it through the hot pan on each side. Place each hot tortilla into a basket lined with a clean cloth, then close the cloth as you heat the next tortilla. Stack them like this, continuing to close the cloth each time. Serve as soon as all of the tortillas are heated through.

Another way of reheating tortillas is to wrap a stack in foil, then steam briefly (about 5 minutes) in the top of a vegetable steamer. Remove from foil, place in cloth-lined basket, and serve.

For many tacos you may warm the tortillas in a hot oiled pan, lightly frying them. For enchiladas, first dip the tortillas into sauce, then fry them and roll them around the filling.

BASIC TORTILLAS

TORTILLAS DE MAIZ
CORN TORTILLAS

Flat, smallish, round corn tortillas are eaten daily throughout much of Mexico (though larger wheat tortillas dominate in the northern Sonora region). They are made from the age-old preparation of soaking field corn in a lime solution to loosen the hull and swell the grain into a mixture known as *nixtamil* (hominy).

For the past several millennia the background music of the entire country has been the pat-pat-pat sound of tortillas being shaped between the sturdy brown hands of ageless women. For all its effortless appearance it is a craft that needs to be practiced often to be mastered—most likely for the first several decades of life. Try it one day when you have enough time to scrape the sticky masa from your fingers.

However, most fresh tortillas in shops and restaurants are prepared on machines or on homemade presses. It is a simple and effective way of getting an even, thinner tortilla. You can purchase a metal press imported from Mexico at shops in Mexican neighborhoods. (see Special Ingredients and Sources).

Fresh masa is used in Mexico, either prepared at home or purchased from the neighborhood tortilla factory or market. In the absence of fresh masa, use dried masa flour, moistened with water to make a pliable dough.

**2 cups masa harina (see Special
Ingredients and Sources)**   **1 ¼ to 1 ⅓ cups warm water**

❶ Mix masa flour with enough warm water to make a dough that holds together and is moist. If it is too dry the tortillas will be crumbly and dry and possibly not hold together at all. If the dough is too wet it will be difficult to handle and possibly fall apart. Experience is your fiend in this endeavor—if your first batches are not perfect, keep at it.

❷ Let the dough sit, covered, for about 15 minutes.

❸ Divide the dough into 12 pieces. Roll each into a ball with your hands.

❹ Place a piece of plastic wrap on each side of the tortilla press, then place a ball of dough in the middle. Close the press, flattening the dough ball between the plastic-sheeted sides of the press.

❺ Place the tortillas on a medium-hot, ungreased heavy frying pan (I turn a cast-iron pan upside down and use the bottom). It is easiest to first peel one side of the plastic off the tortilla, then use the other sheet of plastic to ease it into the pan and peel it off directly onto the hot surface.

❻ Cook 1 to 2 minutes, turning frequently from side to side. It should be speckled light brown and appear dry and undoughy, yet still soft. It may puff up briefly.

❼ Remove from pan and place in a clean cloth-lined basket or plate, covering each warm tortilla as you prepare the rest.

❽ Serve them immediately, warm and fragrant. Store any leftovers well-wrapped in the refrigerator. To reheat, sprinkle with a few drops of water and heat on a hot ungreased pan, turning quickly to cook both sides. If they seem to be sticking, moisten the pan with a tiny bit of oil. **Makes 10 to 12 tortillas, about 6 to 8 inches in diameter**

···

·························· **VARIATION:** ··························

MEMELAS—OAXACA

Memelas are thick tortillas, about 6 inches in diameter. They are usually served in Oaxaca as a pizzalike appetizer, drizzled with savory seasoned lard or other meat drippings, and topped with crumbled cheese, chillies, avocado, and so on (see Appetizers chapter).

Follow the above recipe for basic corn tortillas but press out only until about $1/8$-$1/4$ inch thick and 6 inches in diameter. Cook on the comal or ungreased skillet and use as desired.

Since they are so thick and sturdy, leftover *memelas* keep their shape well when cut up and added to meat, fish, or vegetable hash mixtures. They add their rich, ancient flavor to otherwise simple dishes, such as the following two.

···

PICADILLO DE LEGUMBRES CON MEMELAS
SPICY VEGETABLE HASH WITH DICED THICK TORTILLA CHUNKS

1 tablespoon vegetable oil
4 or 5 small to medium waxy potatoes, peeled and cut into small chunks
2 small to medium carrots, diced
1 or 2 small to medium turnips, cut into small chunks or diced, or 1 cup green beans in 2-inch lengths
4 to 6 cloves garlic, coarsely chopped
1 teaspoon cumin

1 tablespoon pure New Mexico/California chilli powder, or to taste
½ red pepper, diced
½ teaspoon oregano, marjoram, or thyme
1 to 1½ cups diced tomatoes and their juice (canned are fine)
Salt to taste
4 or 5 leftover Memelas, cut into 1-inch pieces

❶ In the oil, lightly brown the potatoes for a few minutes, then add carrots and turnips and continue cooking until vegetables are almost tender, tossing every so often for even cooking.

❷ Add garlic, cumin, chilli powder, red pepper, and oregano. Sauté a minute or two with the vegetables, then add the tomatoes and continue simmering another 5 minutes or so. Add salt and adjust seasonings.

❸ Add Memelas and warm through. Serve hot or at room temperature.
Serves 4

MEMELAS CON QUESO
MEMELAS WITH WHITE CHEESE AND CRISP SAVORY GARNISHES

Memelas are traditionally served drizzled with hot seasoned lard; any sort of meat drippings are good, but so is the mild red oil left over from sautéing the chillies. In Oaxaca you'll often be served these thick tortillas as an appetizer or first course, with the topping varying wildly. One of my favorites is the simple melted *queso Oaxaqueno al Forno*; creamy fresh mozzarella works equally well.

Following is a slightly more complex cheese topping: crumble fresh feta-type cheese over the top, along with chopped onions, *chicharrones*, avocado, thin strips of crisply fried mild red chillies such as ancho, New Mexico, pasilla, or guajillo, and a fresh spunky salsa to taste. ***Serves 4 to 6***

························· **TORTILLA VARIATIONS** ·························

TORTILLAS NEGRAS
BLACK TORTILLAS

Use the inky black cooking liquid from black beans, along with a small amount of mashed black beans in mixing the masa dough. Proceed as with basic tortillas, or memelas.

TORTILLAS ROJAS
RED TORTILLAS

Add about 1½ teaspoons mild chilli powder (such as New Mexico) to the basic masa dough. Proceed as above.

OAXACAN THIN TORTILLAS
AND NEW MEXICO PIKI BREAD

This is more a description than a recipe: These paper-thin discs are both prepared in a similar manner. The dough is dabbed in a huge circle onto a hot heavy pan, the excess scraped off. When the dough is cooked through, it is exquisitely thin, like tissue paper, and is eaten rolled up into a scroll, either stuffed or simply rubbed with a little chilli paste. In New Mexico piki bread may be tinted with somewhat garish colors of red, yellow, and blue, while in Oaxaca, the dough may be gray from ashes used in place of lime for soaking the corn.

BLUE CORN TORTILLAS
CENTRAL AND WEST CENTRAL MEXICO AND NEW MEXICO

Blue corn has a rustic flavor that conjures up the rugged, austere land-scape it grows in. Its startling blue-gray color has been a part of the diet of this region most likely since the Stone Age. In New Mexico blue corn tortillas are part of the everyday diet, but in Mexico they are usually reserved for special occasions.

On the stalk the ears grow blue-black-purple but they dry to a grayish blue and are usually treated as hominy: cooked in lime, then ground into flour. At this stage it looks somewhat like powdered concrete; moistened and patted into tortillas, it can cover a range of blue hues. A dash of baking soda turns it a darker blue to a greenish color; a dash of acidic liquid tints it toward purple.

Fried into *tostaditos* or corn chips, the result is crunchier and more brittle than regular corn chips and particularly pleasing dipped into salsa as an appetizer or served with hot cheese-topped beans, nacho style.

Blue corn may often be purchased in specialty shops and supermarkets. To prepare your own tortillas using blue masa instead of regular yellow masa, proceed as for regular tortillas but keep in mind that the blue ones will be sturdier and less flexible. You will likely need more water than for regular ones (2 parts blue masa to 1 part water).

Some prepare blue corn tortillas a bit more like crêpes, adding milk, salt, and egg to the dough. It makes a lighter, more delicate, and pliable tortilla that lends itself more hospitably to the making of enchiladas. Blue corn tortillas are especially good in stacked enchiladas, a New Mexican specialty, layered with cheese and mild chilli sauce and crowned with a fried egg or two, or served rolled around Chile Colorado or Pollo en Mole Verde con Nopales, with the chicken off the bone and cut into bite-sized pieces. For a vegetarian version, the tortillas are delicious with just the sauces, no meat or chicken.

TORTILLAS DE HARINA
FLOUR TORTILLAS—SONORA AND THE U.S. SOUTHWEST

Hot off the griddle, warm flour tortillas are chewy, fragrant, and eminently satisfying. Homemade ones are thicker and sturdier than storebought ones, best for eating immediately rather than for use in any delicate dishes.

Though they are traditionally prepared with lard or vegetable shortening, I often use oil and find the results fine. Sometimes I use olive oil for a flatbread that is more like the Italian *piadine*, good with cheeses, cold meats, or jam for breakfast. Bean burritos, beef *chimichangas*, or fruit *chimichangas* are all made with flour tortillas.

1 ½ cups flour	1 ¼ cup lard, solid vegetable
1 ½ teaspoons baking powder	shortening, or oil
1 ½ teaspoons salt	¾ cup hot water

❶ Combine flour, baking powder, and salt.

❷ Cut in the shortening or oil until mixture resembles coarse meal. Add water and mix with fork until liquid is absorbed. Gently knead with your hands for 10 to 15 seconds. If dough is too sticky and wet, add a spoonful or two of flour; if too dry, add more water. Cover bowl and let sit for at least 15 minutes.

❸ Divide dough into 10 pieces. Roll each piece in flour and let sit 15 to 20 minutes.

❹ Pat each dough portion into a flattish round, then roll, using strong pressure, until the dough is quite thin, about ¹⁄₁₆ to ⅛ inch thick.

❺ Heat ungreased well-seasoned or lightly oiled heavy frying pan or griddle until very hot, then cook each tortilla until bubbles appear all over the surface. Turn and lightly brown the other side (do not overcook or it will be dry and cracked). Place each tortilla in a cloth-lined basket as you cook the others. Serve as soon as possible. ***Makes 10 tortillas***

TOSTADAS OR TOSTADITAS
CRISP FRIED TORTILLAS OR TORTILLA CHIPS

Warm, crisp wedges of fried tortillas in napkin-lined baskets along with a bowl of fresh salsa are among life's great temptations. They disappear effortlessly, as does the *cerveza*, while you're left with a bit of grease on your fingers and a sense of well-being all around. Perhaps guilt as well, but that has no place here, amidst the pleasure of indulgence.

The tortillas may be cut into strips or wedges. (It is easier to do this with a pair of strong scissors than with a knife; cut through no more than 3 or 4 at a time.) They're crisply delicious in soups, as a garnish to saucy dishes, or to dip into salsa. Tortilla wedges may be arranged in a baking dish, topped with cheese and/or beans, and baked into a savory appetizer, to be dipped into and splashed with salsa.

Tostadas, too, are based on crisp fried tortillas, layered with savory fillings, then piled high with fresh greens and vegetables.

This is the basic recipe for either tostadas or *tostaditas* (in Michoacán *tostaditas* are called *totopos*.)

About 1 lb. lard or shortening, or 2 cups vegetable oil	**12 corn tortillas, cut into 6 wedges per tortilla for *tostaditas* or left whole for tostadas**

❶ Heat fat in heavy frying pan until a tiny bit of bread dropped into it fries golden immediately.

❷ Fry tortilla wedges or whole tortillas, about 6 wedges or 1 whole tortilla at a time, until just crisp.

❸ Drain on absorbent paper.

·· **VARIATION** ··

FRIED FLOUR TORTILLAS

Savory: Flour tortillas, cut into large wedges, are delicious fried golden and topped with a spoonful of mole sauce and sprinkling of chopped green onions for an unusual appetizer.

Sweet: Crisp, golden-fried star or flower shapes can be dusted with cinnamon and sugar and eaten as a cookie, perhaps alongside a simple fruit dessert or ice cream. Flour tortillas may be stuffed with fruit and fried, or the hot golden tortillas may be sprinkled with chocolate and left to melt. See the desserts chapter for complete recipes.

A whimsical idea: Cut the tortillas, either flour or corn, into shapes such as stars, arrows, abstracts, or leaf shapes, then deep-fry until crisp and light golden.

Tacos

Tacos are probably most Americans' first introduction to Mexican food. They are eaten in one form or another throughout the Republic and north of the border as well. Tacos may be soft, consisting of savory ingredients wrapped up in a fresh, warm and pliable corn tortilla, or they may be crisp, having been stuffed and then fried until golden brown, or the tortillas may first be fried into crisp shells, then stuffed.

Throughout Mexico, tacos reflect the regional cuisine. The marketplace is the best place to sample them, especially when the tortillas are soft and warm, pulled off the griddle and wrapped around some sort of saucy or crisp morsel. The fillings are often displayed in brightly colored *cazuelitas*, or in utilitarian stainless steel bowls.

Almost any stewed, grilled, fried, or dressed mixture can be used for filling a taco. *Tacos al carbón* contain shreds of charcoal-grilled meats, unforgettably delicious. Mexico City *carnitas* taste of the very essence of Mexico, especially when eaten as you wander through the Merced market (a market not much different from its Aztec ancestor that flourished for millennia, long before the appearance of the conquistadores). In the south coast areas, tacos are apt to be filled with seafood, while in the central area pork is favored. Yucatán tacos may be filled with exquisitely refreshing *fiambres*, cool vinaigrette-dressed mixtures of seafood, poultry, or meat. Probably any sort of savory meat, fish, or vegetables can be turned into taco filling, seasoned with a spoonful of spunky salsa.

TEN SIMPLE FILLINGS FOR SOFT TACOS

◆ *Fiambre de Jaiba*: Toss cold cooked crabmeat with a cilantro-rich salsa, generous squeeze of lime, and a bit of raw onion. Garnish with thinly sliced lettuce.

◆ Chorizo and potatoes: Brown together, then wrap in soft tortillas.

◆ *Carnitas*: The marketplace classic. Wrap soft warm tortillas around *carnitas*; garnish with Salsa Cruda, chopped onion, cilantro, wedges of lime.

◆ *Flores de Calabacitas* (Squash Flower Tacos): Remove the petals from the stems of 25 to 30 squash flowers. Chop coarsely, then sauté in butter with 1 to 2 cloves chopped garlic and 1 thinly sliced jalapeño or serrano chilli. Season with salt; a bit of shredded Jack or mozzarella cheese is optional.

◆ Chile Colorado: Wrap in soft corn tortillas along with slices of chipotle chilli, sour cream, and avocado.

◆ Chunks of cooked fish, either baked with spices or simply steamed, wrapped in a corn tortilla and splashed with a fresh, invigorating salsa.

◆ Grated cheese and chopped onion: Heat in pan until bubbly, then serve with salsa, avocado, and sour cream.

◆ Diced lobster and avocado wrapped in warm, soft tortillas along with chopped onion and tomato salsa of choice.

◆ Nopale cactus with shredded cooked meat (browned ground beef, or a soy-based meat substitute). Garnish with chopped raw onion, tomatoes and cilantro; roll in soft corn tortillas.

◆ Sautéed red, yellow, and green peppers with tomatoes, cumin, chilli, melted cheese, and sour cream.

TACOS DE POLLO
CHICKEN TACOS WITH GUACAMOLE

An excellent use for cooked chicken that has simmered in a soup pot. The boiled chicken is shredded and quickly browned with a bit of cumin, garlic, and chilli, then a few spoonfuls are wrapped up in corn tortillas. They're good soft, and equally good fried to a crisp.

Salsa verde, that tangy green tomatillo-based hot sauce, is especially delicious with this simple taco.

½ lb. boiled chicken, cut or shredded into bite-sized bits (about 1 to 1½ cups)
Oil for browning chicken and tortillas
½ to 1 teaspoon cumin seeds
2 cloves garlic, chopped
½ teaspoon mild chilli powder, or to taste
Salt and pepper to taste
4 corn tortillas
2 tablespoons chopped cilantro
2 tablespoons finely chopped onion

Handful shredded lettuce
Sour cream (optional)
Extra salsa or finely chopped raw chillies
1 recipe Guacamole (or make a simple one by mashing 2 avocados with lots of lemon or lime juice, adding a chopped tomato and enough flavorful salsa to give it spirit)

❶ Quickly brown the chicken in a little oil with cumin seeds and garlic, then sprinkle in chilli powder. Season with salt and pepper.

❷ Heat tortillas, one at a time, in oiled pan until pliable, then place on plate to stuff. Place several spoonfuls of the chicken mixture on each tortilla and roll up.

❸ Serve as is, topped with cilantro, onion, lettuce, sour cream, salsa, and guacamole, or fry until crispy. To fry, heat pan until quite hot, add an inch or so of oil, then quickly fry the tacos until golden brown. You may need to use toothpicks to secure the edges of the tacos to prevent the filling from leaking out. ***Serves 2 as a main course, 4 as an appetizer***

TACOS DE TINGA POBLANA
SMOKY-FLAVORED SHREDDED PORK TACOS WITH AVOCADO—PUEBLA

In this simple fragrant dish, the earthy corn flavors play against the richness of the meat and smoky heat of the sauce. Like so many other of Mexico's savory, robust dishes, this one begins with a pot of simmering meat. The broth is used in soup, the meat in this dish the next day. The meat must be cooked enough so that it can be shredded with two forks. Pork is the usual choice.

Throughout Puebla you'll find tostadas and *tacos de tinga*. *Tingas* (spicy, sautéed hash) were invented in that area during colonial times and are a good example of the combining of Old World/Spanish and New World/Indian ingredients, prepared with the European technique of sautéing onions and garlic rather than the Indian technique of grinding these into a paste. Along with the distinctive chipotle, sometimes a *tinga* will contain chorizo as well. Since *tingas* are so richly seasoned, I think they are at their best rolled into a soft tortilla for a taco.

2 shallots or 1 onion, chopped
½ to 1 tablespoon vegetable oil, or as needed
1 to 1½ tablespoons mild chilli powder, either ancho, New Mexico, or mixed chilli spice mixture
1 lb. simmered pork, cooled, shredded into small pieces
2 tomatoes, seeded, peeled, and diced (canned are fine)

About ¾ cup broth from cooking the meat
1 to 2 chipotles, mashed, plus a bit of the marinade
8 fresh warm corn tortillas
2 avocados, sliced
½ cup sour cream
¼ cup chopped cilantro
¼ cup sliced or diced radishes and/or
½ cup thinly sliced lettuce

· ·

❶ Sauté shallots or onion in vegetable oil until softened.

❷ Add the meat and sauté for a few more minutes with the onion. Add the chilli powder, tomatoes and broth and cook until it reduces into a sauce, mashing the meat a bit as it cooks. Add the chipotles and continue to cook and mash until the sauce and meat are nearly one.

❸ Serve warm tortillas topped with or rolled around several spoonfuls of the meat mixture, adding a slice of avocado, and a dollop of sour cream to each. Eat immediately, garnished with a sprinkling of cilantro and chopped radishes and/or shredded lettuce. **Serves 4**

· ·

CON CHORIZO

Often Mexican chorizo is added to the Tinga Poblana mixture. Add one or two plump chorizo sausages, skinned and broken into pieces, along with the sautéing onion. Since chorizo can be quite spicy you may want to decrease or omit chilli powder.

TACOS DE CARNERO
CRISP TACOS OF SAVORY ROASTED LAMB AND ONIONS

Chipotles, along with onions, garlic, and a bit of cumin, season this rich lamb taco filling; wrapped in a crispy corn tortilla, freshened with a shredding of raw cabbage, this makes a deliciously lusty taco.

Cooking the lamb in a heavy pot helps it roast away unwatched until it is very tender and browned; a lighter-weight pot will require periodic checks to be sure the meat is not burning.

For the Lamb Filling:

1 to 1½ lbs. lamb chops or lamb stewing meat, including bones
2 onions, sliced or diced
3 to 5 cloves garlic, coarsely diced
1 to 2 chipotles, diced

1 to 2 teaspoons chipotle chilli marinade
½ to 1 teaspoon cumin seeds
¾ to 1 cup broth of choice
Salt and pepper to taste

❶ In a heavy (preferably cast-iron) pot with a tight-fitting lid, place all of the ingredients. Add salt and pepper if needed. Cover tightly with the lid.

❷ Place in 350°F oven and bake for at least 1 hour. Check occasionally to see that meat is browning nicely, turning if necessary.

❸ Remove meat from bone, cut into small pieces and keep warm. May be prepared a day ahead and defatted before reheating.

For the Tacos:

8 to 12 tortillas
½ head cabbage, thinly sliced

Jalapeños *en escabeche* to taste

❶ Warm tortillas until soft and pliable.

❷ Wrap tortillas around hot, tender lamb mixture, strew with cabbage, garnish with jalapeños *en escabeche*, then roll up. For crisp tacos or tostadas, first fry tortillas until crisp, then top (or stuff) and serve immediately. **Serves 4 to 6**

··

TACOS DE LANGOSTA Y AGUACATE
LOBSTER AND AVOCADO SOFT TACOS

Sweet lobster and creamy avocado, combined with a bit of chilli spice, a chopping of raw onion, and a sprinkle of cilantro and salsa, all wrapped up in the earthy flavor of a soft, warm corn tortilla, make the most elegant taco you'll find.

Serve as a first course, followed by Pescado en Adobo.

10 to 12 oz. cooked lobster meat
Oil for heating tortillas and lobster meat
1 teaspoon (or to taste) mild chilli powder such as ancho, pasilla or New Mexico
8 corn tortillas
2 tablespoons finely chopped onions

2 tablespoons finely chopped cilantro
1 avocado, peeled and diced
Juice of ¼ lime or lemon
Salt and pepper to taste
Salsa of choice (or finely chopped chillies)
¼ cup sour cream

··

❶ Gently sauté lobster in a tiny bit of oil with the chilli powder. Remove from heat and set aside.

❷ Heat tortillas in a tiny bit of oil, keeping them warm on a plate covered with foil until you finish heating all of them.

❸ Fill the warm tortillas with a spoonful of the lobster, a sprinkling of the onions, cilantro, avocado, and a squeeze of lime. Season with salt, pepper, salsa or chillies, and top with a spoonful of sour cream.

❹ Roll up and eat right away, accompanied by extra salsa or chillies *en escabeche*. **Serves 4**

························ **VARIATION** ························

TACOS DE JAIBA Y AGUACATE ❖ CRAB AND AVOCADO TACOS
In place of lobster, use 10 to 12 oz. crabmeat.

TACOS DE LANGOSTA Y FRIJOLES ❖ LOBSTER AND BEAN TACOS
Rich refried beans are delicious added to the sweet meat of either lobster or crab. Spread a few spoonfuls of warm refried beans onto each tortilla, then fill with lobster or crab mixture and roll up. Enjoy immediately.

TACOS DE HUACHINANGO CON SALSA VERDE
RED SNAPPER TACOS WITH GREEN SALSA

Red snapper is extremely popular in Mexico. It is a light-flavored yet firm-textured fish, especially good when combined with the strong, bright flavors of chillies, garlic, or tomatoes. The classic red snapper dish, *huachinango Vera-cruzeana*, comes from Veracruz, and is a zesty combination of tomato and chilli-seasoned snapper with garlic, onions, and green olives.

Chunks of red snapper are especially good splashed with a tangy green salsa, then rolled up into tacos.

2 fillets of red snapper or bass, 10 to 12 oz. total
Salt and pepper to taste
1 teaspoon cumin
1 teaspoon mild pure chilli powder (ancho, pasilla, etc) or commercial chilli powder (with cumin and other spices).
½ teaspoon crumbled oregano leaves

2 cloves garlic, chopped
1 to 2 tablespoons olive oil
Juice of ½ lime or lemon
8 corn tortillas
Oil for heating tortillas
Salsa verde, either homemade or good quality bottled
2 tablespoons chopped cilantro
2 tablespoon chopped onion

❶ Place fish in baking dish, then sprinkle with salt, pepper, cumin, chilli powder, oregano, garlic, olive oil, and lime or lemon juice. Cover tightly and bake in a 450°F oven 15 minutes or until just cooked through. Remove from oven and keep warm.

❷ Heat tortillas by warming them gently one at a time in a small amount of oil in a heavy skillet over medium-low heat. Stack them onto a heavy plate and cover them to keep them warm and pliable.

❸ Assemble the tacos: break fish into bite-sized pieces, spoon onto warm tortillas, sprinkle with salsa, cilantro, and onions before rolling up. Serve immediately with extra salsa for dipping. ***Serves 4***

FLAUTAS DE CAMARONES CON GUACAMOLE
CRISP TACOS OF PRAWNS WITH GUACAMOLE

Flautas are thin, flutelike tacos, filled when the tortilla is soft, then rolled and fried to a golden crisp. Often two tortillas are used, one laid on top overlapping a bit to form a much longer surface and more flutelike shape.

Flautas may be filled with chicken, crab, or any other filling in place of the prawns. Since they are fried, however, choose a filling that is not too moist or rich.

Guacamole, cooling and fresh, makes a lively counterpoint to the crisp fried tacos, as does a bowl of a mild relish like salsa or Pico de Gallo.

12 oz. prawns or shrimp, cooked and diced	Salt to taste
1 teaspoon pure mild chilli powder such as ancho or pasilla, or a combination mild chilli powder and paprika	8 corn tortillas
	Oil for frying
	Guacamole
½ onion, finely chopped	Salsa or Pico de Gallo
1 tablespoon chopped cilantro	Toppings: chopped onion, chopped tomatoes, and cilantro

❶ Combine prawns or shrimp with chilli powder, onion, cilantro, and salt.

❷ Prepare either 8 small *flautas* or 4 long ones by using either one corn tortilla per flauta or two. If using two, line them up so that they appear somewhat like a flat double bubble (or double circle, slightly overlapping), then fill and roll. If using only one, simply stuff it with the prawn mixture and roll it. Do not stuff too full and do not fold over at the edges to seal—just roll them very tightly and secure with a toothpick if they show signs of coming apart.

❸ Fry in hot oil to a golden crispness. Drain each *flauta* on absorbent paper.

❹ Serve immediately, each *flauta* garnished with guacamole and salsa, a sprinkling of chopped onions, tomatoes, and cilantro. *Serves 4*

TACOS EN ESTILO SAN LUIS
TACOS FILLED WITH BEANS, MEAT, AND NOPALES CACTUS

These tacos are a memorable melange of flavors and textures. They are not as complicated to make as the list of ingredients implies. The three fillings—sautéed nopales; browned meat and potatoes with tomatoes and chilli; and refried beans—are simple on their own, yet they balance brilliantly.

Meat Filling:

1 oz. raw ground beef or tender, cooked, shredded beef

6 green onions, thinly sliced

6 to 8 cloves garlic, coarsely chopped

1 to 3 small to medium-sized boiled potatoes, cooled and diced

¾ cup chopped tomatoes (canned are preferable unless you have very ripe fresh ones)

2 jalapeños *en escabeche*, chopped or thinly sliced

Salt to taste

Nopale Filling:

2 small to medium onions, thinly sliced

2 cloves garlic, coarsely chopped

1 tablespoon vegetable oil

1 cup cooked nopales, cut into 2-inch lengths (canned are fine)

Salt and pepper to taste

2 teaspoons coarsely chopped cilantro

1½ cups refried beans

8 to 12 corn tortillas

Oil to lightly grease the pan when heating the tortillas

❶ Prepare the meat filling by browning the ground beef or cooked shredded meat in a frying pan. Pour off the fat. Add green onions and garlic and continue cooking a few minutes. Add the potatoes and cook a minute or two longer, taking care not to break up the potatoes too much. Add tomatoes and pickled chillies; taste for salt. Set aside and keep warm if possible.

❷ Prepare the nopale filling: Sauté onions and garlic in vegetable oil until softened, then add nopales (drained if canned). Season with salt, pepper, and cilantro. Set aside.

❸ Heat refried beans and keep warm.

❹ To assemble: Heat each tortilla individually in a medium-hot, lightly greased pan. When hot and pliable, spread each tortilla with refried beans, then top with a few spoonfuls of the meat mixture and the nopale mixture. Roll up or fold over.

❺ Either eat immediately, or keep them warm in the oven while you prepare the rest. ***Serves 4 to 6***

··

·················· **VEGETARIAN VARIATION** ·····················
Since this dish has such a wide range of flavors and textures, a good soya-based ground meat substitute would work well.

··

TACOS DE POLLO EN ESCABECHE
CHICKEN TACOS SPLASHED WITH A TANGY SAUCE

Sloshing a bit of mild sauce onto these tacos stretches the definition of tacos. They're not soft tacos, nor are they crisp ones to pick up in the hands; rather they are both crisp and sauced, somewhat like enchiladas. The filling, too, is different from other taco presentations: using raw chicken instead of cooked gives an almost Asian result.

The sauce is more reminiscent of a French reduction rather than a Mexican salsa. While simple to prepare, this is a sophisticated dish.

Chicken Stuffing:

3 cloves garlic, chopped
1 onion, chopped
1 to 3 roasted medium to hot green chillies, peeled and seeded, then chopped (or to taste)
2 ripe tomatoes (canned are fine), seeded and chopped

1 tablespoon chopped cilantro
About 1 lb. boned raw chicken chunks, coarsely chopped (use food processor or chop by hand)
Salt to taste

··

Mix all ingredients and set aside.

Sauce:

3 cloves garlic, chopped
1 onion, chopped
4 tomatoes, quartered or chopped
(canned are fine)

1 tablespoon vegetable oil
2 cups chicken broth
1 tablespoon vinegar, or lemon or
lime juice

··

❶ In blender or processor, whirl garlic, onion, and tomatoes to make a paste.

❷ Heat oil in frying pan, then add garlic-onion-tomato and fry a few minutes
to concentrate the flavors. Add broth and cook a few minutes longer. Remove
from heat and add vinegar or lemon or lime juice.

To Assemble Tacos:

8 corn tortillas
Vegetable oil for frying

Chicken Stuffing
Reserved Sauce

Toppings:

¼ head cabbage, shredded (or
Enchilado de Col)
Jalapeños *en escabeche* (the kind
with vegetables added)

½ onion, thinly sliced or chopped

··

❶ One at a time, heat the tortillas on a lightly greased frying pan over medium
heat until pliable, then fill with Chicken Stuffing and fold in half, taco style.

❷ When all tortillas are filled, fry them several at a time until they are golden
and crisp. Drain on absorbent paper.

❸ Serve each portion of two tacos splashed with a bit of the warmed reserved
sauce and a garnishing of the shredded or pickled cabbage, the jalapeños and
vegetables *en escabeche*, and onions. *Serves 4*

·································· **VARIATION** ··································

TACOS DE PESCADO EN ESCABECHE
Substitute diced raw fish fillets for the chicken.

··

TOSTADAS WITH TOPPINGS

Tostadas at their most basic refer to fried tortillas, but the word is often used to describe those crisp fried tortillas piled high with a variety of savory fillings and fresh salad ingredients. At a garish extreme they may be deep-fried into gargantuan edible plates and piled high with robust meat and salad ingredients, far too much for one person but too enticing to leave unfinished.

Nearly anything can top tostados, and frequently does. Creamy refried pinto or black beans can act as a delicious "glue" for toppings that range from diced vegetables to seafood, to savory shredded or sauced meats. Piles of fresh shredded cabbage or lettuce, diced radishes and thinly sliced onion, a sprinkling of cilantro and/or diced tomatoes, strips of pickled chillies *en escabeche* or chipotle, slices of avocado, drifts of soft, cooling sour cream—all of these, and more, might be found on a tostada.

TOSTADAS COMPUESTAS
TOSTADAS WITH A SELECTION OF TOPPINGS

The flat, crisp corn tortillas are a natural bed on which to pile toppings. Begin by spreading the tortilla with refried beans (pinto or black), then proceed with a generous spoonful of browned meats or chorizo, then shredded cheese and lettuce, diced tomato, onions, strips of pickled chillies or chipotle, slices of avocado, dollops of sour cream. The tostada is at its best when towering and unwieldy.

Great fun for informal entertaining: the hot bean- and sauce-topped tostadas can be offered on a platter with a selection of toppings for guests to help themselves to.

Meat Mixture:

About 12 oz. chorizo (or use ground meat seasoned with a good mild chilli powder mixture of ancho and pasilla, lots of cumin, and a shot of cinnamon and oregano)

1 onion, chopped
2 cloves garlic, chopped

Tostada Base:

4 corn tortillas, fried to a golden crisp.
About 1 cup warm refried pinto or black beans

About 4 oz. shredded cheese such as Jack or garlic Jack

Toppings:

1 ½ cups shredded lettuce
1 onion, chopped
1 cup diced tomatoes
½ cup roasted mild green chillies
Salsa of choice
1 sliced avocado
Chipotle chillies cut into strips, and/
or chillies *en escabeche*

Any pickled vegetable such as
cabbage or carrots
½ cup sour cream
¼ cup each: chopped cilantro, green
onions, radishes

....

❶ Brown chorizo (or seasoned ground meat) with onion and garlic.

❷ Spread refried beans on tostada shells, then top each with meat mixture, shredded cheese, and shredded lettuce. Offer the other toppings separately in bowls. *Serves 4*

....

TOSTADAS TAPATIA
PIG'S FEET TOSTADAS WITH VINAIGRETTE-DRESSED LETTUCE TOPPING—GUADALAJARA

In Jalisco, tostadas of pickled pig's feet are quite popular. Over the layer of hot beans and cheese, the pieces of boneless pig's feet, fresh vinaigrette-dressed lettuce, and nuggets of crunchy radish make a hearty accompaniment through a night of *cerveza* and mariachis.

4 corn tortillas, fried to a golden
crisp
1 ½ cups refried beans, heated
through
4 to 6 oz. shredded Jack or similar
cheese
6 ounces pickled pig's feet, cut into
bite-sized pieces

2 cups shredded lettuce, lightly
dressed with oil and vinegar
(crunchy Romaine or iceberg is best
here)
6 to 8 radishes, sliced
Several pinches crumbled dried
oregano leaves
Hot chilli sauce such as Tabasco or
salsa of choice

....

Spread tortillas with hot refried beans, then sprinkle with cheese. Broil until the cheese melts. Serve immediately topped with the pig's feet, lettuce, and radishes. Sprinkle with oregano and a dash of hot sauce. *Serves 4*

....

TOSTADAS DE PAPAS
POTATO TOSTADAS WITH *SALSA VERDE DE TOMATILLO* AND SOUR CREAM

The tangy flavor of tomatillo salsa pairs particularly well with the earthy, spicy chillied potatoes. A smoky whiff of chipotle is a delicious counterpoint to this delightfully tart salsa, but if chipotle is unavailable, thin rings of pickled jalapeños are good, too. Sour cream cools it all off, and the crunch of shredded cabbage gives additional textural interest.

3 medium potatoes, peeled and diced
1 small onion, diced
1 tablespoon vegetable oil
2 cloves garlic, chopped
1 teaspoon mild chilli powder
1 teaspoon paprika
4 corn tortillas, fried to a golden crisp

Refried beans (optional)
Salsa verde *de tomatillo*, either homemade or a good commercial one
About ¹/₃ cup sour cream
1 tablespoon chopped cilantro
1 chipotle chilli, or 2 jalapeños *en escabeche*, sliced
Handful shredded cabbage

❶ Lightly brown the potatoes and onion in the oil. When potatoes are nearly tender, add garlic, chilli powder, and paprika. Set aside and keep warm.

❷ Heat tortillas under the grill or in a hot oven, just long enough to heat through. Then spread with refried beans, if desired. Pile with cooked potatoes, garnish with Salsa Verde, sour cream, cilantro, chipotle or jalapeño *en escabeche*, and a sprinkling of shredded cabbage. Serve immediately. **Serves 4**

·············· VARIATION ··············

TOSTADAS DE PAPAS Y CAMARONES ❖ POTATO AND SHRIMP TOSTADAS
Add a handful of warm cooked shrimp to the tostadas, scattered on top of the potatoes.

PICADAS
CARNITAS TOSTADAS WITH *SALSA VERDE DE TOMATILLO* AND CHIPOTLE—PUEBLA

These tostadas combine a layer of rich meat *carnitas* with a dab of fiery smoke-tinged chipotle salsa and a spoonful of tart tomatillo salsa. The contrast is superb.

4 corn tortillas, fried to a golden crisp
Several spoonfuls of refried beans, sour cream, or guacamole (to flavorfully anchor the chopped meat to the tostada)
About 1½ cups chopped or diced *carnitas* or other tender cooked meat

About ½ cup mild Salsa verde *de Tomatillo*, (fresh or bottled)
¼ cup Salsa de Chiles Chipotles
½ onion, finely chopped

Spread refried beans (or sour cream or guacamole) thinly over each tostada. Pile with meat, then garnish with Salsa Verde and Salsa de Chiles Chipotles. Sprinkle onion over the top and serve immediately. *Serves 4*

SEVEN SIMPLE SAVORY TOSTADAS

TOSTADAS DE FRIJOLES Y HUEVOS
TOSTADAS OF BLACK BEANS AND SCRAMBLED EGGS

Spread 4 hot crisp tostadas with 1½ cups mashed Frijoles Negros Enchilados. Top with 4 to 6 eggs scrambled Mexican style: butter-sauté 2 to 3 cloves coarsely chopped garlic, ½ to 1 thinly sliced serrano or jalapeño, 1 diced tomato, and 2 tablespoons chopped cilantro. Scramble the eggs in this mixture. Salt and pepper to taste. *Serves 4*

TOSTADAS DE FRIJOLES Y CREMA
REFRIED BEAN AND CHEESE TOSTADAS TOPPED WITH ROASTED GREEN CHILLI CREAM

Spread 4 crisp-fried corn tostadas with refried beans (about 3 tablespoons per tostada), then with shredded Jack, mozzarella, white cheddar, queso fresca, or fresh pecorino cheese and a sprinkle of cumin or red chilli powder. Broil until cheese melts. Meanwhile, blend 1 cup sour cream with ¼ cup finely chopped roasted mild green chillies (or more, to taste). When hot tostadas emerge from broiler, spread with chilli cream and serve immediately. *Serves 4*

TOSTADOS DE PATO
DUCK AND CHIPOTLE TOSTADAS

Spread 4 corn tostadas with Frijoles Refritos made with black beans. Top
each with several spoonfuls shredded roast duck, a tablespoon or so chopped
onion, salsa, sour cream, a few drops of either chipotle marinade or Salsa de
Chiles Chipotles and a sprinkling of cilantro. *Serves 4*

PANUCHOS
BLACK BEAN TOSTADAS OR STUFFED TORTILLAS
TOPPED WITH PICKLED ONION RINGS

In the Yucatán, tortillas are slit open to form a pocket, then stuffed, fried
crisp, and topped with a variety of savory ingredients. A simplified version is
the following tostada.
Spread each of 4 crispy fried tostadas with about 3 tablespoons mashed
Frijoles Negros Enchilados, then top with several spoonfuls torn or shredded
simmered chicken or several slices of hard-boiled egg; garnish with Cebollas
en Escabeche a la Yucateca (or thinly sliced onion marinated in lemon juice
for 15 to 30 minutes). Top with a handful of shredded lettuce and sliced jalapeños *en escabeche*. *Serves 4*

TOSTADAS DE LEGUMBRES ENCHILADOS
POTATO, CARROT, AND GREEN BEAN TOSTADAS
WITH SALSA RANCHERA AND SOUR CREAM

Onto each of 4 crisp fried tostadas, spread several tablespoons hot Salsa
Ranchera, then top with several spoonfuls of Legumbres Enchilados and a
dollop of sour cream. Add Salsa Picante Verde or a scattering of cilantro as a
garnish. *Serves 4*

TOSTADAS DE PESCADO Y CALABAZA EN VINAGRETA
TOSTADAS OF VINAIGRETTE-DRESSED ZUCCHINI AND FISH

Onto each of 4 crisp fried tostadas, spread a thin layer of warm refried beans. Top with a layer of diced cooked whitefish fillets or shellfish, then a layer of Ensalada de Calabaza y Jitomate. Top with a flurry of shredded lettuce and chopped cilantro. Offer salsa of choice on the side. *Serves 4*

TOSTADAS DE LENGUA DE RES CON SALSA DE CHIPOTLES
TONGUE TOSTADAS WITH CHIPOTLE SALSA

Spread about 3 to 4 tablespoons warm refried beans on each of 4 crisp fried tostadas; top with about ¼ cup julienned tongue (see recipes in the Meat chapter) and Salsa de Chiles Chipotles. Add chopped cilantro and lettuce as desired.

Flour Tortilla Dishes

Tortillas made of wheat flour rather than corn are favored in Mexico's northern regions such as Sonora, as well as in the American Southwest, especially Arizona. Introduced by the Spaniards, wheat added a new dimension to the previously corn-dominated Mexican diet.

Many simple meals are based on warm flour tortillas rolled around mixtures of beef or pork in sauces of brick-red ancho or pasilla chillies or green tomatillos. In such dishes the flour tortillas are the perfect partner to the robust stew. I cannot think of any other dish that is equally satisfying.

Flour tortillas are used for a variety of burritos, *chimichangas*, and layered savory tarts. They may also be used for sweets—fry them until golden and dust them with sugar and cinnamon for impromptu buñuelos (fried sweet cakes). Refer to the Desserts chapter for other ideas.

BURRITOS DE NOPALES Y FRIJOLES
BEAN AND CACTUS BURRITOS

Tangy nopales, rich creamy beans, melted cheese, and bits of crisp raw onion wrapped into a soft warm flour tortilla: delicious and so simple. Browned chorizo makes a good addition.

²/₃ to 1 cup cut-up or diced nopales, cooked and drained (bottled or canned are fine)
2 tablespoons vegetable oil, plus a tiny bit more for heating tortillas
4 large flour tortillas
1 to 1¹/₂ cups refried beans, heated through

4 to 6 oz. mild cheese such as Jack, shredded
Salsa of choice, either green or red
¹/₂ medium to large onion, chopped
1 medium-sized chorizo sausage, skinned and browned, broken into bits as it browns (optional)

❶ Lightly sauté nopales in 2 tablespoons oil; set aside and keep warm.

❷ Spray or lightly brush tortillas with a bit of water, then place in a lightly oiled hot frying pan and quickly cook on both sides until pliable.

❸ Stuff the warm tortillas with the sautéed nopales, hot refried beans, shredded cheese, salsa, chopped onion, and chorizo if desired. Roll up and enjoy immediately, or place in baking dish, cover with foil, and keep warm in a medium oven until all burritos are prepared. *Serves 4*

BURRITOS DE HUEVOS A LA MAYA
WARM FLOUR TORTILLAS WRAPPED AROUND SCRAMBLED EGGS AND PIPIAN SAUCE

Eggs are a favorite food in the Yucatán region—you find slices of eggs tucked into enchiladas and tacos, as a topping for tostadas, decorating salads and platters of sauced foods, as well as scrambled and layered into dishes like these burritos.

In this dish the eggs are scrambled into soft creamy curds and rolled into warm flour tortillas along with a good spoonful of Pipián Sauce, a puree of pumpkin seeds and vegetables. Sprinkle in a little chopped chilli or hot salsa since the sauce is quite mild.

Enjoy accompanied by platters of black beans, Arroz Mexicana, and sautéed chorizo.

½ recipe Pipián Sauce
8 eggs, lightly beaten
3 tablespoons butter
Salt and pepper to taste
8 small to medium flour tortillas or 4 large ones

Few drops vegetable oil (if needed)
2 to 3 green onions, thinly sliced
1 jalapeño, chopped (seeded if desired), or salsa to taste

❶ Prepare Pipián Sauce and set aside.

❷ Scramble eggs softly in butter with salt and pepper to taste.

❸ Heat flour tortillas in hot pan, sprinkling with a drop or two of water as you go along. If the tortillas stick, add just a few drops of oil to the pan.

❹ As each tortilla is warmed, spoon in the scrambled eggs, then several spoonfuls of Pipián Sauce and a sprinkling of green onions and jalapeño or salsa. Enjoy immediately. *Serves 4*

BLACK BEAN BURRITOS WITH FETA CHEESE, SOUR CREAM, AND FRESH MINT

Not an authentic Mexican dish, rather one I put together from ingredients on hand. It is amazing how lovely a combination the feta cheese, fresh mint, and black beans are, especially contrasted to the soft, white flour tortilla. A variation I am especially fond of is using a pizza-type dough base or fresh bread dough fried into flat rounds or baked into a sort of *focaccio* in place of the flour tortillas.

4 flour tortillas, preferably homemade and a bit thicker than storebought ones, warmed through; or fresh bread dough rolled flat into pancakelike shapes and pan-fried until golden and cooked through.
About 1½ cups Frijoles Negros Enchilados or Frijoles Refritos made with black beans, heated through

4 oz. crumbled feta cheese
Salsa Cruda
2 tablespoons chopped fresh mint
1 tablespoon chopped onion
2 tablespoons chopped cilantro
3 tablespoons sour cream

Spread tortillas or flatbreads with warm beans, then top with crumbled cheese, salsa, mint, onion, cilantro, and sour cream. Serve immediately. *Serves 4*

CHIMICHANGAS ❖ CRISP FLOUR TORTILLA—WRAPPED PARCELS, ARIZONA AND SONORA STYLE

Chimichangas are burritos plunged into hot oil and fried to a golden crisp. The most common filling is shredded meat or poultry rather than the refried beans or cheese often used in tender soft burritos. Other fillings for *chimichangas* include picadillo (hash) made with the traditional beef, or made with the less traditional shredded dark meat of turkey or chicken; browned shreds of simmered pork; browned and crumbled chorizo (or mild chilli-spiced minced beef) mixed with refried beans; diced potato and chorizo; or spicy fish. For a sweet twist on the genre, try the Chimichangas de Frutas in the Desserts chapter.

Chimichangas originated in the region that is now the state of Sonora, as well as across the border into Arizona. A good *chimichanga* is a contrast of textures: the crisp outside, soft flour-tortilla inside, and savory stuffing, slathered with cool sour cream and/or guacamole and spicy-hot salsa.

Chimichangas make excellent do-ahead party fare; the filling may be prepared up to a day ahead and kept refrigerated, or the whole parcels may be fried earlier in the day and reheated in a 400°F oven until heated through and crisp, about 10 minutes.

CHIMICHANGAS DE RES
BEEF *CHIMICHANGAS*

Hearty Southwestern fare, this is a classic rendition—the shredded meat encased in a golden, crisp tortilla shell, green chilli salsa and sour cream blanketing the whole thing.

8 large flour tortillas
1 recipe Ropa Vieja
Oil for frying
Green Chilli Salsa, Sonora Style
Sour cream
1 diced avocado or 1 batch
Guacamole of choice

Hot salsa of choice or chopped jalapeños
4 green onions, thinly sliced, or 2 tablespoons chopped cilantro
16 ripe black olives (oil-cured or Greek-style) pitted and halved

❶ Heat tortillas one at a time in a lightly greased heavy skillet or frying pan. When softened, place several spoonfuls of Ropa Vieja in the middle of each tortilla along a vertical line, leaving a border at the top and at the sides to seal the edges.

❷ Fold the top and bottom over to encase the filling, then roll the sides into neat parcels.

❸ Heat oil and fry stuffed parcels, about 2 at a time, depending on the size of the pan, and cook until golden brown. (Alternatively, they may be pan sautéed, then placed in a baking dish and baked in a 375 degree oven. This method is best for serving a large group.)

❹ Serve the *chimichangas* hot, each crisp golden parcel topped with a dollop of sour cream, avocado or guacamole, a spoonful of salsa, a sprinkling of green onions or cilantro, and a few olive halves. *Serves 8*

CHIMICHANGAS DE PAPAS
POTATO *CHIMICHANGAS*

Flour tortilla parcels filled with cheesey and sour creamy, chilli-spiked mashed potatoes, then fried to a golden crisp, are an unexpected treat. Serve with a splash of salsa, a sprinkle of chillies, and sour cream.

4 flour tortillas
**Filling from Enchiladas de Papas,
omitting the mild chilli powder**
Oil for shallow frying

2 to 3 chopped green onions
About ½ cup sour cream
Salsa of choice

❶ Gently heat the tortillas, one by one, in an ungreased or lightly greased pan to soften. Remove to a plate and fill each with several spoonfuls of the potato filling. Fold the tops over, then roll up the sides to make an oblong parcel. Set aside until all tortillas and filling have been used up.

❷ Heat the oil until hot enough for frying. Add the parcels and cook on medium-high heat until lightly golden brown. Drain on absorbent paper.

❸ Serve garnished with green onion, sour cream, and salsa. *Serves 4*

TORTA CON QUESO Y TOMATILLO
TORTE OF CHEESE AND GREEN CHILLI SALSA

Butter 6 flour tortillas and broil until crisp. Layer with 2 to 3 cups shredded Jack, fresh mozzarella, or similar cheese and 1 to 2 cups Mole Verde, ending with a layer of cheese. Bake in 375°F oven about 15 minutes, or until cheese is melted and bubbly-browned. Serve cut into wedges topped with cilantro, sour cream, and diced tomatoes. *Serves 4 to 6*

SINCRONIZADAS
CRISP STUFFED FLOUR TORTILLAS

Like burritos, *sincronizadas* are a specialty of Arizona and Sonora, Mexico. The flat discs are crisp and golden and oozing melted cheese; the name refers to the synchronization of the two flour tortillas, held together with the melted cheese like so much delicious glue.

Other savory bits may be added to the cheese filling: slices of salty pink ham, spicy salami, browned and crumbled bits of chorizo, pureed black beans, even a little bit of cooked and well-squeezed chopped spinach mixed with a few dabs of creamy ricotta or similar cheese. A good salsa spread on the tortillas before sandwiching them individualizes the dish: try a rich dark pasilla chilli paste, and splash the finished product with a fresh and tangy tomato salsa. Or spread the tortillas with a bit of fiery chipotle salsa, then use a creamy mozzarella type cheese and dress the sandwich with a freshly tart tomatillo salsa. They make a zesty snack; cut into polite wedges they make good dinner party nibbles. For each *sincronizada*:

2 large flour tortillas
Salsa or spice paste of choice (a thick, unrunny one works best)
About 3 oz. sliced cheese (Jack, mozzarella, Cheddar, etc.)
Optional Additions: **1 or 2 oz. sliced ham, spicy salami, or browned crumbled chorizo; pureed spiced black beans; or a tablespoon or two of cooked spinach squeezed dry, mixed with a bit of creamy ricotta or goat-type cheese**

Several tablespoons vegetable or bland seed oil for frying
Fresh salsa of choice (preferably green tomatillo salsa)
About 1 tablespoon sour cream
¼ cup shredded lettuce
1 green onion, chopped
2 radishes, diced

❶ Spread the tortillas lightly with salsa or spice paste of choice. Arrange the cheese on top of one tortilla, then top with your choice of the optional savory bits.

❷ Top with the other salsa-spread tortilla, the spread side inward, to make a sort of disclike sandwich.

❸ Heat the oil in a heavy frying pan. When hot enough for frying, place the sandwich in the hot pan carefully, so that the filling doesn't plop out. Over medium-high heat, cook the disc until golden brown and cheese begins to melt. Turn over and repeat. The sandwich will be done when both sides are golden, leaning toward brown in places, crisp, and the cheese is melted. Any bits of cheese that melt out of the sandwich will fry in the hot oil and become crispy and luscious.

❹ Drain a minute on absorbent paper, then serve immediately, piled with the toppings: spicy salsa, sour cream, lettuce, green onion, and diced radishes. *Serves 1 as a snack or light meal*

....

QUESADILLAS
SAVORY TURNOVERS

Quesadillas are uncooked tortillas that are stuffed and folded, then either fried in oil or cooked on an ungreased heavy pan. A dough of straight masa gives a good flavor but the consistency is a bit sticky; using the basic dough for antojitos gives a more manageable pastry.

Traditional fillings include meat, vegetables, mole or adobo mixtures, chorizo, potatoes, beans, and cheese. Simple cheese and chillies is possibly the best to my taste, the rich turnover topped with a fresh relish of diced tomato, chilli, onion, and cilantro.

Stuffed with cheese and topped with avocado or guacamole, quesadillas are delicious for breakfast. Smaller versions make an excellent first course or appetizer.

For each quesadilla: Take either a freshly made uncooked tortilla or a storebought corn tortilla, lightly warmed in a bit of oil to make it pliable. Place a few spoonfuls of the filling of choice in the center, fold over, then fry on both sides either in oil or in an ungreased frying pan. Serve immediately, garnished with strips of fresh or pickled chilli or a good quality salsa, chopped onions, and guacamole or diced avocado.

....

Three Simple Quesadillas

QUESO Y CHILE VERDE
CHEESE AND GREEN CHILLI

Fill each quesadilla with several spoonfuls of shredded cheese (Jack, mozzarella, queso fresca, etc). and a spoonful or so of roasted mild green chillies, cut into strips. Fry the quesadillas until the cheese melts and oozes out of the edges. Serve topped with Pico de Gallo, or Salsa de chillies y ajo, or other salsa of choice. *Serves 1*

MACHACA DE CAMARON
SHRIMP HASH

Sauté 1 chopped onion and several cloves garlic in vegetable oil, then add 1 chopped jalapeño and 1 cup diced tomatoes. Cook until no longer watery but thick and saucy. Season with ½ teaspoon cumin, a pinch of cinnamon, and ¼ teaspoon oregano, then add about 12 ounces diced raw shrimp. Cook a few minutes longer over low heat until it is relatively dry, full of savory flavors. Season with salt and pepper, then spoon into uncooked tortilla and proceed as for Quesadillas. *Serves 4*

SESOS
BRAINS

Soak one pair lamb or beef brains in cold water to cover for one hour, then remove outer membrane and veins. Place in boiling water with several cloves garlic, 1 bay leaf, a spoonful of vinegar or juice of ½ lime, and sprinkle of salt. Reduce heat and simmer on very low heat for 30 minutes. Cool in its liquid, then drain and cut into large dice or mash coarsely. Season with fresh home-made salsa of choice, along with a few sprigs of chopped epazote, if available.

Stuff into quesadillas (makes a good taco filling as well) and serve garnished with shredded lettuce and salsa of choice. *Serves 4*

Enchiladas

Enchiladas are corn tortillas dipped first in a savory sauce, then into hot oil, and rolled up. The word *enchilada* translates to "chillied up," referring to the spicy sauce in which the tortillas are dipped. Usually, but not always, they are wrapped around a filling of some sort: meat, fish, cheese, poultry, vegetables, or simply chopped onion, chillies, and herbs. Most commonly rolled, enchiladas may also be stacked, as in New Mexico, or folded, as in Oaxaca. They may be served as is, or slathered with sauce and cheeses and baked into a savory casserole.

I will never forget the first simple countryside enchiladas I tasted in Mexico. On a second-class bus journey through the mountains in which I shared my seat with several chickens and one snake, our vehicle came to a stop in a rustic village. There were no amenities, no café, rest stop, or souvenir stand. Instead there was a flock of plump brown women bearing huge platters of enchiladas. They came up to the windows of the bus offering their wares. The freshly made tortillas tasted of field-grown corn, dipped into a vibrant chilli sauce. There was only a bit of onion for filling—this was a poor village—yet it was as memorable as any more elaborate and complicated dish could have been.

A practical note: Good authentic enchiladas should be prepared with slightly stale corn tortillas.

ENCHILADAS DE PAPAS
POTATO AND CHEESE ENCHILADAS

Corn tortillas filled with a mild, cheesey potato mixture, then baked in an unusual cilantro sauce, make a surprisingly delicate flavored though hearty and filling dish. Since it is not dipped into a chilli sauce, this is not an authentic enchilada but more a baked taco.

Serve a small portion as a first course, Mexican style, followed by a mild chilli-grilled fish, or accompany with a large salad for a cozy supper.

Filling:

6 to 8 large, mealy potatoes, boiled until tender, then mashed

8 to 10 oz. crumbled cheese such as *queso fresco*, fresh pecorino, or a not-too-salty feta

1¼ cups sour cream

8 green onions, thinly sliced

3 or 4 jalapeños, roasted over an open flame and peeled, then stem and seeds removed and chilli flesh chopped

Generous pinch mild chilli powder (optional)

Salt and pepper to taste

Oil for frying

8 corn tortillas

Sauce:

2 cloves garlic, chopped
6 ripe tomatoes, roasted, seeded, and peeled (canned are fine)
1 poblano or Anaheim chile, charred and peeled, then diced

1 to 2 serranos or jalapeños
1 cup chicken or vegetable broth
½ cup coarsely chopped cilantro
Juice of 1 lime
1 tablespoon vegetable oil

Toppings:

4 oz. sharp cheese of choice, coarsely shredded

Shredded lettuce
Salsa of choice

....

❶ Mix mashed potatoes with cheese, sour cream, green onions, chopped chillies and mild chilli powder. Season with salt and pepper and set aside.

❷ Heat oil, then warm tortillas in the oil one at a time. Place several spoonfuls of filling in the center of each tortilla and roll up. Place in a casserole baking dish.

❸ Make sauce: In blender or food processor, puree garlic, then add tomatoes, chillies, broth, cilantro, and lime juice. Whirl until it reaches a sauce consistency.

❹ Heat 1 tablespoon oil in heavy frying pan. Add the sauce, several spoonfuls at a time at first, then the rest, letting it fry and reduce in volume until it darkens somewhat and intensifies in flavor. This should only take a minute or two.

❺ Pour sauce over potato-stuffed tortillas and sprinkle with cheese.

❻ Bake in a 400°F oven about 10 minutes, just long enough for cheese topping to melt and ingredients to meld and heat through.

❼ Serve sprinkled with shredded lettuce and offer salsa of choice. *Serves 4*
....

ENFRIJOLADAS
BEAN-TOPPED ENCHILADAS

This hearty casserole consists of enchiladas topped with a layer of refried beans, a layer of cheese, then baked until melty. It is the sort of rib-sticking dish that could warm any winter's evening. Though the filling in the recipe is a simple one of browned beef or pork, any browned meat bits make a good filling.

1 ¹/₄ lb. ground beef or pork
3 small to medium onions, chopped, divided
2 tablespoons chopped cilantro
2 jalapeños, (roasted, peeled, and chopped if hot; raw and chopped if mild)
Salt and pepper to taste
8 corn tortillas

Oil for frying
About 3 cups refried beans, canned or homemade
12 oz. sharp creamy cheese such as Jack or Cheddar, grated coarsely
²/₃ cup sour cream
About 6 leaves lettuce, shredded
Salsa of choice

* * *

❶ Brown the meat and 2 of the onions, crumbling the meat as it cooks. Pour off excess fat, then add cilantro, jalapeños, and salt and pepper. Set aside.

❷ Heat tortillas in a tiny bit of oil to soften. Stuff with the meat mixture and place stuffed enchiladas in the bottom of a casserole.

❸ Top with a layer of beans, spread somewhat evenly. Then top with shredded cheese.

❹ Bake in a 400°F oven until cheese is melted and all ingredients are heated through.

❺ Serve topped with sour cream, the remaining chopped onion, and shredded lettuce. Offer hot salsa of choice. **Serves 4**

* * *

VEGETARIAN VARIATION

Omit meat and dip each tortilla in a mild red chilli sauce, then roll around a bit of chopped onion, cilantro, and jalapeños. Top with refried beans and cheese, bake and garnish as above.

* * *

PAPA-DZULES
PUMPKIN-SEED SAUCED ENCHILADAS—YUCATAN

Papa-dzules are Yucatán enchiladas, flavored with pumpkin seeds and spicy tomato sauce. Often the tortillas are dipped in a *pipián* sauce, then garnished with a rich green oil pressed from pumpkin seeds. This recipe is a less demanding version, with hard-cooked egg filling seasoned with chopped pumpkin seeds rather than a *pipián* sauce. It is an ancient dish, once prepared from any seeds at all: squash, sunflower, cucumber. It is said that the Aztecs served a similar dish to Cortés and his Spanish entourage.

8 hard-boiled eggs, peeled and
coarsely chopped
Salt, cumin, oregano, and black
pepper to taste
1 to 2 green onions, thinly sliced
Several tablespoons pumpkin seeds
Oil for toasting pumpkin seeds and
warming tortillas

8 corn tortillas
Salsa Ranchera
Cebollas en Escabeche a la Yucateca
2 jalapeños or serranos, seeded and
sliced

❶ Season egg with green onion, salt, cumin, oregano, and pepper. Set aside.

❷ Lightly toast pumpkin seeds in a heavy frying pan, adding a tiny bit of oil if needed until they are golden. Remove from pan and in food processor or blender chop coarsely. Add to the egg mixture.

❸ Warm tortillas in a tiny bit of oil. Spoon a bit of the egg mixture down the center of each, then roll up.

❹ Heat Salsa Ranchero and pour over the enchiladas. Serve immediately, garnished with pickled onions and sliced chillies. *Serves 4*

·········· **VARIATION** ··········

PAPA-DZULES CON CARNE
Stuff the tortillas with browned ground pork and scrambled eggs instead of the hard-cooked egg, and season with either ground pumpkin seeds or Pipián Sauce, then top with Salsa Ranchera.

DOS ENCHILADAS VERDES ❖ TWO GREEN CHILE ENCHILADAS

ENCHILADAS VERDES SUIZAS
CLASSIC GREEN ENCHILADAS WITH SOUR CREAM

Dip 8 corn tortillas, one at a time, into either a little hot oil or warmed Mole Verde to make them pliable. Fill each with about ¼ cup cooked shredded chicken or grated cheese. Roll up and place in casserole. Spoon on lots of Mole Verde, top with about 1 cup shredded cheese, and bake briefly in a hot oven until cheese melts. Serve topped with sour cream, shredded lettuce, and cilantro. *Serves 4*

ENCHILADAS VERDES EN ESTILO SONORA
SONORA-STYLE GREEN CHILLI ENCHILADAS

You wouldn't think that just the difference of rolled versus stacked enchiladas would change the flavor, but in some inexplicable way it does.

Often stacked enchiladas are topped with a fried egg, as they are north of the border in New Mexico. The contrast of rich, spicy layers tortillas, meats, and cheese with the purity of a slightly soft egg is exquisite.

Dip 12 slightly stale corn tortillas, one at a time, into warmed Green Chilli Salsa, Sonora Style. Layer into a lightly greased baking dish, spooning a layer of meat and vegetables from the sauce, then top with another sauce-dipped tortilla. Continue with half of the tortillas, then top with shredded cheese; repeat for a second stack. Bake in a hot oven until cheese is melted and enchiladas heated through, then serve immediately, each portion topped with a lightly fried egg. **Makes 2 stacks, to serve 4 people**

Chilaquiles—Tortilla Casserole

Chilaquiles refers to a casserole of torn stale tortillas, fried until crisp and layered with chilli sauce or broth, cream, cheese, and bits of savory ingredients such as meats and chicken. Authentically, if the dish contains chillies it is called *chilaquiles*; if not, it is called a *sopa seca*. To further confuse things, a *sopa seca* may be made with chorizo or ingredients already spiced with chillies, so the name is almost irrelevant. Whichever name it goes by, this casserole is versatile, economical, and delicious in an earthy, hearty way. It is quintessentially Mexican in taste, texture, and appearance.

Traditionally, *chilaquiles* are prepared with old tortillas that have gone stale in the sultry weather. Any sauce may be used: a tomato sauce, green chilli and tomatillo, creamy cheese sauce, and so on. (I've been served *chilaquiles* topped with a red chilli sauce, a green tomatillo sauce, and a splash of sour cream, to approximate the three colors of the Mexican flag.) Additions to the hearty dish might include chorizo, ground or shredded meat, diced vegetables, chunks of chicken or turkey, or prawns in a mild rich chilli sauce.

Once the sauce is made and the tortillas fried, the casserole is quick and easy to assemble. It doesn't keep its texture long, however. In marketplace cafés (*fondas*) throughout Mexico, pots of *chilaquiles* are prepared freshly for the lunch crowds; by the end of the afternoon, these dishes have become the consistency of breakfast porridge. In fact, leftover *chilaquiles* are often served for breakfast, accompanied by fried eggs and hot chilli salsa. Try preparing *chilaquiles* for brunch in individual ramekins, topped with a poached or fried egg, or with a raw egg to bake on top of the casserole. Accompany with beans, either black or pinto/pink ones, crusty bread, a platter of lush fruits, and lots of strong cinnamon-scented coffee with milk. A pitcher of tequila and tropical fruit juice enhances the spirit of the morning.

CHILAQUILES DE LEGUMBRES
VEGETABLE *CHILAQUILES*

This consists of broken fried tortillas, cooked zucchini, and mashed potatoes, baked for a short while in an enchilada-type sauce of cinnamon-scented tomato and pasilla chilli with a dash of chipotle. Serve it topped with diced potatoes, carrots, and peas tossed with vinegar, handfuls of shredded lettuce, and a sprinkling of cilantro.

Since the recipe is divided into so many steps, I've divided the ingredients accordingly. Despite the long list of ingredients and steps, it is simple to prepare.

Sauce:

6 pasilla or guajillo chillies
2 cups hot vegetable broth
1 small to medium onion, chopped
2 cloves garlic, chopped
½ teaspoon oregano
1½ cups chopped tomatoes (canned are fine)

1 to 2 chipotles
Generous pinch cinnamon
2 to 4 tablespoons oil of choice
Juice of ¼ lime

❶ Place pasilla chillies in bowl and pour the hot broth over them. Cover with a plate and let them sit and steam until soft, at least 30 minutes.

❷ Remove stems and seeds from the soaked chillies, then scrape the softened flesh from the skin with a blunt knife. Reserve the soaking liquid and any juice from the chillies.

❸ Put the chilli flesh, onion, and garlic into blender or food processor and whirl together briefly to chop and combine. Add all remaining ingredients except the oil and lime juice, and blend until well mixed. Add reserved chilli soaking broth.

❹ In a heavy frying pan, heat the oil. Pour the sauce into the hot oil. It might sputter, so stand back and protect your face until it calms down. Cook down over relatively high heat 5 minutes or so. Remove from heat and add lime juice. Set aside.

Tangy Vegetable Topping

2 or 3 small to medium-sized cooked potatoes, peeled and diced
4 cooked but still firm carrots, sliced or diced

½ cup cooked peas (or use frozen and simply defrost)
2 teaspoons white wine or sherry vinegar, or to taste

....

Combine all vegetable topping ingredients. Set aside to marinate.

Filling:

4 to 5 small to medium-sized cooked potatoes, mashed coarsely
2 zucchini, steamed or boiled and diced

Large pinch cumin seed or ground cumin
About 6 oz. crumbled *queso fresco*, fresh pecorino, or not-too-salty feta cheese
¾ cup sour cream

....

Combine all filling ingredients. Set aside.

Tortillas and Garnishes

24 stale tortillas
Oil for frying
8-10 oz. Jack or similar cheese, shredded

Salsa of choice
6 to 10 lettuce leaves, shredded
¼ cup coarsely chopped cilantro

....

❶ Break or cut tortillas into strips, then fry in oil until golden brown and dry on absorbent paper.

❷ To assemble, arrange half the fried tortilla strips in a large baking dish. Cover with a layer of the potato and zucchini filling, then the rest of the tortillas. Pour the sauce over tortillas.

❸ Top with a layer of Jack cheese, then bake in a 400°F oven about 10 minutes, or just long enough to melt the cheese. If the casserole bakes for too long it sinks into a mushy consistency.

❹ Serve immediately, garnished with a little salsa, the marinated vegetables, lettuce, and cilantro. *Serves 6*

....

CHILAQUILES DE CHORIZO
CHORIZO *CHILAQUILES*

This makes a luscious brunch dish, accompanied by scrambled eggs and a sassy homemade salsa, frijoles on the side, and a pitcher of sangria.

2 to 3 chorizo sausages
¾ cup tomatoes, peeled, seeded and diced (canned are fine)
2 cloves garlic, chopped
12 crisp-fried tortilla strips
About 1½ cups broth of choice: beef, chicken, vegetable, turkey, etc.) (homemade if possible)

Generous pinch dried mint, crumbled, or 1 to 2 teaspoons fresh mint, chopped
6 oz. *queso fresco*, not-too-salty feta, or fresh pecorino cheese, crumbled; or 8 oz. shredded Jack cheese
1 small onion, chopped

❶ Brown chorizo in frying pan, crumbling the sausage as it cooks. Pour off any excess fat.

❷ Add tomatoes and garlic, cook a few minutes, then add tortilla strips. Pour in half of the broth, cover, and simmer a few minutes, then add the rest of the broth. You might need a little more than 1½ cups broth. Don't, however, stir it all into a mush. Let the pieces of tortilla soften but still retain their shape.

❸ When tortillas are softened and most of the liquid has been absorbed, serve in shallow soup plates, topped with a sprinkle of mint, cheese, and onion. *Serves 4*

Tamales

The *tamal* is among the most ancient of foods; its name is derived from the Aztec *tamalli*, meaning patty or cake. Tamales were served by the Aztecs, Mayans, and other Indian nations, and were greatly enhanced by the Spanish introduction of pork and cooking fat.

Can anyone who has ever eaten them hot, fragrant, and freshly made not be passionate about them? They might look lopsided and lumpy and not nearly as perfect as the storebought version, but their flavor is earthily delicious.

This dish of wrapped and steamed corn dough—either masa harina or ground hominy—is popular throughout the Republic. In city and town streets, village squares, and marketplaces, street vendors as well as special *tamal* shops sell them, hot and fragrant in ollas, clay pots set over charcoal braziers. The same vendor often sells an accompanying mug of atole (a cornmeal beverage) or black coffee.

Tamales are frequently prepared in quantity for family fiestas at great tamale-making parties know as *tamaladas*. When I was growing up our neighbor prepared a huge vat of tamales for every holiday and proudly brought us a platterful each time. I barely remember the neighbor, but I'll never forget those huge, corn-redolent tamales and the seemingly bottomless pot she fished them out of.

What tamales are wrapped in depends upon the area they hail from: corn husks in the north and the central mountain regions and banana leaves in the south and coastal regions. Regionality, too, influences the type of corn or masa used, whether it is a dried mixture or a wetter grind. Occasionally tamales are prepared from fresh sweet corn, or from dough mixed of mashed potatoes or even rice flour. One of my favorites is a dough with lots of fresh corn kneaded in, surrounding a chunk of cheese and strip of green chilli in the center. As the corn masa cooks, the cheese melts and it makes a very delicate tamale.

Tamale fillings vary widely: meat, chicken, turkey, duck, rabbit, iguana, fish or seafood, pumpkin seeds; indeed, tamales are perfect vehicles for leftovers in the thrifty Mexican kitchen, with leftover mole, adobo, *picadillo, salsa de chile pasilla* or *ancho* used to bind the bits of meat or fish. Diced potatoes and browned bits of chorizo, strips of sautéed chillies and cheese (*rajas*), squash blossoms, mushrooms, or corn fungus (*huitlacoche*; see Special Ingredients) might be used as fillings as well. The flavor combinations are further expanded by the sauces; green *salsa de tomatillo*, mild *chile pasilla, salsa de chile chipotle*.

Then there are the "blind" tamales that have been left unfilled to serve as an accompaniment for saucy dishes such as mole or barbecued lamb, or eaten for breakfast with a glass of hot chocolate, coffee, or atole.

Tamales may be tiny, one-bite nibbles, or they may be gargantuan, almost unreasonably plump parcels that make a full meal. They may also be made in sweet versions, the masa kneaded with sugar and fruit juice, the dough filled with fruit.

The dough must be beaten to a light, fluffy consistency or else the tamales will be heavy; the word *leaden* comes to mind. A food processor does the job well but not as effectively as beating by hand.

SAVORY TAMALES
PORK, BEEF, CHICKEN, OR TURKEY TAMALES

This makes a hearty, rustic dish, very classic and peasant. Though it is a basic chillied-meat–stuffed tamale, its flavors vary greatly depending on the type of masa and lard or vegetable shortening used.

This tamale may be made either central/southern Mexican style, in small parcels, or Sonora style, in big, plump packets of masa-spread corn husks layered into one huge tamale. (The diner peels off layer after layer of the corn husks, scraping the cooked masa from each layer. Many of us think this is the best part of tamale-eating.)

Meat Filling:

1 lb. boneless pork or beef, cut into stew meat; or 2¼ lb. meat with bones; or poultry meat with bones such as thighs or breasts	1 quart broth 1 head garlic 1 onion, halved 5 bay leaves

....

Place meat in pot with other ingredients. Bring to boil, cover, and simmer until meat is tender, about 2 hours, adding water as needed to keep it simmering. Set aside.

Chilli Sauce for Meat Filling:

1 onion, chopped	1 tablespoon bland vegetable oil
2 cloves garlic, chopped	Generous pinch cumin seed or
3 tablespoons New Mexico chilli powder	ground cumin
	Salt to taste
1 tablespoon paprika or ancho chilli powder	Juice of ½ lime
1½ cups reserved broth from cooking meat	

....

❶ In blender or processor, whirl onion, garlic, chilli powder, paprika, and a bit of the broth until it forms a pastelike mixture, then thin it with a bit more of the broth.

❷ Heat oil in frying pan. Add the onion-chilli paste and fry until it concentrates a bit, about 5 minute. Add the remaining broth and cumin seed and cook a few minutes longer.

❸ Season with salt and lime juice.

Masa:

⅓ **cup softened lard or vegetable**
shortening
1 teaspoon salt
2 cups masa harina (preferably a
white type such as the Quaker brand)

About 1½ to 2 cups broth from
cooking the meat
1 teaspoon baking powder

....

❶ Whip the lard or shortening until somewhat fluffy, then whip in the salt and masa harina until mixture looks like tiny crumbs.

❷ Add the broth in several batches, whipping as you go along. Then let the dough sit and rest for a few minutes before you commence with whipping it into fluffiness. Beat in the baking powder. When it is ready it will be the consistency of a light cookie dough.

Serving Sauce:

12 cooked green tomatillos, pureed
1 cup broth from cooking meat
Homemade salsa to taste

....

Combine all ingredients and warm when ready to serve.

To assemble:

About 16 dried corn husks (the
number needed will depend on their
size), soaked in warm water to cover
for at least 3 hours or overnight

Masa mixture
Meat and chilli sauce for filling
Serving sauce
Salsa of choice

....

❶ Remove corn husks from the soaking water and pat dry. Lay 2 large or 3 smaller husks out on a work surface, slightly overlapping to form a rectangle, and "glue" the seams with a bit of the masa mixture. Spread a layer of masa over the husks. (If you are preparing large northern-style tamales, continue layering masa-spread corn husks to form a larger surface, then roll the tamales instead of folding them.)

❷ Spoon a bit of the meat and chilli sauce onto the masa-spread corn husks. Make a parcel by folding the corn husk over to enclose both the masa and filling, somewhat like an envelope: first fold over the long sides, then tuck the top and bottom under. Repeat until masa and filling are used up (reserve some of the chilli sauce for use in step 6 below).

❸ Layer the stuffed tamales in a steamer and cover with a layer of corn husks, then with a clean dish towel to absorb excess steam and moisture and keep the tamales from becoming soggy. Fill the pot with water high enough to steam but not high enough for the water to reach the tamales.

❹ Steam over high heat for about an hour, checking every so often to be sure the pot has not boiled dry.

❺ When tamales are ready, serve each one resting on a portion of the serving sauce, with a drizzle of the red chilli sauce (from the filling) over the top and a spoonful or two of salsa as well. *Serves 4 to 6*

LEFTOVERS

You've made exactly the right amount of tamales when you have leftovers. Layer them into a casserole much like *chilaquiles*: unwrapped, cut into pieces, sauced, layered, then topped with cheese and baked.

··

···························· **VARIATION** ····························

TAMALES CAMARONES ❖ SHRIMP OR PRAWN TAMALES

Prepare the above masa mixture, using a flavorful fish stock in place of the broth. Fill with any shrimp mixture such as Machaca de Camarón, or combine sautéed onion and garlic with the flesh of 1 or 2 mild soaked chillies, a few tomatoes, and a dash of cumin. Add a cup or so of shrimp. *Serves 4*

··

TAMALES DE VERACRUZ
BANANA LEAF-WRAPPED TAMALES, VERACRUZ STYLE

Banana leaf-wrapped tamales are prepared with a moister filling, one made from pureed hominy rather than masa. Chillied meat or poultry fillings are best for these tamales, especially with bits of chipotle chilli added for a smoky nuance.

Considerably larger than corn husks, banana leaves can be cut up for individual tamales or left in large pieces for tamales huge enough for a whole family to share.

Masa Filling:

2 cups cooked hominy, drained well
⅓ cup lard or vegetable shortening

2 teaspoons pure mild chilli powder
1 teaspoon salt

Meat Filling:

1½ lb. pork, beef, turkey, or chicken chunks, simmered in broth until tender
About 1 cup Salsa de Chilli Rojo
1 chipotle chilli, chopped (optional)
10 pimiento-stuffed green olives, sliced

1 green pepper or poblano chilli, roasted, peeled, and cut into strips
1 ripe tomato, peeled, seeded, and diced
¼ cup raisins
1 or 2 banana leaves
Salsa of choice

❶ Prepare masa by pureeing hominy in processor with lard or shortening, chilli powder, and salt.

❷ Dice meat and mix with mild chilli sauce, chipotle chilli, green olives, green pepper strips, tomato, and raisins.

❸ Make banana leaf pliable by heating over a stove top. Cut into pieces about 10 to 12 inches long. Spread each piece with masa, then place several spoonfuls of the meat mixture in the center. Fold up the sides first, then tuck in the top and bottom to enclose meat mixture.

❹ Stack tamales in steamer. Steam for 40 to 50 minutes or until masa is cooked firmly. Serve immediately, accompanied by a flavorful hot salsa. *Serves 4*

VARIATION

TAMAL DE CAZUELA ❖ LARGE BANANA LEAF-WRAPPED CASSEROLE-STYLE TAMALE

Prepare this casserole by lining a baking dish with the warmed banana leaves, a layer of the masa, then the meat filling and more masa. Close up the whole thing with more banana leaves folded over. Cover with foil and bake in a 350°F oven about an hour. *Serves 4 to 6*

TAMALES DE DULCE
·····································
SWEET TAMALES

Before the Spanish conquest, Mexico had few sweet dishes. Without sugar, butter, and wheat flour, their sweet tooth was satisfied by the wide array of luscious tropical fruits and fragrant honey. Often these were combined with ground corn and wrapped into corn husks for sweet tamales.

Sweet tamales are still enjoyed throughout Mexico, often for breakfast or supper, accompanied by cups of strong hot coffee or chocolate or sweet corn-based atole. Strangely, though they are sweet, they are moistened with broth. Somehow it works, despite the hefty amount of sugar in the tamales. The chicken broth brings out the earthy flavor of the corn masa.

Like their savory counterparts, sweet tamales may be made either unfilled or filled. Simple sweet fillings are best: a spoonful of apricot or strawberry preserves, Dulce de Coco (coconut fudge), diced candied fruit mixed with pine nuts, candied pineapple, papaya or other tropical fruit, quince jam (*ate*). Sometimes canned or poached fruit is used: the fruit diced and used as filling, the sweet juice mixed with the masa in place of broth.

¾ to 1 cup lard, or mixture of half lard and half unsalted butter	1 teaspoon salt
2 cups cooked hominy, drained	1 teaspoon cinnamon
About ½ cup lightly salted or unsalted chicken broth	1 teaspoon baking powder
1 cup sugar	About 16 dried corn husks, soaked in warm water to cover at least 3 hours or overnight

··

Filling of choice (see above) or a handful of raisins

❶ Beat lard or lard-butter combination until it is the consistency of whipped cream. Set aside.

❷ Grind hominy in a food processor or blender. In batches, add the ground hominy to the whipped lard along with a little of the broth, sugar, salt, cinnamon, and baking powder. Continue to add broth gradually and beat or whip the mixture into extreme fluffiness. The classic test is to drop a small amount of this mixture into a cup of cold water; if it floats, it is fluffy enough. (If you are using raisins as a filling, they may be mixed into the dough.)

❸ Drain the corn husks and pat dry. Spread out the husks as for Savory Tamales. Fill each with a spoonful of jam or other filling. Fold as for Savory Tamales.

❹ Steam according to the directions given for Savory Tamales. Tiny *tamalitos* will take about 30 minutes; larger ones an hour or longer. ***Serves 4 to 6***

HUEVOS

··

EGGS

I can think of few cuisines that offer as dazzling an array of enticing egg dishes as does Mexican cookery. Yet, before the conquest, chicken eggs were unknown in Mexico. The eggs that were available—from turkeys and other wild birds—were strongly flavored and not easily obtained.

Now, however, the Mexican table offers splendid dishes based on egg. There are several reasons why Mexican cuisine favors eggs. First, eggs are economical. Almost any family can keep a chicken or two, feeding them on bits of leftover tortillas and bread crumbs.

Second, few flavors enliven eggs as well as does chilli—indeed, all of the staples of the Mexican diet: lime, tomatoes, cheese, tortillas, beans, vegetables, onions, garlic, sausages. The ancient sauces of pureed tomatoes, vegetables, chillies, and aromatics bring out the best in the gentle egg.

Scrambled eggs are served with salsa and warm tortillas to roll up into tender tacos; soft boiled eggs are eaten with a squeeze of lime and a sprinkle of fiery cayenne pepper. Eggs are softly poached in the rich dark adobo sauces or red chilli and meat sauces, or baked in *cazuelitas* with hearty chilli stews until the eggs are just set. Fried eggs might be topped with cheese, grilled until the cheese melts, then served on a bed of spicy browned meat and a blanket of *salsa ranchera*, with a scattering of sliced fresh chillies.

Throughout the Republic, eggs are scrambled with a variety of ingredients: browned chorizo or strips of spicy dried beef; nopales or green beans; tomatoes and shrimp; peas and pimientos; potatoes and chillies. One of the most exotic omelet fillings is from the state of Hidalgo: sautéed ant eggs with lots of cilantro or epazote. You'll find scrambled eggs as fillings for tacos: stuffed into flour or corn tortillas, splashed with a mild chilli, pumpkinseed, or tomatillo sauce. *Chilaquiles*, the delicious casserole of ragtag bits of leftover tortillas, is traditionally served with an egg or two alongside, or layered with softly scrambled eggs. The variety is endless.

In the countryside, egg dishes are traditionally eaten at *almuerzo*, the hearty midmorning meal that follows the early morning coffee and sweet rolls, *desayuno*. These dishes make gorgeous brunch and lazy weekend breakfasts, docile enough to begin a day with, lively enough to awaken your taste buds and open your eyes.

HUEVOS RANCHEROS
FRIED OR POACHED EGGS WITH RUSTIC TOMATO SAUCE

Huevos Rancheros is one of those simple, utterly memorable dishes— spicy tomato sauce blanketing fresh eggs on a bed of fragrant corn tortillas. Cut into the eggs and let the soft golden yolk run into the spicy sauce. Fork up each zesty bite, adding a dash of extra salsa if the flavor is too mild. The tortilla on the bottom becomes a bit soggy and sauce-laden—the best part of the whole dish. Huevos Rancheros can be blissfully good; like all simple dishes, it depends upon its main components for its character: good fresh eggs and tortillas, a zesty, full-of-life sauce.

Huevos Rancheros is served all over the country, its flavor depending on the chillies of the region: poblanos, jalapeños, smoky chipotles, fresh serranos. It can be mild and only slightly picante, or it can be fierce, with thinly sliced fresh hot chillies lying in wait to assault your palate.

Huevos Rancheros is awfully good following a few shots of tequila with salt and lime. Finish the meal with lush tropical fruits and Café con Leche.

About 2 cups Salsa Ranchera	**8 eggs**
4 corn tortillas	**1 tablespoon chopped cilantro**
Oil for heating tortillas	

❶ Heat or prepare sauce and keep warm.

❷ Heat tortillas in hot oil in heavy skillet. Keep warm, covered, in oven or on back burner of stove.

❸ Poach or pan-fry eggs to desired doneness.

❹ On each plate, place a tortilla; top with 2 eggs, then spoon over with Salsa Ranchera. Sprinkle with cilantro and serve immediately. **Serves 4**

·· **VARIATION** ··

HUEVOS MOTULEÑOS—YUCATAN

This is the Yucatán version of Huevos Rancheros. Typically the dish is prepared with a stack of several crisp-fried tortillas spread with black beans; in between the layers are sandwiched several fried eggs. The dish is given a carnival-like appearance by a sprinkling of green peas, bits of pink ham, strips of roasted red peppers, cilantro leaves, cubes of mild cheese, and sometimes slices of fried banana. I find it a bit unwieldy layered like this and have streamlined it into a one-layer spectacular.

Fry 4 tortillas until crisp. Spread each with Frijoles Negros Enchilados. Top each with 1 or 2 poached or lightly fried eggs, then spoon about ¼ cup hot Salsa Ranchera over each portion. Sprinkle with tender green peas (briefly cooked or frozen and defrosted), diced ham, cubes of mild cheese, and chopped cilantro. Offer salsa of choice on the side. **Serves 4**

HUEVOS EN SALSA VERDE
EGGS IN GREEN TOMATILLO-CHILLI SAUCE

Tart tomatillos and nippy green chillies, enhanced with a generous amount of pungent cilantro, combine to make a forceful sauce to blanket mild eggs. Either pan-fry the eggs or poach them in the simmering green sauce. One chilli should make a spicy but gentle heat, while three chillies may propel you to the nearest glass of beer. The choice is yours.

Serve on rustic pottery, accompanied by crusty bread or warm corn tortillas to scoop up the savory sauce and runny yolk. I like to serve this dish for brunch or supper, accompanied by pinto beans mashed into a refried bliss with bits of melted cheese, and a bowl of simple steamed rice. Hot salsa of choice on the side, and Bananas al Horno as dessert.

2 medium-small onions, chopped
3 cloves garlic, chopped
1 to 3 jalapeños, chopped (remove
seeds and membranes for more
flavor, less heat)
2 tablespoons vegetable oil
1½ cups cooked tomatillos, cut or
coarsely mashed (canned are fine)
1 cup chicken or vegetable broth

1 teaspoon cumin
Salt to taste
¼ to ⅓ cup chopped cilantro
4 or 8 eggs
2 tablespoons butter

....

❶ Sauté onions, garlic, and chillies lightly in vegetable oil until soft.

❷ Add tomatillos, broth, cumin, and salt; simmer until tomatillos are tender, 5 to 8 minutes, or for just a moment or two if using canned tomatillos. Add cilantro.

❸ Puree in blender or food processor and keep warm while you cook the eggs.

❹ Lightly fry the eggs in the butter, allowing 1 or 2 eggs per person, then serve topped with several spoonfuls of the sauce. Alternatively, you could poach the eggs in the simmering tomatillo sauce or bake in individual ramekins. **Serves 4**

....

HUEVOS CON CHORIZO
SCRAMBLED CHORIZO AND EGGS

Deliciously simple, crumbled chorizo and eggs can be memorable beyond reason. It is a comfort dish, ridiculously easy to prepare and full of spicy flavor. The chorizo itself is so forcefully spiced that you don't need to add anything else: just crumble and cook the zesty sausage, pour off any excess grease, and pour in the eggs to scramble.

I remember the first time I ate this, having been dragged into the most dismal-looking restaurant I had ever seen in my life, past tables filled with faces not altogether friendly. The paint on the wall was peeling, the calendar was several years old, the walls were adorned with near-naked ladies painted on black velvet. The chairs, creaky constructions of spindly arms and legs, were hanging together for dear life. This was the sort of place my mother had always told me never to enter.

The rest of the story is predictable: The food was exceptional. The *cerveza* was cold and plentiful, and soon the faces in the room grew less menacing. We ate chorizo and eggs, with an endless stack of the palest, most ethereally delicate corn tortillas fresh from the comal.

This makes a delicious brunch dish, accompanied by pan-browned potatoes seasoned with lots of garlic and a bit of mild chilli powder, salsa on the side. Chilled *cerveza* makes the perfect drink.

About ½ lb. chorizo
8 eggs, lightly beaten

Sprinkling of chopped cilantro or
green onions

❶ Remove the casing from the chorizo and brown the sausage in a frying pan, crumbling it as it cools. Pour off excess fat, leaving a little to cook the eggs in.

❷ Pour in the eggs and cook over medium heat, scrambling as you go along. Cook to desired doneness and serve immediately, sprinkled with cilantro or green onions. *Serves 4 to 6*

······· VARIATION ·······

TACOS DE HUEVOS Y CHORIZO
Warm corn tortillas in a very lightly greased frying pan and roll each with a portion of the chorizo and scrambled egg. Serve immediately.

······· VARIATION ·······

HUEVOS CON PAPAS Y CHORIZOS ❖
EGGS WITH POTATO-CHORIZO HASH
A sort of spicy hash of chorizo and diced potatoes, with indentations in which to simmer or poach whole eggs. Serve accompanied by a rambunctious salsa and lots of chilled *cerveza* or mugs of strong, steamy coffee.

4 large potatoes, peeled and diced
1 lb. Mexican chorizo
2 to 3 small to medium onions,
coarsely chopped
1 green or red pepper (or half of each),
coarsely chopped
1 mild fresh chilli, red or green, diced
(optional)

4 tomatoes, diced (peeled and seeded
if desired; canned are fine)
4 or 8 eggs
2 tablespoons chopped cilantro
Salt and pepper to taste

❶ In a heavy frying pan, slowly brown the potatoes with the chorizo, onions, green or red pepper and chilli. Cook about 10 minutes, or until potatoes are nearly tender and chorizo nearly cooked through. (In a fair and just world, they will be ready at the same time.) Add tomatoes and continue cooking until potatoes and chorizo are cooked through and tomatoes have reached a saucy consistency. Pour off excess fat.

❷ Make indentations for the eggs, then break the eggs open and plop them in.

❸ Cover and simmer, or bake covered in a 375°F oven until the whites are firm and the yolks still runny, about 6-8 minutes.

❹ Serve sprinkled with cilantro, salt, and pepper. *Serves 4 to 6*

....

MIGAS
....
SPICY SCRAMBLED EGGS WITH BITS OF TORTILLAS— TEXAS AND NORTHERN SONORA

In Spanish, *migas* refers to bits of fried bread. In northern Mexico and parts of Texas, *migas* refers to crisp-fried bits of tortillas added to a spicy scramble of eggs. Often restaurants will offer a list of optional additions: spicy fried chorizo, diced avocado, strips of sautéed chillies, shredded cheese, chopped onion, tomatoes, and so on. *Migas* is occasionally found in Mexico proper, but without the fanfare, and called not *migas* but *huevos con tostaditos*.

Whatever one calls it, the savory chilli blends with the other spicy flavors, and the creamy scrambled eggs slightly soften the crisp-fried tortilla pieces. This makes a robust brunch dish accompanied by black beans. You could start with avocado halves stuffed with lobster and a spoonful of salsa verde.

10 to 12 corn tortillas, cut into
1/2-inch strips
1/2 cup vegetable oil for frying
(Or, in place of both tortillas and oil,
use restaurant-style crisp and not-
too-salty tortilla chips)
6 cloves garlic, chopped
2 poblano or Anaheim chillies,
roasted, peeled, and sliced
3 tablespoons unsalted butter,
divided

1 1/2 teaspoons cumin
6 ripe small to medium tomatoes,
coarsely chopped (canned are fine)
8 eggs, lightly beaten
1/2 cup chopped cilantro
3 to 4 green onions, thinly sliced
Salsa of choice

....

❶ Fry tortilla strips in oil until golden brown but not dark. Drain on absorbent paper. (If you use restaurant-style chips, omit frying.)

❷ Sauté garlic and chilli in 1 tablespoon butter for just a minute. Do not let garlic brown. Sprinkle in cumin, then add tomatoes and cook over medium heat 3 to 4 minutes, until tomatoes are no longer runny. Remove from pan and set aside.

❸ Over low heat, melt remaining butter in the pan. Pour in beaten eggs. Cook over low heat and stir until eggs begin to set. Add reserved chilli-tomato mixture and tortilla strips, and continue cooking, stirring once or twice until eggs are the desired consistency. The tortilla strips should be neither crisp nor soggy but pliable and chewy. Top with cilantro and green onions. Serve immediately, accompanied by a fresh hot salsa or other spicy condiment. ***Serves 4 to 6***

VARIATION

SPICY EGG-FILLED SOFT TACOS

Instead of serving the eggs scrambled with the fried tortillas, roll the spicy cooked eggs into soft corn tortillas and serve as tacos.

HUEVOS EN SALSA JITOMATE CON FRIJOLES NEGROS
EGGS POACHED WITH A SAUCE OF TOMATOES AND BLACK BEANS—CENTRAL, BAJIO REGION

The eggs are poached, then placed in ramekins filled with tomatoes and mashed black beans, topped with cheese, and baked until the cheese is creamily melted on top. You want the whites firm and the yolks sensuously runny. I find the combination of rich egg yolk running into a spicy sauce almost unbearably good. Actually, the sauce is only mildly spicy—pass a fresh chilli salsa for each diner to spoon on.

This makes a delectable dish, much like the classic Huevos Rancheros but a bit more complex. Adding mashed black beans to a simple tomato-chilli sauce is a flash of brilliance—try the mixture added to a simple sauté or simmer of zucchini and corn, topped with melted cheese.

In a Mexican kitchen there is always a pot of beans cooking. In North American kitchens this is unlikely, but they are often available in cans. One trick is to freeze small amounts of cooked beans in ice cube trays, then place the frozen cubes in a plastic bag and seal well. Whenever you need a small amount of black beans, there they are.

Serve this delectable egg dish for a simple supper accompanied by a stack of warm corn tortillas; or for a more elaborate brunch, accompanied by Ensalada de Piña con Pimientos Morrones, roast potato chunks seasoned with mild chilli spices and lots of garlic, crusty bread, and a salsa of choice. Accompany with a pitcher of tequila and icy grapefruit juice.

2 onions, coarsely chopped
3 cloves garlic, coarsely chopped
2 jalapeños, seeded and chopped
2 tablespoons vegetable oil
2 cups diced tomatoes (canned are fine)
Several generous pinches dried oregano leaves
³/₄ cup cooked and pureed black beans

Salt and black or red pepper to taste
4 or 8 eggs
About 6 oz. grated white cheese suitable for melting (Jack, etc.)
Fresh salsa to taste
Chopped fresh cilantro or green onions (optional)

....

❶ Lightly sauté onions, garlic, and chillies in vegetable oil until softened. Add tomatoes and cook until saucy. Add oregano, black beans, and salt and pepper to taste; set aside.

❷ Poach the eggs until still quite soft on the inside, firm on the outside. (I find that adding a dash of vinegar to the water helps keep the egg together.)

❸ Remove poached eggs from hot water and drain briefly.

❹ Spoon the tomato and black bean sauce into individual ramekins (or into one large skillet). Make indentations for the eggs, then place the eggs in. Top with the cheese.

❺ Place under the broiler or in a 450°F oven for several minutes or until the cheese melts and browns to a bubbly and appealing topping (remember that you have delicate eggs underneath—if it becomes a choice between a lovely, runny yolk and a topping of cheese that has melted but not browned, go for the runny yolk. Serve immediately, accompanied by warm corn tortillas.
Serves 4
....

HUEVOS OAXAQUEÑOS
STRIPS OF OMELET IN A SAUCE OF TOMATOES AND PUREED, ROASTED ONIONS—OAXACA

Few egg dishes are as strikingly different as this one: the sauce is made from roasted tomatoes pureed with onions, garlic, and chilli, then the whole thing is tossed into a bit of very hot oil in a heavy skillet and cooked down to a concentrated flavor. It has the texture of a pre-Hispanic sauce, a smooth paste without bits and chunks.

Into this smooth, thick sauce are tossed strips of freshly cooked, hot, tender omelet, the whole topped with chopped cilantro and chillies. It is deliciously unique. Serve with warm corn tortillas for an unusual brunch dish or first course, and accompany with potatoes that you have first parboiled, then tossed with Recado de Ajo y Salpimentado and olive oil, then roasted in an 400°F oven until crusty and golden.

The dish calls for quite a few chillies, but depending on the chillies, it shouldn't be terribly hot. Removing the seeds and roasting the chillies first cuts down their sting; if your chillies are hot, however, reduce the amount called for considerably.

6 small to medium onions, peeled and cut into chunks
9 cloves garlic, whole and unpeeled
3 poblano or Anaheim chillies
3 to 5 jalapeños, or to taste
About 2 cups diced tomatoes (canned are fine)
⅓ cup vegetable oil

Pinch cumin and oregano (optional)
6 eggs, lightly beaten
Salt and black pepper to taste (plus pinch of sugar or honey if tomatoes are too acidic).
2 tablespoons coarsely chopped cilantro

❶ Roast onions, garlic, poblanos, and half the jalapeños on an ungreased heavy skillet until they char, turning so that they blacken evenly. Remove from stove and let cool.

❷ When cool enough to handle, chop onion and place in blender. Squeeze the garlics out of their papery skins and add to blender. Peel the chillies, remove seeds, and chop. Add to blender and puree together to form a paste. Add tomatoes and whirl until it forms a saucy mixture.

❸ Heat ¼ cup of the oil in a heavy skillet or frying pan. When hot, add the saucy mixture and cook until it reduces in volume and the sharpness of the raw onions recedes.

❹ Remove seeds from one of the remaining jalapeños and chop the raw flesh. Add half to the sauce, season with salt and pepper (and sugar if needed), and set aside. If sauce seems to need a little extra flavor, season with cumin and oregano, or increase amount of tomato and/or chillies.

❺ Cook beaten eggs in 3 or 4 batches in a flat omelet shape removing each to a plate, then rolling up, pancake fashion. Slice each of these rolls into ¾-inch widths.

❻ Reheat sauce in frying pan, then add the egg strips, tossing carefully so that they do not fall apart. Serve immediately, sprinkled with cilantro and remaining jalapeños if desired. **Serves 4**

SOME SIMPLE MEXICAN EGG DISHES

Essentially Mexico: Soft boiled eggs with a squeeze of lime juice and a sprinkle of cayenne pepper.

GREEN CHILI AND CHEESE OMELET

The bland egg, slightly picante chillies, rich melty cheese, and cooling sour cream are delicious in this simple omelet.

Fill French-style rolled omelets with several tablespoons mild roasted green chilli strips and shredded Jack or garlic Jack cheese, letting the cheese melt as the egg cooks. Serve each tender omelet topped with a spoonful of sour cream. **Allow 2 to 3 eggs per person**

HUEVOS CON FRIJOLES NEGROS Y PLATANOS
EGGS WITH REFRIED BLACK BEANS AND FRIED PLANTAINS—YUCATAN

Heat about 3 cups refried black beans with shredded mild white cheese such as mozzarella or Jack melted in. Serve each portion of beans topped with 2 poached or fried eggs, pan-browned ripe plantain slices, and season with Salsa Ranchera and a bracing *salsa picante*. Bacon, ham, or spicy sausages make a good accompaniment for this robust brunch dish. Serve with warm tortillas. **Serves 4**

HUEVOS TAPATIOS
CORN TORTILLAS TOPPED WITH CHORIZO, EGG, MELTED CHEESE, AVOCADO AND SALSA—JALISCO

Top each of 4 warmed corn tortillas with about 3 tablespoons crumbled browned chorizo, then with one or two pan-fried eggs and a sprinkling of shredded cheese (it should melt onto the hot eggs). Garnish with guacamole or diced avocado and a fresh homemade salsa such as Salsa Cruda, Salsa con Limón y Cilantro, Salsa de Chillies y Ajo, or Salsa Verde de Tomatillo. *Serves 4*

HUEVOS EN CALDO
EGGS POACHED IN BROTH

Prepare a strongly flavored broth by sautéing some chopped garlic, then cooking a seasoning paste of choice in the hot oil, concentrating its flavors, for about 5 minutes. Add broth and simmer together to meld flavors.

Poach 1 egg per person in this highly seasoned broth, and serve each person a bowlful of the broth topped with the egg. A slice of toasted garlic-rubbed bread placed under the poached egg is delicious, as are a sprinkling of chopped cilantro and a drizzle of hot vinegary salsa. *Allow 1 egg per person*

ARROZ CON HUEVOS
RICE TOPPED WITH EGGS AND SALSA

The combination of egg and rice is delicious simplicity, much more so than its few humble ingredients suggest. Prepare any rice dish (such as Arroz Verde), or even simple steamed white rice. Serve topped with a poached or lightly fried egg and spoonfuls of Salsa Ranchera or other mild flavorful salsa. Sprinkle with chopped cilantro and/or fresh chillies if desired. *Allow 1 cup rice and 1 egg per person*

MOCHOMOS CON HUEVOS
SHREDDED MEAT SCRAMBLED WITH EGGS

Savory shreds of browned meat, seasoned with tomatoes, chillies, onions, and garlic, all scrambled into creamy soft egg and served with refried beans.

Prepare 1 to 2 cups Mochomos or Ropa Vieja. Beat 8 eggs and pour into the browning meat mixture. Serve sprinkled with thinly sliced serranos, chopped cilantro, and creamy refried pinto or *bayo* beans. **Serves 4 to 6**

PESCADOS Y MARISCOS

···

FISH AND SHELLFISH

To first-time visitors in Mexico, who may be familiar only with tacos, enchiladas, nachos, and the occasional tamale, the dazzling array of impeccably fresh, briny-sweet fish and shellfish comes as a revelation. With over 6,000 miles of relatively unspoiled coastline there is scarcely an area of Mexico where seafood does not figure prominently in the local diet.

Sea creatures abound: spindly-legged crabs, great tentacled squid and octopus, sweet conch, robust shark meat, oysters and clams, the ever-present snapper and hearty swordfish, frogs' legs, and beeflike steaks of terrapin. In mountain regions, myriad lakes offer freshwater fish, most notably the sweet-fleshed tiny white *pescado blanco* of Lago Pátzcuaro.

Seafood combines brilliantly with Mexico's dominant seasonings: chillies, garlic, tomatoes. Rarely is the fish blanketed with cream and butter, European style; rather it is brought to life with zesty spices and clean-tasting seasonings.

There is no one favored way to prepare seafood in Mexico. The collection of techniques is varied: simmered into chilli-spiked stews; rubbed with spice paste and grilled or smoked; quickly steamed and served with chopped onions, chillies, and wedges of lime as a cocktail appetizer; wrapped into fresh tortillas for soft tacos. Tamales are as likely to be stuffed with lobster, crab, shrimp, or fish chunks as they are to be stuffed with meat or poultry. Sometimes, especially on the Gulf Coast, a big cauldron of chilli-scented broth will collect whatever fish and crustaceans are dredged from the sea that day, simmering into a spicy soup-stew. In addition to ocean fish and freshwater fish, dried fish are eaten—occasionally salted cod, more commonly tiny dried shrimp. Sometimes the shrimp are cooked with rice or with other bland foods that need a helping hand with flavoring. A classic Lenten dish is fried patties of dried shrimp, often served with nopales or *romeritos*, a green resembling rosemary. In macho cantinas in Mexico City, a traditional snack is a chilli-seasoned broth made from these tiny salty shrimp.

OSTIONES CON SALSA DE LIMA
OYSTERS WITH LIME-CILANTRO SALSA

The startlingly tart flavors of lime and chilli are as welcome on raw oysters as the traditional shot of Tabasco or dab of mignonette (classic French spicy vinegar dip for seafood).

Serve oysters on the half-shell, resting on a bed of ice or tendrils of tender seaweeds. Top each oyster with a judicious dollop of Salsa con Lima y Cilantro.

CEBICHE OR CEVICHE
RAW FISH "COOKED" IN A CITRUS MARINADE

At its best it is pristinely fresh seafood, marinated in enough lime juice to almost pickle it, then dressed in a chunky salsalike salad or sauce. At its worst it is mediocre, even inedible, a last-ditch attempt to disguise over-the-hill fish in ceviche flavors.

Many recipes call for combining the fish with lime juice and sauce ingredients all at once. I think this is a mistake. A bath first in undiluted lime juice—and plenty of it—"cooks" the fish, firms it up, and readies it for its submersion into the tomatoes, onions, and chillies.

In Mexico ceviche may be made from any sort of fish or seafood: prawns, crab, scallops, or that great sea-snail the conch, in addition to white-fleshed fish fillets.

1 lb. white-fleshed fish fillets
Juice of 7 limes
2 to 3 ripe tomatoes, seeded and diced
3 fresh jalapeños or serranos, or 4 jalapeños *en escabeche*

½ teaspoon crumbled oregano
Salt to taste
⅓ cup olive oil
1 small onion, chopped
2 tablespoons chopped cilantro

....

❶ Cut fish into bite-sized pieces and place in a glass bowl. Pour on the lime juice and mix well. Let sit, refrigerated, for at least 5 hours, or until mixture looks opaque. Turn every so often so that lime juice evenly permeates the fish.

❷ When fish is opaque, add tomatoes, chillies, oregano, salt, and olive oil. Chill another hour or so.

❸ About 15 minutes before serving, remove from refrigerator so that olive oil has a chance to warm slightly and uncongeal. Serve sprinkled with onion and cilantro. *Serves 4 to 6*

.... **VARIATION** ....

Drain fish of its lime bath before adding the other ingredients. This makes for a clean-tasting, though less tangy, ceviche.

....

CAMARONES A LA PARILLA
GRILLED CHILLIED PRAWNS WITH PAPAYA

The combination of lime and orange juice with the citrus rind and chilli powder imparts a distinctive zest to seafood, a flavoring particularly suited to the smoky taste of outdoor grilling. Accompany by sweet and cool juicy papaya or other tropical fruits and garnish with edible blossoms such as nasturtiums or pansies.

Note that the shells are left on the prawns—this protects the flesh during grilling and keeps it juicy. It is admittedly a mess to eat, unfortunately—be sure to provide bowls for the discarded shells. If this is too messy to contemplate, used shelled prawns with their tails intact and take care not to overcook.

1 orange
2 limes
3 cloves garlic, chopped
1 jalapeño or serrano, chopped
(or to taste)
2 tablespoons mild red chilli powder
such as ancho, New Mexico, or
combination (for less heat, use half
chilli powder, half paprika)
1 teaspoon cumin

½ teaspoon crumbled oregano leaves
1 teaspoon salt
2 tablespoons olive oil or vegetable
oil
2¼ lbs. prawns or large shrimp, with
shells left on
Bamboo or metal skewers
1 firm but ripe papaya, peeled and cut
into bite-sized pieces
Fresh salsa of choice

❶ Grate the rind from the orange and one of the limes, then squeeze the juice from both. (Reserve other lime.) Combine the juice and rind.

❷ Add garlic, jalapeño or serrano, chilli powder, cumin, oregano, salt, and oil.

❸ Mix with prawns and let marinate for 30 minutes to 1 hour.

❹ Skewer and grill over a charcoal fire if possible; otherwise grill or sauté on a stove.

❺ Serve immediately, each skewer garnished with chunks of papaya and the remaining lime cut into wedges, accompanied by salsa of choice. *Serves 4 to 6*

CAMARONES "COCTEL"
YUCATECAN PRAWN APPETIZER

In shellfish food stalls in the Yucatán, plump, robust prawns, exquisitely fresh and full of their sea-juice and briny flavors, are served in a soup plate, four or five large specimens arranged in a sunburst or flower pattern. They have been cooked and cooled, then seasoned with a shake of olive oil and vinegar, a sprinkling of chopped onions, cilantro, tomatoes, and pungent fresh green chillies. Their spicy simplicity captures the essence of sun-drenched Mexican eating.

(Note: The best way of cooking prawns is by a Chinese method known as steeping. Place the unshelled prawns in a saucepan along with ½ lemon and water to cover. Bring to boil, cook a moment or two, then remove from heat. Cover and let steep until water is cool. Remove shells, legs, and veins, but leave the tails. The prawns should emerge pink and juicy-tender).

**4 or 5 large prawns per person,
cooked as described above**
Cruet each of olive oil and vinegar
**Small bowls, each filled with a
separate ingredient: chopped onions,
diced tomatoes, chopped cilantro,
and chopped or thinly sliced
serranos or habaneras (breathtakingly hot, but with a distinctive
flavor)**
Lime wedges

....

Arrange prawns in shallow soup plates in a sunburst or flower shape. Pass cruets of olive oil and vinegar and bowls of raw condiments, letting each diner help himself. *Allow 4 to 5 prawns per person*

....

CAMARONES EN FRIO
PRAWNS SAUTEED WITH ONIONS, GARLIC, AND VINEGAR, TOPPED WITH LEMON-MARINATED-ONIONS

The charm of this dish is its contrast of tastes and textures. The prawns are earthy, rich-tasting, with soft sautéed onions and garlic, yet tangy with a splash of vinegar and topped with crunchy, lemon-pickled onions. It is provocative but not shocking, a dish that could be enjoyed as part of an appetizer selection or picnic lunch. Follow with Arroz Negro and a selection of sliced vegetables that you've marinated in a bit of olive oil and vinegar, then grilled; serve with dabs of mayonnaise seasoned with garlic, olive oil, and mild chilli powder such as New Mexico or mulatto.

2 onions, thinly sliced
Juice of 1 lime
2 cloves garlic, coarsely chopped
2 tablespoons vegetable oil
1 lb. prawns

**Pinch each: black pepper, cayenne
pepper, paprika, oregano**
3 tablespoons white wine vinegar
Salt (optional)

....

❶ Combine half the sliced onions with the lime juice and chill for at least 30 minutes.

❷ Sauté the remaining onion with the garlic in vegetable oil; when softened, add the prawns. Sprinkle with black pepper, cayenne, paprika, and oregano and stir. Splash the vinegar into the pan and let it cook out as the prawns firm up—it should only take a few minutes. If the prawns are done but the vinegar still sharp, remove the prawns and let the vinegar cook a moment longer, becoming a concentrated essence rather than a sauce. Toss the prawns in it and remove to a plate to cool.

❸ Serve the cool prawns and cooked onions topped with the tangy lime-marinated onions. *Serves 4*

··

··· **VARIATION** ·······························

Other seafood or firm white-fleshed fish fillets cut into bite-sized pieces are equally delicious in place of the prawns. I often make it with chicken, too; turkey would probably by good as well.

··

PESCADO CON DOS SALSAS
FISH FILLETS WITH GREEN SALSA AND RED CHILLI PUREE

The sauces should be bright and direct in both color and preparation: sea-green tomatillo sauce and brick-red chilli sauce.

In the following dish, simple fillets of fish are poached, then placed on a bed of pureed green tomatillos and cilantro; mild red chilli puree is drizzled on top. Its visual appeal and great flavor belies its easy preparation.

Instead of whole fillets, you could dice the fish before poaching and then serve the nuggets of fish scattered on the sauce's surface. While the recipe calls for the dish to be served at room temperature as an appetizer, by all means serve it warm if you like. Follow with Arroz con Elote and Chayote Relleno or Chiles Rellenos filled with goat cheese.

For the Fish:

2 cups fish broth
2 bay leaves
5 cloves garlic, whole
1 cup dry white wine or water
1 teaspoon pure chilli powder of
choice, or pureed chilli flesh

1 lb. fish fillets—red snapper, bass,
rock cod, or any firm-fleshed mild-
flavored whitefish, each cut into
several large pieces or lots of bite-
sized nuggets

....

❶ Place the fish broth, bay leaves, garlic, wine or water, and chilli powder in a saucepan. Bring to boil and simmer until the garlic cloves are tender.

❷ Place the fish fillets, cut as desired, into the broth. Simmer a few minutes, only until the fish begins to turn opaque, then remove from heat and let cool to room temperature. Remove fish from liquid and refrigerate it, tightly covered, until ready to eat.

Salsa Tomatillo:

4 green onions, sliced
1 to 3 jalapeños or serranos, chopped
(to taste)
2 cups cooked tomatillos, drained
(canned are fine)

½ teaspoon cumin (or to taste)
¼ cup coarsely chopped cilantro
1 cup cool fish broth from above
recipe

....

❶ In blender or food processor, place green onions and green chillies and whirl until finely chopped or pureed. Add tomatillos and continue pureeing until saucelike, then add cumin and cilantro and continue to puree.

❷ Thin the mixture with broth, whirling until the sauce is pale bright green with darker green flecks of cilantro throughout.

Red Chilli Puree:

⅓ to ½ cup pure pasilla, New Mexico,
or combination chilli powder, or a
mixture of about 2 parts paprika and
1 part mild chilli powder

½ to ⅔ cup fish stock from above
recipe, heated to just boiling

....

Mix chilli powder with the hot broth gradually, making first a paste, then a smooth, lump-free, rather thin and paintlike sauce.

To Assemble:
Cover the bottom of each plate with some of the green sauce, then place a fish fillet (or scatter fish nuggets) on top. Drizzle with a tiny bit of the red chilli puree. **Serves 4 as a light main course or first course**

....

.... **VARIATION** ....

In place of fish fillets and fish broth, used boned chicken breast and chicken broth. Poach chicken whole and let cool in broth. Serve sliced, fanned out on top of the green sauce, garnished with a bit of the red chilli puree.

....

TORTAS DE CAMARON
FRIED SHRIMP PATTIES

These patties are traditional for Lent and Christmastime. Certain restaurants are known for their *tortas de Camarón* and people come especially during the holidays to sample them.

The patties are usually made with dried shrimp only, but I find that adding fresh shrimp lightens them and makes them juicier, more interesting. They are usually served in a sauce of either tomatoes or mole; sometimes they are simmered with *romeritos*, a rosemary-like green vegetable, or shredded spinachlike greens. Nopales, too, are a traditional accompaniment.

1 recipe Salsa Ranchera or Mole sauce from Mole Poblano de Guacamole
About ²⁄₃ to 1 cup sliced cooked nopales, rinsed and drained; or lightly cooked green beans; or cooked, squeezed-dry spinach

2 oz. dried shrimp
4 oz. fresh shrimp, cooked and cooled
4 medium eggs, separated
Pinch salt
About ¼ cup flour
Oil for frying

....

❶ Heat sauce, cover and keep warm. Add nopales, green beans, or spinach, and heat in the sauce.

❷ Whirl dried shrimp in blender until it is mealy or crumblike in consistency. Set aside.

❸ Chop cooked shrimp, then mix with ground dried shrimp.

❹ Beat egg yolks until thick and lemon-colored. Whip egg whites with a pinch of salt until stiff peaks form, then gently fold the whites into the yolks. Sprinkle flour atop the eggs and gently fold it in, along with the shrimp.

❺ In a heavy frying pan or wok, heat enough oil to reach a depth of 1½ to 2 inches.

❻ Spoon 2 tablespoons batter into the hot oil for small fritters, or ¼ cup for large fritters. Fry until golden.

❼ Drain on absorbent paper and serve immediately, accompanied by the warm sauce. **Makes 8 to 10 large fritters, 15 to 20 smaller ones**

LANGOSTA ROSARITA
GRILLED LOBSTER WITH REFRIED BEANS

Not long ago, Rosarita Beach was about as far south as one could drive from the U.S. into Baja California. Beyond that lay hazardous terrain; travelers told of rough roads frequented by remorseless *banditos*.

Because of its accessibility from Los Angeles, its lush exotic landscape, and its proximity to Agua Caliente racetrack, Rosarita Beach at one time was a favorite getaway spot for old-time Hollywood stars and wanna-be's. Only a short distance past tawdry Tijuana, the charm of Rosarita seemed a lifetime away from the demands and dreams of the movie world.

They came to the Rosarita Beach Hotel, a place that always struck me as a romantic outpost at the edge of the world. There diners tucked into the local specialty: briny sweet lobster, slathered with garlic-herb butter and served with creamy refried beans. The elegant lobster meats combined with the humble, earthy beans in an unexpected and joyous way.

Begin the meal with Caesar salad (created in Tijuana) to which you've added thin strips of fried mild red chillies and diced avocado. Serve the lobster and beans with a stack of fresh, warm flour tortillas and a bowl of crisp chunky cilantro-flecked chilli-and-tomato salsa.

This is one of those dishes that is best eaten sitting on a terrace overlooking a warm beach, as the oppressive heat of the day disappears into a breezy evening.

4 to 6 oz. (1 to 1½ sticks) unsalted
butter, softened at room temperature
1½ teaspoons crumbled dried
oregano leaves
½ teaspoon salt (or to taste)
3 to 5 cloves garlic, coarsely chopped
(or to taste)
Generous coarse grindings of black
peppercorns

4 large lobster tails, split into halves,
the flesh loosened with a knife
1 batch Frijoles Refritos or Frijoles
Mexicana, kept warm
Salsa Cruda
Warm flour tortillas

....

❶ Mix butter with oregano, garlic, salt, and pepper. Spread over the lobster flesh, reserving a bit to baste the lobster with once it is finished cooking.

❷ Grill the lobster over an open flame for about 10 minutes, or heat it on a griddle or frying pan, or broil it. (Since the lobster is most likely already cooked through, you just need to heat it with the seasonings. Any more cooking will make it tough.) Spread reserved herb butter over the lobster.

❸ To serve, place a lobster tail and a portion of the beans on each plate. Offer tortillas and salsa as desired. *Serves 4*

....

CAMARONES CON NOPALES Y CHIPOTLES
PRAWNS WITH CACTUS IN A SMOKY CHILLI SAUCE

The combination of chipotle chilli with its rich, smoky fire and the sea flavor of shrimp or prawns—or any seafood—is a brilliant one, especially with strips of tangy nopales to balance it all. This dish is similar to one traditionally prepared with dried shrimp for Lent.

Serve this rich and savory simmer with crusty bread, blind (unfilled) tamales, or soft, warm corn tortillas to dip into the seafood-tomato-chipotle mixture; or ladle the saucy seafood over thinly sliced lettuce and herbs such as cilantro, green onions, and oregano for a warm salad. Begin the meal with a selection of several masa *antojitos*, and serve a *cazuela* of black beans on the side. For dessert: Helado de Chocolatl with tiny cups of strong black coffee.

3 onions, chopped
5 cloves garlic, chopped
2 tablespoons vegetable oil
4 tomatoes, diced
½ to 1 chipotle chilli, chopped, plus a bit of its marinade
About ½ cup peeled, sliced, and parboiled nopales

2 cups fish broth
1 lb. raw shrimp or prawns, peeled and deveined
2 tablespoons chopped fresh cilantro
1 lime, cut into wedges
Handful shredded lettuce (optional)

••

❶ Lightly sauté onion and garlic in oil until softened. Add tomatoes and cook several minutes until somewhat saucy.

❷ Add chipotle chilli and marinade, nopales, and fish broth. Bring to boil, reduce heat, and simmer for a few minutes to combine flavors.

❸ Add shrimp or prawns and cook only a minute or two, then remove from heat and let the shrimp sit in the hot liquid to finish cooking. When they have turned bright pink they are ready.

❹ Serve immediately, each portion garnished with cilantro, lime, and lettuce. Add a drizzle of extra chipotle marinade if dish is not already spicy enough for your tastes. ***Serves 4***

••

•••••••••••••••••••••••••• **VARIATION** ••••••••••••••••••••••••••

TOSTADAS DE CAMARON Y NOPALES ❖ SHRIMP AND CACTUS TOSTADAS

Serve the hot sauced prawns and nopales on crisp-fried tortillas, then top with shredded iceberg lettuce and diced tomato, dressed with lemon juice or vinegar.

•••••••••••••••••••••••••• **VARIATION** ••••••••••••••••••••••••••

MARISCOS MARIACHI

Increase the chipotles to two. Choose a selection of seafood—scallops, squid, bite-sized pieces of bass—in addition to the prawns. Nopales may be omitted.

Rather than simmering the seafood in the sauce, combine the raw seafood with the sauce, then wrap up into parcels of banana leaves (see instructions for wrapping tamales). Steam over dark (preferably Mexican) beer for about 6 minutes, or long enough to just cook the seafood through. Served with lime wedges and a sprinkle of cilantro.

••

MEJILLONES A LA MEXICANA
MUSSELS STEAMED OVER LAGER WITH TOMATOES, CHILLIES, AND ONIONS

The slight bitterness of the beer combines with the acidic tomatoes, sweet onions, and biting chilli to form a sort of spicy court bouillon for steaming briny mussels. It's a nice way of using up any leftover beer.

Serve as a first course or appetizer, followed by Arroz Verde con Mariscos and Ejotes con Pimientos Morrones, crusty bread, and a spunky salsa on the side.

2 cups lager or beer
2 small onions, chopped coarsely
1 jalapeño or serrano, seeded and diced
¼ to ½ cup chopped tomatoes (canned are fine)

2¼ lbs. mussels in their shells, scrubbed and trimmed of their "beards" (or clams in their shells)
Fresh salsa of choice

Place lager, onions, chilli, and tomatoes in the bottom of a steamer. Bring to boil, then add mussels or clams and steam until their shells pop open. Discard any that have not opened. Serve immediately, accompanied by salsa. *Serves 4 as a first course*

PESCADO EN TAMAL
CORN-HUSK-WRAPPED CHILLIED FISH, TOLUCA STYLE

The plump tamale is placed on the plate before you. Gingerly you fork open the corn-husk wrapping, and to your delight the insides are filled not with doughy tamale filling but with what seems like a school of tiny fish, fragrant with spices, pouring out onto your plate.

Fish—in bite-sized chunks or small and whole—have been wrapped in corn husks and steamed, much like a tamale, since pre-Hispanic times. The wrapped parcels were stacked into a sort of steamer device based on corncobs, then water was poured in and the parcels steamed.

Serve each diner several parcels, so that when the tamales are unwrapped the tantalizing aromas hit with their full force. Accompany with warm corn tortillas, avocado slices, and jalapeño *en escabeche* or salsa of choice, so that those who wish to can make their own soft tacos. You could begin the meal with Caldo del Papas prepared with fish broth, and finish with Flan de Café.

About 16 corn husks, depending on size
1 recipe Recada Rojo Enchilado
1 lb. firm white-fleshed fish, cut into bite-sized pieces, or 1 ½ lbs. tiny whole sardines, cleaned

2 tablespoons chopped fresh cilantro
1 avocado, peeled and sliced
Jalapeños *en escabeche*
Warm corn tortillas

❶ Soak corn husks in warm water to cover for 30 minutes.

❷ Meanwhile, mix chilli paste with fish and toss to coat well.

❸ When corn husks have become pliable, lay out two at a time, making a flat oblong surface, then top with a spoonful or so of the chilli-seasoned fish. Fold over to enclose the fish well.

❹ Stack parcels in steamer and steam over boiling water for 10 minutes. Serve immediately, accompanied by avocado, jalapeños, and warm corn tortillas. *Serves 4 as a first course*

VARIATION:

In place of corn husks, use banana leaves as they do in the Yucatán for a subtly different flavor. Cut the leaves into a workable size, and heat over medium-low heat on top of the stove to render them pliable. Place a generous spoonful of fish in the middle of each leaf and fold the leaf over to enclose completely. Steam and serve as above.

CALDO LARGO CON LIMA
SOUP-STEW OF FISH, SEAFOOD, ROASTED GARLIC, AND CITRUS FRUIT—YUCATAN

Roasted garlic gives a complex, slightly smoky aroma to the broth. Despite the large quantity of garlic, it is cooked beyond sharpness and its flesh has mellowed and sweetened as it has toasted. A sprinkling of raw onions, chillies, and lime juice adds tangy freshness.

This is a seafood rendition of the classic Yucatecan soup, *sopa de lima*, more usually prepared with shredded chicken and tortilla strips. While the original is one of the brilliant soups of the Mexican kitchen, I find the deliciously sharp flavors even better suited for a variety of seafood. This bowlful makes a full meal.

Serve with crusty bread or soft corn tortillas and several savory appetizers: guacamole, a plate of fresh cheese such as pecorino or string cheese with roasted mild green chillies, and cactus topped with shrimp or diced hard-cooked egg. Fresh fruit ice creams, splashed with a little tequila and orange liqueur such as Gran Marnier or Triple Sec, would be a deliciously simple dessert: Chimichangas de Frutas a more ambitious one.

2 onions, coarsely chopped
1 jalapeño or serrano, seeded and chopped
15 large garlic cloves, unpeeled
1 tablespoon olive oil
4 cups chicken broth
2 cups fish broth or clam juice
1 cup water
6 medium clams, scrubbed
12 medium mussels, scrubbed and trimmed of their "beards"
8 ripe tomatoes, peeled, seeded, and coarsely chopped (canned are fine)

¼ teaspoon crumbled dried oregano leaves
1 teaspoon finely grated zest from 1 grapefruit
1 teaspoon finely grated zest from 3 limes
8 oz. medium shrimp or prawns
8 oz. firm-fleshed whitefish, cut into bite-sized pieces
Salt and black pepper to taste
⅓ cup lime juice (juice of approximately 2 limes)

❶ Mix a third of the onions with half the chopped chilli; reserve for garnish.

❷ Roast the garlic on an ungreased heavy skillet over medium-heat until the skins are charred and the cloves slightly softened, about 4 minutes. Cool slightly, then slip the skins off.

❸ Heat oil in large saucepan and sauté remaining onions and chilli until softened, about 5 minutes. Add roasted garlic, chicken broth, fish broth or clam juice, and 1 cup water. Simmer to blend flavors, about 15 minutes.

❹ Add clams, mussels, tomatoes, oregano, and grapefruit and lime zests. Cook over medium heat until clam and mussel shells open, 5 to 10 minutes. Discard any that have not opened.

❺ Add shrimp or prawns, cut-up fish, and salt and pepper. Simmer until shrimp and fish turn opaque, just 2 or 3 minutes.

❻ Remove from heat and stir in reserved onion-chilli mixture and lime juice. Serve immediately. ***Serves 6***

PESCADO YUCATECA
CHILLIED BASS WITH COCONUT MILK

I tasted this dish along a seemingly endless stretch of beach in the Mexican tropics. It was at once tropical and exotic, as delicious as the palm tree-fringed scenery.

Almost any red chilli paste makes an excellent coating for this fish; in the Yucatán achiote seasoning is traditional, but I often use Recado Rojo Enchilado or the red chilli and tequila paste from Pato con Naranja y Yerbabuena. Roasted garlic gives a distinctive Yucatecan flavor to the dish, and slices of orange gently perfume the flesh of the fish. The drizzle of cool, rich coconut milk is a delicious surprise against the slightly acidic spiced fish.

Begin the meal with Tostadas del Papas and accompany the fish with Arroz Mexicana. For dessert, enjoy something refreshingly tropical: a platter of juicy fruit splashed with a bit of tequila and fruit liqueurs, or perhaps as simple as diced mango mixed with peach frozen yogurt and served with crisp shortbread cookies.

1 whole bass or rock cod, about 3 lbs., inside cleaned
1 lemon, halved; leave one half intact and slice the other
4 to 5 cloves garlic, unpeeled
Recado Rojo Enchilado, or seasoning paste from Pato con Naranja y Yerbabuena, Pollo Pibil, or Camarones a la Parilla

Several slices of orange, unpeeled
1/4 cup coconut milk
Garnishes: shredded lettuce, chopped chillies, chopped cilantro, diced tomato

❶ Place fish in baking pan. Rub it inside and out with lemon half.

❷ Toast garlic cloves in an ungreased skillet until lightly charred, about 5 to 7 minutes.

❸ Coat fish inside and out with chilli paste, then place the charred garlic, orange slices, and several slices of lemon into its cavity.

❹ Cover pan with foil. Bake in a 325°F oven 1 hour, then remove foil.

❺ Place under the broiler and let top brown and crisp a bit.

❻ Serve drizzled with coconut milk and garnished with shredded lettuce, chopped chillies, cilantro, and diced tomato. *Serves 4 to 6*

EIGHT SIMPLE FISH DISHES

CHIPOTLE GRILLED SALMON

Brush salmon steaks with a little oil, lime juice, salt, and pepper. Grill over an open fire, then top with dabs of chipotle marinade mixed with sour cream. Chunks of grilled salmon, seasoned with chipotle marinade, are delicious wrapped up into a soft corn or flour tortilla, along with a dollop of sour cream and a sprinkling of onions.

SMOKY ROAST FISH WITH PICKLED JALAPEÑOS OR SERRANOS

Roast a whole fish such as snapper or bass slowly over a low fire, preferably covered like an old-fashioned barbecue, letting the fish develop a smoky flavor. Serve with sliced pickled jalapeños or serranos, wedges of lime, and warm corn tortillas, and roll up into tacos while you knock back glasses of tequila followed by chilled Mexican beer.

PESCADO CON AJO
FISH WITH GARLIC

Marinate fish fillets in lots of lime juice to firm the flesh. Top with an exceedingly garlicky garlic butter such as that from Langosta Rosarita, then grill until lightly browned and fish approaches firmness. Serve with more garlic butter and a sprinkle of parsley. No chillies in sight, but a little freshly chopped serrano and diced tomatoes are always welcome.

PESCADO FRITO A LA CAMPECHE
FRIED FISH WITH ONION-VINEGAR SAUCE

Serve any crisply fried fish fillets with the following pickled onion sauce: Combine 2 thinly sliced onions with 1 cup cider vinegar, ½ cup water, a large pinch oregano, and salt to taste. Cook until onion is transparent. Let sauce cool.

PESCADO CON NARANJA Y LIMON
FRIED FISH FILLETS WITH CITRUS WEDGES, CHOPPED ONION, AND CILANTRO

Sprinkle fried fish fillets (that have a light flour or batter coating before frying) with mild chilli powder. Accompany with wedges of orange, lime, and lemon, letting each diner squeeze a bit of each over his or her portion. Sprinkle with cilantro and chopped onion.

PESCADO CON GUACAMOLE
POACHED OR GRILLED FISH WITH GUACAMOLE

Simply spoon Guacamole of choice over poached or grilled fish fillets or steaks.

PESCADO EN ADOBO
FISH MARINATED AND BAKED IN MILD, TART CHILLI SAUCE

Marinate fish fillets or steaks for about an hour in Salsa Adobo. Bake, still in its marinade, until fish is just firming up and cooked through.

AVES

··

POULTRY

Before the conquest, Mexico had little in the way of poultry. Wild birds and rabbits were hunted, turkeys and a sort of large duck (now extinct) were both kept as food, but none could be depended on for steady nourishment. The introduction of the domestic chicken as well as the domestication of the turkey proved monumental in the development of Mexican cuisine. The ancient sauces of pounded and pureed chillies adapted brilliantly to poultry.

Much of Mexican chicken cookery is based on long, slow simmering, using the liquid for soup, then stewing the now-tender creature in a richly spiced sauce. The long cooking time is necessary because chickens in Mexico lead a long, full life before meeting the stewpot. You see these wiry birds pecking around gardens, wandering down village streets, and clucking in parking lots.

A simmered chicken or turkey might be rubbed with a spice paste—moles, *escabeches*, or recados—then baked or stewed until fork-tender. If a chicken is not to be simmered first, it may be tossed with a selection of varied seasonings and popped into the oven for a slow bake, the fragrant sauce permeating the flesh. In addition to main courses, chicken shows up in a wide variety of other guises: shredded and added to soups, piled into tostadas, stewed into taco fillings, and so on and on.

Turkey is probably Mexico's favorite bird, though, its great bulk stretching to feed many mouths. You'll find its agreeably versatile flesh in the same sorts of sauces used for chicken. It is the traditional choice for the spicy sauces known as moles.

Duck is less common, yet its richness is offset brilliantly by the spiciness of Mexico's seasonings. Wild birds are enjoyed as well, usually marinated and grilled over a charcoal fire, the smoky flavors enhanced by the chilli in the marinade.

As with other meats, no part of the fowl goes to waste in the Mexican kitchen. Chicken feet enrich stock; livers, gizzards, and hearts are sautéed into savory taco fillings. Even the blood is used: that unfortunate turkey whose fate is intertwined with the Sunday Mole Poblano will have its neck slashed, its blood collected, to be poached into a quivering brown puddinglike delicacy.

POLLO PIBIL
SPICE-COATED, BANANA-LEAF-WRAPPED ROAST CHICKEN, YUCATECAN STYLE

Achiote flavors this dish with its subtle aroma while the wrapping of banana leaf keeps the chicken moist as it gently perfumes. It comes to the table an exotic parcel of graying-green leaves; when unwrapped it releases a fragrant steam. The chicken inside is meltingly tender.

When making the paste, you must allow time to soak the rock-hard achiote seeds overnight, then simmer them. Once done, they are soft enough to mash or puree and form the basis of the bright red paste.

Make-Ahead Note: Achiote seasoning paste may be frozen and kept almost indefinitely.

The dish may be made from pork instead of chicken; the name *pibil* refers to the type of stone-lined pit oven, called a *pib*, used for the dish. Serve a heady citrus- and chilli-seasoned broth to begin with, such as Caldo Largo con Lima, prepared without seafood and using chicken broth instead of fish. Accompany the Pollo Pibil with steamed rice or Arroz Blanco garnished with sliced bananas, a *cazuela* of savory black beans with creamy cheese melted in, a stack of warm flour or corn tortillas (or *naan* or similar breads), and a platter of shredded cabbage, sliced radishes, diced avocado, sliced tomato, Cebollas en Escabeche a la Yucateca, and a sprinkle of oregano, or Escabeche de Col along with a bowl of fresh salsa. Pollo Pibil is also excellent the next day, all moist and flavorful: delicious as a salad, or shredded and wrapped into tacos.

Recado Rojo con Achiote
Seasoning Paste:

3 tablespoons achiote seeds
2 cups water
3 mild chillies such as ancho, New Mexico, guajillo, pasilla, or combination (or equivalent in pure chilli powder)
3 cloves garlic, chopped
1 to 2 jalapeños, chopped
1 tablespoon paprika

2 teaspoons cumin
½ teaspoon crumbled oregano leaves
1 teaspoon salt
3 tablespoons chopped cilantro
1½ teaspoons chopped fresh orange rind or a generous pinch dried rind
Juice of 1 orange, 1 lemon, and 1 lime

....

❶ Combine achiote seeds with 1 cup water and bring to a boil. Reduce heat and simmer over low heat 5 minutes, then remove from heat, cover, and let soak at least 2 hours, preferably overnight.

❷ Half an hour before you are to grind the achiote seeds, prepare the chillies. Lightly toast each chilli by holding over an open flame or in an ungreased skillet. Tear into pieces and cover with remaining cup of hot water. Cover and let soak for 30 minutes to 1 hour.

❸ Puree achiote seeds and chillies together with the soaking liquid in a blender. (The bright coloring of the achiote seeds will stain the plastic container you use. The harmless discoloring will fade and disappear within several days of using and washing.)

❹ When pureed as smoothly as possible (it will still have texture), put mixture through a strainer, pushing against the strainer to extract all the goodness from the ingredients, leaving behind the skins and other hard bits. Discard them.

❺ Combine strained achiote-chilli paste with the remaining ingredients.

Cooking and Serving:

1 package banana leaves (see Special Ingredients)
1 whole chicken, about 3½ lbs.
3 to 4 green onions, whole

3 to 4 slices bacon
2 limes, cut into wedges for garnish
¼ cup whole cilantro leaves

....

❶ Rub the seasoning paste all over the chicken, inside and out. Heat each banana leaf briefly over a flame to soften, then wrap chicken in about 2 thicknesses of banana leaves. Place wrapped chicken in baking dish, cover with foil loosely, and marinate overnight in the refrigerator.

❷ Next day, partially unwrap the chicken, just enough to insert the green onions into the cavity and top the chicken with the bacon. Rewrap using the same leaves, rearranging them as tidily as possible. Wrap tightly in foil, then bake in 325°F oven 2 to 2½ hours.

❸ Unwrap leaves and remove chicken to serving platter. Garnish with lime wedges and cilantro leaves. **Serves 4**

···

······················· **VARIATION: PUERCO PIBIL** ·······················

Use pork instead of chicken; choose a boned loin or shoulder cut, and cut into 2-inch chunks. Prepare according to the basic recipe but increase cooking time to 3–3½ hours.

···

POLLO EN ESCABECHE DE VALLADOLID
CHICKEN BREASTS COATED WITH SPICES, IN A SAUCE OF ONIONS, VINEGAR, AND STOCK

While variations of this dish are eaten all over the Yucatán, it is associated with the hot and dusty town of Valladolid, where chicken dishes of all sorts are a specialty; as often as you are to find pork tacos in the central area of Mexico, beef in the north, or fish on the coasts, you are likely to find your taco stuffed with shredded chicken in Valladolid.

This particular dish is called *escabeche*, or pickled, in honor of the vinegar used in the sauce. Its piquant presence is reminiscent of Spanish and French vinegar-based sauces, but with an unmistakable New World interpretation.

Traditionally the dish is prepared with a whole bird long-simmered. I like the delicacy, however, of white chicken flesh only, cooked until just tender, then paired with the tangy vinegar-onion broth. Serve in shallow soup bowls, the chicken pieces topped with onions, the whole sitting in spoonfuls of tangy stock, accompanied by crusty bread or warm corn tortillas.

Since this is a light and sprightly dish, begin with a selection of hearty masa *antojitos* such as Garnachas de Frijoles Negros or Picadas. For dessert, try tea-steeped prunes spooned over coffee ice cream sprinkled with cinnamon.

4 large or 8 small chicken breasts, with or without bones
Chicken broth to cover
About ½ cup Recado Escabeche
4 small to medium onions, sliced lengthwise
½ to 1 jalapeño, seeded and chopped

2 to 3 güero wax peppers, or similar mild fresh yellow chillies
About ½ cup vegetable oil
⅓ cup cider or sherry vinegar
Pinch cumin seeds
About ½ cup flour

....

❶ Place chicken breasts in saucepan with broth. Bring to boil, reduce heat, and simmer 5 minutes (if using boned chicken breasts, cook only 2 or 3 minutes). Remove from heat and let cool in broth. (Chicken may be simmered ahead of time and then kept refrigerated up to 2 days.)

❷ Remove chicken from broth (you should have about 3 cups broth; add water and bouillon cube if needed). Reserve broth.

❸ Dry the chicken and remove and discard the skin. Remove chicken from the bone in one or two pieces if it is still on the bone. Smear the chicken with ⅔ of the spice paste. Let it sit at room temperature for 30 to 45 minutes.

❹ Sauté onions and chillies in a tiny bit of the oil until browned in places and softened; pour in vinegar and cumin seeds, let cook down a bit, then add reserved broth and remaining spice paste. Boil until somewhat reduced in volume and richly flavored. Set aside and keep warm.

❺ Dredge chicken in flour. Heat remaining oil in heavy frying pan. Fry chicken until lightly browned and somewhat crusty. Remove from pan and serve immediately, each portion topped with some of the onions and swimming in a small pool of the broth. *Serves 4*

.... **VARIATION** ....

PESCADO A LA VALLADOLID

Substitute fish fillets or steaks for the chicken; adjusting cooking time accordingly.

....

POLLO A LA MERIDA
·······························
CHICKEN IN AN ORANGE, OLIVE, ALMOND, RAISIN, AND CAPER SAUCE—YUCATAN

The sauce is strongly Mediterranean accented, with bits of olives, raisins, capers, orange, and olive oil. Cinnamon adds a Moorish touch, with a scattering of the ubiquitous Mexican chopped chilli and cilantro.

Serve with Arroz Verde, Frijoles Negros Enchilados, and a salad of shredded romaine lettuce garnished with sliced red onions, diced avocado, and Seville oranges, dressed in olive oil and oregano-seasoned vinaigrette.

1 chicken, 2½ to 3 lbs., cut into serving pieces	15 blanched almonds, coarsely chopped
2 limes	15 pimiento-stuffed green olives, coarsely chopped
1 to 2 onions, coarsely chopped	
1 red, yellow, or green pepper (or a little of each), diced	2 cups orange juice (sweet, hand-squeezed juice is best)
About 2 tablespoons olive oil	¼ cup chicken broth
8 tomatoes, peeled, seeded, and diced (canned are fine)	¼ teaspoon ground cinnamon
	Salt and pepper to taste
2 tablespoons capers	½ to 1 jalapeño, coarsely chopped
1½ tablespoons raisins	2 teaspoons chopped cilantro

···

❶ Place chicken in a shallow pan or bowl and squeeze lime juice over it. Let set for 30 to 60 minutes.

❷ Lightly sauté onions and pepper in half the olive oil until softened, then add tomatoes, capers, raisins, almonds, and olives. Let cook until the liquid has evaporated and the mixture is beginning to brown. Add orange juice, then remove from the pan.

❸ Wipe the lime juice off the chicken and discard excess juice. Brown chicken on high heat in a heavy skillet in the remaining olive oil, adding more if needed.

❹ Pour off any fat. Add the sauce plus the broth to the pan. Reduce heat and simmer, covered, until chicken is tender, about 35 minutes.

❺ Season with cinnamon, salt, and pepper. Serve immediately, sprinkled with chopped chilli and cilantro. *Serves 4*

······················· **VARIATION** ································

PESCADO EN NARANJA

Fish fillets are delicious instead of chicken in this spicy citrus olive sauce.

Prepare the sauce as above. Serve spooned over sautéed fish fillets in a baking dish or frying pan. Heat together for 10 minutes or so, long enough to meld flavors. Serve sprinkled with chopped chilli and cilantro, accompanied by lime wedges.

··

CHICKEN PAILLARD WITH CITRUS-RED CHILLI PASTE AND PASILLA GUACAMOLE
PECHUGAS DE POLLO CON GUACAMOLE

Not a traditional dish, rather the sort of elegantly simple, highly spiced food that is becoming a modern classic both in contemporary Mexican cookery and in America's Southwest. The flat medallions of tender chicken are superb lightly marinated in the mild and tangy spice mixture accented with a squeeze of tart lime. A dollop of Pasilla Guacamole brings it all to life.

Serve following Caldo del Papas and accompany with a salad of thinly sliced romaine garnished with fried strips of mild chilli, a handful of crumbled fresh goat cheese, and a flurry of chopped herbs: cilantro, green onions, mint, marjoram. For dessert, Helado de Yerbabuena con Tostadas de Chocolatl.

4 chicken breasts, bones and skin removed, pounded lightly to an even ½-inch thickness.
Recado Rojo Enchilado, or spice paste mixture for Pato con Naranja y Yerbabuena

Vegetable oil or olive oil
1 lime, cut into wedges
1 recipe Pasilla Guacamole

···

❶ Coat chicken breasts in spice mixture and let sit for about 30 minutes.

❷ Quickly sauté chicken in a lightly greased pan, or brush with olive oil and grill over an open fire. In either case, do not overcook it.

❸ Serve the chicken accompanied by lime wedges and spoonfuls of Pasilla Guacamole. *Serves 4*

························ **VARIATION** ························

GRILLED CHILLIED CHICKEN BREAST TORTAS

Stuff each grilled chicken breast into a crusty pan-grilled roll, then dress the plump sandwiches with Pasilla Guacamole and shredded lettuce splashed with mild salsa.

························ **VARIATION** ························

POC CHUC—YUCATAN

Marinate flat, tender, pounded-thin beefsteaks in the chilli-citrus paste from the above recipe, then grill over an open fire. In the Yucatán the meat would authentically be venison; beef is equally good. Serve garnished with wedges of Seville orange or lime. Accompany with rice, black beans, warm tortillas, marinated cabbage, and chipotle salsa.

···

POLLO DE PLAZA
CHICKEN IN CHILLI-TOMATO SAUCE WITH ENCHILADAS—MICHOACAN

The picture book village of Pátzcuaro is nestled in a valley in the lush Michoacán region, next to the lake also called Pátzcuaro. The area is mild and fertile, well-known throughout Mexico for its crisp white fish from the lake, and its fragrant, sweet strawberries (and known in California for its illegal smoke).

Life in Pátzcuaro, as in most other villages, centers around the plaza. The marketplace thrives by day; food vendors and social street meetings are the focus in the evening. Dusk is filled with the enticing aroma of simple foods cooking over a charcoal brazier, ready to be wrapped into tacos and devoured with shots of tequila.

One of the town's specialties is the following dish of chicken served with enchiladas. Traditionally the chicken is pan-fried and seasoned only with a little sauce. In my less traditional versions the chicken is coated with sauce, then roasted along with a handful of whole garlic cloves; lightly cooked potatoes and carrots are tossed into the pan at the end.

The whole robust platter of chicken, vegetables, and enchiladas makes a festive Sunday lunch. You could begin with a soup, such as Sopa de Aguacate or Rich Spicy Broth, offer crusty bread and vinaigrette-dressed lettuce, then end with coffee ice cream splashed with brandy or blanketed indulgently with thick chocolate sauce.

Sauce:

3 dried mild red chillies such as New Mexico or California
1 mulatto, negro, or ancho chile (optional)
1 onion, coarsely chopped
1 tablespoon vegetable oil
1 tablespoon cumin seeds or 2 tablespoons ground cumin

2 cloves garlic, chopped
1 cup chicken broth
6 ripe tomatoes, diced or coarsely chopped (canned are fine)
¼ cup tomato paste
1 cup orange juice

....

❶ Lightly toast the chillies in a hot, ungreased pan until they begin to change color; this will take only a few moments. Place in deep bowl and pour hot water over the chillies, then leave to steep until they are tender and water has cooled, an hour or so. (This can be done up to 2 days ahead of time; store the chillies in the refrigerator.)

❷ Scrape flesh from chillies to make a puree; reserve the soaking liquid for soups or stews.

❸ Sauté onion in oil until softened. Add cumin seeds and let heat through, toasting somewhat, then add pureed chillies.

❹ In a blender, puree onion and spice mixture along with the garlic, adding chicken broth to smooth it. Continue to puree, then add tomatoes, tomato paste, and orange juice.

Chicken:

1 whole chicken, about 3 lb.
2 heads garlic, broken into cloves but left unpeeled
Sauce from above recipe
3 to 4 green onions

1 cup orange juice or chicken broth
8 to 10 small to medium potatoes, preferably waxy ones
4 to 6 carrots, halved
2 tablespoons vinegar

....

❶ Place chicken in roasting pan. Stuff several cloves of garlic inside it. Dip the green onions into the sauce and stuff these into the chicken as well.

❷ Pour half the sauce over the chicken, letting it run down into the bottom of the pan. Reserve remaining sauce for enchiladas. Scatter the remaining garlic cloves throughout the bottom of the pan.

❸ Roast in a 350°F oven for one hour, adding orange juice or broth occasionally so that there is always an inch or two of liquid at the bottom of the pan.

❹ Meanwhile, prepare the vegetables: Boil potatoes until half-tender, then add carrots and continue cooking until both vegetables are just tender. Drain and toss with vinegar. When cool enough to handle, cut into bite-sized pieces and set aside.

❺ When chicken is just tender, add potatoes and carrots to the pan and toss with the sauce and whole garlics. Return to oven and let cook slowly another half hour or so while you make the enchiladas.

Enchiladas:

12 corn tortillas (slightly stale ones work best)
Remaining half of sauce, warm
Hot oil for frying tortillas

6 oz. crumbled cheese such as *queso fresco*, fresh pecorino, not-too-salty feta, or a creamy Jack
1 onion, chopped
Chicken broth if needed

....

❶ Dip each tortilla into the warm sauce, then into the hot oil. Quickly remove to plate, sprinkle with crumbled cheese and onion, then roll up and place in baking dish. Repeat until all tortillas are used up. If sauce threatens to run low, add a bit of broth.

❷ Pour any remaining sauce over the rolled tortillas.

❸ Cover baking dish with foil and place in oven with the chicken for about 10 minutes, to heat through.

❹ To assemble: Place chicken on platter and surround with the sauce-cloaked vegetables. Accompany with the enchiladas and lots of chilled beer. **Serves 4 to 6**

....

POLLO EN MOLE VERDE CON NOPALES
CHICKEN WITH TOMATILLOS AND NOPALES

The tart tomatillo and the slightly viscous nopale make a particularly good sauce for chicken. Without the nopales, this is a very basic dish, *mole verde*, eaten throughout many regions of Mexico in varying levels of spiciness. The distinctive flavor of this delicious dish depends upon the tomatillos.

Serve with corn or flour tortillas and a *cazuela* of beans. Begin the meal with a platter of sweet papaya with a sprinkle of dried red chilli flakes, wedges of lime, and thin slices of prosciutto. For dessert, serve pecan tartlets and fresh creamy cheese (such as *fromage frais* or fresh goat cheese), and tiny cups of dark coffee.

2 small to medium onions, coarsely chopped
3 cloves garlic, chopped
2 tablespoons vegetable oil
1 lb. cooked tomatillos, pureed or mashed with a fork (or about 2 cups canned)
About 2 cups rich chicken broth
About ⅔ cup cooked and drained nopales, cut into strips (canned are fine)

½ cup chopped cilantro
3 to 4 jalapeños or 2 to 3 serranos, coarsely chopped (for less heat, cut down on amount of chillies and/or remove the seeds and membranes)
1 medium chicken, about 3 lbs., cut into serving pieces
Salt to taste

Lightly sauté onion and garlic in oil until softened and translucent. Add remaining ingredients and simmer, covered, until chicken is tender, about 45 minutes, adding more broth as needed. *Serves 4*

VARIATION

PESCADO VERDE CON NOPALES
Follow the basic recipe but omit the chicken. Choose firm-fleshed fish fillets such as bass. Place in a baking dish and top with sauce. Bake at 350°F 20 minute or until fish is desired doneness.

VARIATION

POLLO CON CALABACITAS Y MAIZ
Omit the nopales from the basic dish and instead add 2 zucchini, in chunks or large dice, and ½ cup corn.

MOLE POBLANO DE GUAJALOTE
PUEBLA-STYLE MOLE OF TURKEY

Perhaps the single greatest festive dish of Mexico, *mole poblano* is often thought of outside the country as a curiosity: turkey with chocolate sauce? Don't, however, expect a sweet chocolate sauce slathered over the bird—not unless it is badly made (as I encountered one unfortunate evening in a London Mexican restaurant).

A mole is a complexly layered sauce of toasted and ground nuts, crushed raisins, soaked and pureed chillies, spices, and a final simmer with a bit of semisweet chocolate—not enough chocolate to make it sweet, only enough to set off the rest of the rich, spicy ingredients. A final sprinkle of toasted sesame seeds gives a nutty crisp contrast to the sauce.

Though the nuns of the 17th-century Puebla convents are often given credit for the creation of this dish, it is likely to have originated in ancient times in the state of Chiapas, once a part of the Mayan empire. The region has a tradition of savory chillied stews seasoned with chocolate. Women were forbidden to taste the chocolate dishes; the only men who were allowed to eat them were the emperor, military nobility, important merchants, and clergy. Though the name is usually indicated as derivative of the Spanish *moler*, meaning to grind, it could also reflect the Aztec word *molli*, meaning chillied foods.

Mole poblano is often sold in Mexico as a thick reddish-blackish paste, ready to be mixed with broth to transform into a rich sauce. Sometimes it is very good this way, other times not. Traditionally mole is served with unfilled tamales, but I prefer corn tortillas to roll up into little tacos, or flour tortillas to make plump burritos. Serving mole with a bowl of steamed rice and a selection of fresh vegetable condiments—cilantro, radishes, onions, tomatoes, fried plantains, and salsa—makes a deliciously festive presentation.

The list of ingredients is long, but the preparation is easy. Just soak, simmer, toast, then grind it all together and simmer it merrily to meld the flavors. Several bouillon cubes are added to enrich the broth, since mass-market poultry may be a bit pale in flavor. As with many simmered complex dishes, mole is best at least a day after preparation.

Turkey (or Chicken):

½ small turkey (about 3 lbs.), or	2 onions
1 whole chicken (3-3½ lbs.)	2 cloves garlic
2 bay leaves	3 or 4 bouillon cubes

....

❶ Place turkey or chicken in large pot with bay leaves, onions, and garlic. Fill the pot with water and add the bouillon cubes.

❷ Bring to boil, skim off the scum that rises to the surface, and reduce heat. Let simmer on low heat for 2 to 3 hours, or until the bird is tender and the soup rich.

Mole Sauce:

10 New Mexico or California chillies
4 ancho chillies
4 dried negro or mulatto chillies
⅓ cup raisins
⅓ cup unblanched almonds
¼ cup sesame seeds
¼ cup shelled pumpkin seeds
1 corn tortilla, broken or cut up
1 large slice French bread or crusty whole-wheat bread, torn into bite-sized pieces
1 onion, chopped
4 cloves garlic, chopped

1½ cups chopped tomatoes (canned are fine)
3 tablespoons vegetable oil or lard
Pinch fennel seeds
¼ teaspoon ground cloves
About ½ teaspoon ground cinnamon
2 to 3 tablespoons crunchy peanut butter
1 to 2 squares (1 to 2 oz. in total, to taste) semisweet chocolate
Several drops vanilla extract (optional)
Salt and black pepper to taste
Toasted sesame seeds

....

❶ Pour hot broth from the simmering turkey over the chillies to cover. Place a plate over the bowl and let the chillies sit about an hour, long enough to let their flesh soften completely.

❷ Meanwhile, pour about ½ cup hot broth over the raisins and let them sit and plump.

❸ Place the almonds, sesame seeds, pumpkin seeds, tortilla pieces, and bread chunks on a baking sheet. Bake in a 350°F oven 15 minutes, or long enough to lightly toast it all, tossing the mixture several times with a spoon.

❹ When the mixture is toasted, place it in a blender and grind into a mealy consistency. Set aside.

❺ When raisins are tender, puree in blender along with their soaking liquid. Set aside.

❻ In blender, whirl the onion and garlic, then add the tomatoes and whirl together into a sauce. Set aside.

❼ When chillies have softened, cut open, saving their liquid for the sauce, and use a butter or similar knife to scrape the tender flesh away from the tough skin. If the chillies have softened well enough, the flesh should pull away relatively easily. Add the flesh to the tomato mixture and puree, then combine this with the pureed raisins and ground nut mixture.

❽ Heat the oil in a heavy skillet or frying pan, then add the sauce. Let mixture fry-simmer, then add the reserved chilli soaking liquid to thin it out a bit. Simmer about 10 minutes, then add the spices, peanut butter, chocolate, and vanilla extract. Continue to cook another 10 minutes or so.

❾ Taste for seasonings and adjust as desired.

❿ To serve: Reheat the turkey or chicken by either simmering it in its broth or by browning it in a heavy frying pan. Heat the mole separately and ladle it over the hot turkey or chicken. Serve immediately, sprinkled with toasted sesame seeds. **Serves 4**

·················· **VARIATION** ··················

BURRITOS DE MOLE POBLANO

Cut or tear the simmered turkey or chicken into bite-sized bits. Brown them in a frying pan using a tiny bit of the fat from the broth. Add several ladlefuls of the mole sauce and simmer a minute or two to heat through, then roll up in warmed flour tortillas along with shredded lettuce and green onions.

POLLO ESTILO MAZATLAN

MAZATLAN-STYLE CHICKEN

At umbrella-shaded tables set out under the broiling Mexican sun in the open-air marketplaces of Mazatlán, tourists and locals alike tuck into platters of chicken, cooked and raw vegetables, all splashed with a zesty salsa. The weather is sultry and the chicken is tepid rather than piping hot, somewhat like a warm salad. (Beef is often served the same way, and I suspect anything already cooked and tender would also be a good candidate.) While it is an easy-to-prepare dish, you really do need a good salsa, preferably homemade.

In Mazatlán this unpretentious platter is likely to be served with a *cazuelita* of creamy refried beans and a stack of warm corn tortillas, a bowl of fiery salsa on the side.

2 cups ripe tomatoes, peeled and diced (canned are fine)

Homemade salsa, such as Salsa Picante Verde, Salsa con Lima y Cilantro, or Salsa de Jalapeños en Escabeche y Jitomate

1 cooked chicken, cut into serving pieces

Oil for frying

Several cloves garlic (optional)

Salt and black pepper to taste

4 large waxy potatoes, boiled and cooled in their jackets

½ teaspoon crumbled oregano leaves

3 large zucchini, cooked, then tossed with a few shakes of wine vinegar

About 1 cup green beans, steamed until just tender

Shredded lettuce

1 avocado, sliced

Small whole radishes, or larger sliced ones

1 onion, chopped

2 tablespoons chopped cilantro or parsley

....

❶ Combine tomatoes with several tablespoons of salsa, the amount depending on the heat of the salsa. Reserve the rest of the salsa.

❷ Brown chicken in a small amount of oil. Add several cloves garlic if the chicken was not originally cooked with garlic. Sprinkle with salt and pepper and place on a platter to keep warm.

❸ In same pan, brown potatoes, adding a little more oil if needed. Sprinkle oregano over potatoes and chicken.

❹ Arrange hot chicken and potatoes on a platter, along with zucchini, green beans, and shredded lettuce. Splash the tomato-salsa over it all.

❺ Serve garnished with avocado, radishes, chopped onion, and cilantro or parsley, with extra salsa on the side. *Serves 4*

·························· **VARIATION** ··························

Any tangy, savory, and not-too-hot salsa can be splashed over a platterful of browned chicken, meat, fish, and vegetables. Try the tangy Salsa con Limón y Cilantro, prepared with the chillies drastically reduced and the lime juice increased to make a more liquid sauce.

....

PATO CON NARANJA Y YERBABUENA
RED CHILLI-SEASONED DUCK ROASTED
WITH ORANGES AND MINT

Fresh mint has an amazing affinity with mild chilli, especially when combined with the classic duck and orange.

This duck is worthy of a place in a celebration meal. For a traditional Mexican *comida*, start with the lush and invigorating Sopa de Frijole Negro con Tortillas, and follow with Arroz Verde. A salad of nopales sprinkled with feta or goat cheese would be a good accompaniment to the duck; of course, add a stack of corn tortillas and salsa of choice.

1 medium duck, whole	**2 tablespoons tequila**
Salt and black pepper to taste	**1¼ cups orange juice**
1 orange, halved	**3 cloves garlic, chopped**
1 head of garlic, whole and unpeeled	**Juice of 1 lime**
2 tablespoons ancho chilli powder	**2 to 3 tablespoons coarsely chopped**
2 tablespoons New Mexico chilli powder or paprika	**fresh mint**

❶ Cut off excess fat from neck of duck; reserve it to make cracklings (see recipe for Pato en Pozole). Prick duck all over with a fork, then place on a rack in a roasting pan (this will give an all-over crispness to the duck; letting it sit in its own juices won't). Sprinkle with salt and pepper, then stuff its insides with orange halves and garlic.

❷ Roast duck in a 450°F oven for 30 minutes, then remove from oven and let cool. This preliminary roasting may be done the day before; in this case you can defat the drippings when they are cool and solidified.

❸ Meanwhile, make the chilli paste. Combine the chillie powders with the tequila, ¼ cup orange juice (enough to make a paste), and the chopped garlic. Rub well onto the duck.

❹ Roast the chilli-coated duck in a 350° F oven for 40 to 50 minutes or until duck is tender, its skin crispy and not fatty, with juices that run clear when the fleshy part of the leg is deeply pricked with a fork.

❺ Remove duck to platter and keep warm. Spoon off fat from bottom of pan, then pour in remaining orange juice. Stir over high heat, taking care to get the brown bits of pan drippings mixed into the juice. Cook until reduced to about ⅓ cup of savory sauce. Stir in lime juice. Taste for salt and adjust seasonings.

❻ Serve duck with this intensely flavored pan sauce, sprinkling the whole thing with chopped mint. Accompany by warm corn tortillas, Arroz Negro, and a plate of chopped onions and raw chillies or Ajos y Chillies Chipotles. *1 medium duck serves 2; a large one, 3 to 4*

·········· **LEFTOVERS** ··········

RICE WITH DUCK, PINEAPPLE, SWEET RED CHILLIES, AND PEANUTS

Toss bits of the diced chilli-coated duck into cooked rice, along with sautéed pineapple chunks, slices of ripe red fresh chillies, and a sprinkle of coarsely chopped toasted peanuts.

THREE SIMPLE MEXICAN POULTRY DISHES

CHILLI-COATED AND ROASTED, SPOON-TENDER CHICKEN

Take simmered or boiled chicken or turkey thighs or legs. Rub with Recado Rojo Enchilado or the seasoning paste from Pato con Naranja y Yerbabuena. Roast in a 450°F oven 15 minutes, or just long enough to heat through and give a crispy edge. Serve sprinkled with cilantro.

POLLO EN MOLE COLORADO—OAXACA

Combine 2 to 3 cups Salsa Verde de Tomatillo that you have prepared omitting the green chillies with 3 to 4 toasted, rehydrated, then pureed ancho chillies. Season with 2 to 3 cloves chopped garlic and ½ to 1 teaspoon cumin. Heat a tablespoon or two of oil, then "fry" this mixture to thicken the sauce and concentrate the flavors. When sauce is flavorful, add one cut-up, broth-simmered chicken. Heat through. *Serves 4*

PINEAPPLE SALSA–MARINATED GRILLED CHICKEN
....

Combine ½ cup pineapple juice with Recado Rojo Enchilado or about ½ cup pureed mild rehydrated chillies. Season to taste with salsa, chopped cilantro, and garlic. Marinate flattened small chicken halves or quarters or boned breasts in this mixture. Grill over an open fire, then serve sprinkled with cilantro and chillies. Offer tortillas to wrap up the savory bits. *Serves 4*

CARNES

....

MEAT

Meats of all sorts are used in the Mexican kitchen, though often in tiny amounts and combined with vegetables, starches, or fruits.

Pork is probably the most common meat on the Mexican table, but beef is the meat of choice in the north, and lamb is popular in the central regions, especially in a *barbacoa* or *birria*, as is cabrito, roast kid. Rabbit is occasionally eaten, usually stewed in chilli-based sauces such as adobo or sauces similar to those used with a chicken. Other, more exotic meats appear on the Mexican table: wild deer (a favorite in the Yucatán), iguana (in Guerrero), giant terrapin (on the south Pacific coast), armadillo (in the northern desert regions; said to give "vigor to men").

As in all peasant kitchens and great cuisines alike, no part of the animal is wasted. A whole or half pig's head seasons pozole. The trotters are prized, especially in Jalisco, where they top tostadas. The fat of the pig is rendered into lard, the main ingredient that transformed Indian food into Mexican food. Even the skin and blood are used: the skin to make huge sheets of crisp, deliciously addictive *chicharrones*; the blood for a mint-and-coriander-scented blood sausage, *morcilla*. Brains, especially beef and sheep, are *muy Mexicana*, doted on with a passion probably inherited from the French occupation; they make delicate fillings for tacos or quesadillas. Throughout the land, tripe is stewed into menudo, and livers are spiced vigorously and sautéed into rich brown potfuls, rolled up in warm thin tortillas. The oxtail is sliced and simmered with pink beans for a favorite soup. If you happen to be at a cowboy-style barbecue, the choicest bits are the unmentionable ones.

Whichever beast or cut of meat is chosen, the choice of seasonings and cooking methods is nearly endless. Often meat is rubbed with spices and slowly roasted whole over an open fire; in the central regions, where maguey plants abound, great pits are dug and filled with hot rocks, then parcels of meat wrapped in maguey leaves are left to cook slowly over the hot embers. Sometimes beef, lamb, or pork is pounded, coated with a spicy marinade, then grilled quickly over an open fire, barbecue style; this is called *carne asada*. Chunks of meat may be sautéed, baked, roasted, or simmered with a variety of vegetables, beans, and herbs. The most common way to prepare meat, regardless of the spicing, is to simmer it until tender, then either brown or roast it, and serve it in small amounts, shredded or diced. This gives two dishes or meals from one piece of meat: first soup, then the meat course. Roasting, it is often implied, is wasteful, "a cooking method for rich people."

Puerco—Pork

CARNITAS A LA CASERA
CRISPY, TENDER BITS OF PORK

Carnitas make wonderful fillings for tacos, enchiladas, burritos, tortas, and so on. The name translates as "little meats." The chunks of pork are crispy-edged and meltingly tender. In the marketplace *carnitas* are simmered in great vats, the fat rendered out of the meat almost in the same way as in the French *confit*. The whole pig is usually prepared this way—one orders the bits as desired. Often the chunks of meat are served on a large round of skin crackling, or *chicharrón*, as a rich and crisp edible plate. The pork is traditionally served sprinkled with a dusting of mild pasilla chilli (or a mild chilli powder) and guacamole, fresh salsa, and a bowl of warm, freshly made corn tortillas.

To prepare the *carnitas* homestyle, you first simmer a large pork roast, then roast it in the oven until tender. A bonus to this process is a large pot of broth for soup the next day. Meaty spareribs, with enough fat to produce crispy, crackly brown bits, also make an excellent cut for *carnitas*; allow a larger weight than in the following recipe, about double, to allow for the bones.

Serve the succulent meat with a selection of salsas: a rich mild pasilla or ancho one, a feisty raw one, a tart tomatillo salsa, and a lip-searing fresh chilli mixture.

1 boneless pork leg roast, about 2¼
lbs., or a fattier cut such as pork
belly, cut into small pieces
1 onion, halved
2 garlic cloves

1 teaspoon salt
½ teaspoon crushed oregano leaves
½ teaspoon cumin
Salt, pepper, and mild chilli powder
to taste

❶ Place meat in a large pot and add water to cover. Add onion, garlic, salt, oregano, and cumin. Bring to boil, then reduce heat and simmer, covered, for 2 hours.

❷ Preheat oven to 350°F.

❸ Drain meat, reserving broth for another use (add a bouillon cube or two to *oomph* up the flavor and you have a basis for a delicious soup). Place meat in a baking pan and sprinkle evenly with salt and mild chilli powder.

❹ Bake for 45 minutes. Remove from oven. While still warm, shred meat with a fork. **Serves 4**

·· **VARIATION** ··

MARKETPLACE CARNITAS

This approximates the flavor of street-stall *carnitas*. Use a heavy cast-iron pot with a tight-fitting lid. Rather than boil the meat first, place the bite-sized pieces of meat in pot with seasonings as above. Pour in just enough water to cover. Cover with lid and place in preheated 325°F oven and let roast slowly for 3 hours or so. Remove lid and continue to roast another 45 minutes, or until liquid has evaporated (if there is a lot of liquid when you uncover it, pour out excess). A bit of orange juice and a shake of mild chilli powder may be added to the final roasting.

·· **VARIATION** ··

CARNITAS DUCK

Duck, especially the dark-fleshed thigh and legs with their fatty quality, takes as readily to *carnitas* preparation as it does to the French *confit*. The fat seems to render completely out and is drained away, leaving a succulent lean meat. The tender yet crisp pieces of duck are delicious shredded and added to tostadas, tacos, salads, tortas, and the like.

Follow instructions for Marketplace Carnitas, but use a very small amount of water in the initial cooking (about an inch in depth), and decrease the cooking time to 40 minute initial cooking, and 30 minutes or so without the lid. For a new-wave presentation, serve the hot *carnitas*-style duck on a bed of mixed salad leaves, with a vinaigrette enhanced with salsa verde.

······················ **VARIATION** ·······················

CARNITAS Y MARISCOS ❖ ROASTED PORK BITS WITH CLAMS

Prepare Marketplace Carnitas, then pour off any excess fat. Season well with salt and pepper, then add as many clams as desired—at least 3 per person. Toss with the meat, cover with foil, and return to the oven. Bake about 10 minutes, or until the clams pop open. Discard any that do not open.

Prepare Salsa con Limón y Cilantro, reducing the amount of chillies to one or two. Toss the meat and clams with several spoonfuls of the salsa and offer the rest at the table, along with either a plate of chopped chillies or bottled hot sauce.

CARNE EN OTRO ESTILO
FRAGRANT MARINATED AND ROASTED MEAT FOR FILLINGS

Marinating the pork in lots of garlic, onions, bay leaves, and herbs gives an almost Mediterranean scent to this dish. The meat is coated with a bit of fat before it is left to marinate. Traditionally this fat is seasoned lard, but I use a bland vegetable oil for health reasons and find that it produces a lovely dish; pork is so lean these days that it benefits from a bit of delicate fat. Since you simmer the meat after its browning, the fat can be easily skimmed from the chilled broth.

Use this fragrant meat to layer on top of tostadas or *antojitos*, to grind and stuff into tacos, to shred and use inside tortas, and so on. Or you could serve the meat on a platter, accompanied by chopped onions, cilantro, several salsas, and a stack of soft warm tortillas for do-it-yourself tacos.

1 lb. boneless cut of pork, cut into larger-than-bite-sized pieces	**5 sprigs fresh oregano or marjoram**
Salt and pepper to taste	**Pinch dried thyme or several sprigs fresh thyme**
2 heads garlic, each clove lightly crushed to remove the skin	**¼ cup vegetable oil**
3 onions, sliced	**1½ cups broth**
5 bay leaves	**1½ cups water**

❶ Place pork in a noncorrosive pot or bowl. Mix with salt, pepper, garlic, onions, bay leaves, oregano, thyme, and vegetable oil. Let sit to marinate at least 2 hours, preferably overnight in the refrigerator.

❷ Heat a heavy pot and brown the meat together with the garlic, onion, and seasonings in the marinating oil. When browned in parts, add the broth and water. Bring to a boil, then reduce heat and cover, cooking at a low simmer until tender (about 2 hours).

❸ Serve meat chopped into small pieces, as desired. Reserve broth for soups or sauces (skimming excess fat off the top if needed). *Serves 4*

······················· **VARIATION** ·······················
TACOS DE MERCADO
Pureeing sautéed vegetables with a bit of the meat into a savory paste, then browning it to concentrate the flavors, makes an exquisite, unusual taco filling.

Sauté chunks of diced potato, onion, and zucchini (or carrots, peas, green beans or your choice of vegetables). Whirl some of the meat from the above recipe in a blender, along with enough of the stock to make a paste, and as many bits of tender onion and garlic as you can fish out. Add this meat paste to the browned vegetables, season with mild chilli or fiery/smoky chipotle chilli, and roll up into warm corn tortillas. Sprinkle with a bit of chopped onion if desired.

Lengua
TONGUE
BASIC RECIPE

In Mexico tongue is considered among the choicest of cuts. To be excellent, however, the often-tough tongue must first be simmered into tender submission. It may then be prepared and sauced as desired (see suggestions following basic recipe). *Serves 6 to 8*

1 fresh beef tongue, whole	**5 to 6 bay leaves**
1 onion	**Salt and pepper to taste**
5 to 10 cloves garlic	

❶ Place tongue in a large pot. Fill with water. Add all other ingredients. Bring to boil, then reduce heat and simmer about 3 hours, or until tender.

❷ Let tongue cool in stock, then remove and serve as desired. Reserve stock to use in soups or stews. *Serves 6 to 8*

Suggestions for Cooked Tongue

WITH SMOKY SALSA

Hot tongue is particularly good with a shake or two of hot and sweet Salsa de Chiles Chipotles.

TONGUE PICADILLO

Chop cold cooked tongue and brown in Picadillo in place of ground beef.

LENGUA EN ADOBO

Simmer sliced or diced cooked tongue in Salsa Adobo.

TINGA DE LENGUA

Julienne cooked tongue and use in *tingas* in place of shredded beef.

SALPICON DE LENGUA

Julienne cold cooked tongue and dress in a spicy vinaigrette, *salpicón*-style, garnished with diced oranges, radishes, serranos, and cilantro.

LENGUA EN SALSA VERDE

Tangy salsa verde is particularly good with tongue. Either serve the simmered tongue accompanied by Salsa Picante Verde as a condiment, or simmer sliced tongue together with mild salsa verde as a sauced dish.

LENGUA EN SALSA RANCHERA

Simmer sliced cooked tongue in Salsa Ranchera to which you've added a bit of smoky chipotle marinade. Sprinkle with a garnish of chopped cilantro.

HIGADO MEXICANA
LIVER, MEXICAN STYLE

Sautéed liver and onions, seasoned generously with paprika and a dash of cumin and oregano, is *muy Mexicana* when served with a salsa of choice (such as Salsa de Chilli Chipotle y Jitomate, Salsa de Jalapeños en escabeche y Jitomate, or Salsa Cruda), a sprinkling of shredded cabbage, and a wedge of lemon to squeeze over it all. Offer warm corn tortillas for rolling into soft tacos.

MANCHA MANTELES
"TABLECLOTH STAINER"

This dish probably owes its name to the red chilli-fruit sauce that tends to splash around. The dish is a classic, more a grouping of dishes than one definitive recipe. It may be prepared from chicken, pork, or both; it always has a selection of fruit, though exactly which fruits depends on the recipe and the marketplace. Chorizo is sometimes included for a spicier, richer, and more chilli-redolent sauce; sometimes avocado is used as a garnish. The nuts included can vary, too; almonds or walnuts may be used rather than peanuts.

1 onion, diced
2 cloves garlic, coarsely chopped
2 tablespoons vegetable oil
1 to 2 jalapeños, seeded and diced
1/4 to 1/2 poblano or Anaheim chilli, seeded and diced
1 1/2 cups tomatoes, seeded and diced (canned are fine)
1 teaspoon cinnamon
2 rehydrated ancho chillies and 2 rehydrated New Mexico/California or guajillo chillies, the flesh scraped from the tough skin

5 whole cloves, or a generous pinch ground cloves
1 tablespoon sesame seeds
1/3 cup roasted peanuts
1 1/2 cups broth of choice
1 lb. lean pork for stewing
1/2 small chicken
2 small apples (preferably Fuji, Golden, or Cox), sliced
1/2 orange
1 cup pineapple juice
1 bay leaf

❶ You can simmer the meat first, the layer it with the sauce and simmer or bake to meld the flavors. Or you can simply layer the sauce with the meat and bake away to tenderness. If simmering first, cut down the amount of broth in the sauce.

❷ Prepare the sauce: Sauté onion and garlic in vegetable oil until softened, then add both diced green chillies, tomatoes, cinnamon, rehydrated diced chillies, cloves, and sesame seeds. Cook together until saucy. Add peanuts and broth and puree in blender until smooth.

❸ Return sauce to heavy saucepan and add pork, chicken, apples, orange, pineapple juice, and bay leaf. Cover tightly and simmer over low to medium heat or in a 350°F oven about 2 hours, or until meat is fork-tender. (If using presimmered pork and chicken, cook over low heat about 20 minutes.) *Serves 4 to 6*

·· **VARIATION** ··

CON PLATANOS
Add a diced plantain or banana, allowing 15 minutes cooking time for the plantain, only a minute or two for the banana.

·· **VARIATION** ··

POLLO CON FRUTAS ❖ CHICKEN WITH FRUIT
Prepare the sauce without the pork or chicken. At the end of its cooking, add a diced banana and handful of seedless green grapes. Continue cooking for just a few minutes, then serve alongside the following roast chicken: Season chicken inside and out with a generous amount of mild chilli powder and sweet butter, stuff with lots of whole garlic cloves and bay leaves, then roast to tender succulence.

PUERCO CON VERDOLAGA
PORK WITH PURSLANE

Portulaca is the botanical name for purslane, a ground-hugging weed that is delicious to eat. It grows in gardens, creeping along between the rows of lettuce, carrots, and what-have-you, covering the earth in a carpet of spindly strands with oval, pinkish-green, succulent leaves.

Native to Europe, purslane has grown widespread in North America and Mexico. If you have a garden, it's sure to turn up sooner or later. If not, cultivate your local herb seller. In addition to growing wild, I've found it sold in marketplaces in Southwest France as well as Mexico.

Purslane is delicious raw. I adore it as a generous garnish (a bed, really) for American-style potato salad. Its slightly acidic flavor is good, too, in a simple tomato salad dressed with olive oil and studded with salty black olives.

In Mexico it is frequently served cooked, as in the following pork stew, combining the piquancy of the herb with the equally piquant tomatillos and spicy chillies. One pound may sound like a lot, but much of that is thick stems and stalks that you will discard.

Serve with a *cazuela* of creamy refried beans, and Ensalada de Calabaza y Jitomate, with tortillas or crusty bread.

4 pork chops or 1 lb. boneless pork stewing meat (or meaty spareribs or other meat-and-bone cuts—allow extra weight for the bones)
1 small to medium onion, chopped
3 garlic cloves, chopped
3 cups light chicken or vegetable broth

10 to 12 diced tomatillos (about 1½ cups cooked, canned are fine)
3 jalapeños, chopped (for a milder, subtler flavor, roast, peel, and seed chillies)
Vegetable oil for sautéing
About 1 lb. purslane

❶ Place pork, onion, and garlic in heavy pan along with broth. Cover and simmer about 30 minutes, or until pork is quite tender. Remove pork from broth and set aside.

❷ Add tomatillos and chillies to the broth. Bring to the boil, then simmer until tender, about 5 minutes. Puree in blender and set aside.

❸ Remove the tender, succulent leaves and small stems from the large stems of the purslane. Discard the big stems.

❹ Sauté reserved pork in a tiny bit of oil until well browned and crispy. Add reserved sauce and purslane and bring to the boil, cooking over medium-high heat 5 to 10 minutes, or long enough for the sauce to thicken a bit. Serve immediately, accompanied by warm corn tortillas or unfilled tamales. ***Serves 4***

PUERCO CON PIÑA
PORK IN PINEAPPLE JUICE WITH SWEET PEPPERS AND PRUNES

Moorish influences echo in this spicy-sweet stew, with its sprinkling of sesame seeds as a contrast of taste and texture to the rich, deeply flavored sauce. Traditionally the sauce in this dish would be pureed into a mysterious dark puddle; I like the interest the texture provides: the strands of sweet onion, the tiny bits of winey prune, the sweet bits of red pepper, all awash in the spicy pineapple sauce.

Though the recipe calls for pork, this would be equally good prepared with turkey thighs; or even a meat substitute such as tofu.

Serve following a zesty soup such as Caldo del Papas or Sopa de Tortilla, and accompany the savory, sweet meat with crusty bread and simple pan-browned spinach.

2 onions, sliced
3 cloves garlic, coarsely chopped
1 lb. pork chops or loin, cut into bite-sized pieces
About 2 tablespoons vegetable oil
1 roasted red pepper, peeled and cut into strips
1 to 1½ tablespoons pure mild chilli powder such as ancho or pasilla

3 small to medium tomatoes, coarsely chopped
3 to 4 prunes, pitted and diced
1½ cups pineapple juice
2 to 3 tablespoons toasted sesame seeds

....

❶ Sauté onions, garlic, and pork in the vegetable oil until browned in parts.

❷ Add roasted red pepper, chilli powder, tomatoes, prunes, and pineapple juice. Bring to boil, then reduce heat, cover, and simmer until meat is tender. Remove lid and cook further to evaporate and concentrate the sauce, if needed.

❸ Serve meat with sauce, sprinkled with toasted sesame seeds. *Serves 4*

....

CHILE COLORADO
RED CHILLI STEW, SONORA STYLE

Meat stewed in a sauce made from mild chillies, this is a classic "bowl of red," a simple stew rather than its tarted-up descendants. You'll find *chile colorado* in many guises throughout the U.S. Southwest and in the northern Mexico state of Sonora. It is typical charro (cowboy) fare, a combined effort of Spanish beef with Indian chilli stewing. Note that there are no tomatoes or other fancifications—this could taste as austere and direct as a night spent under a desert sky and equally as satisfying.

Whatever recipe you prepare, chilli is at its classic best when topped with lots of chopped onions, grated or crumbled sharp cheese, shredded lettuce, a spoonful of salsa, and a dollop of sour cream. Some add tender boiled beans (pinto or *bayo*)(Frijoles de Olla), and/or diced avocado.

Serve Chile Colorado in shallow soup plates with soft flour tortillas to scoop up the savory meats and make impromptu burritos.

3 to 5 smooth-skinned red chillies such as New Mexico, California, or pasilla
3 to 5 ancho chillies
1 tablespoon ground cumin
2 small to medium onions, chopped
5 cloves garlic, coarsely chopped
2 tablespoons vegetable oil

2¼ lbs. lean beef, cut into bite-sized cubes or chunks
1 teaspoon salt or 1 bouillon cube
About 1½ cups lager
About 3 heaping tablespoons masa harina
Salsa or cayenne pepper to taste

❶ Pour hot but not boiling water over the chillies and let sit, covered, until they are softened. Remove stems and puree, then put through a strainer or sieve to extract the tough bits of skin.

❷ Toast cumin in a heavy ungreased skillet until fragrant, taking care not to burn it. Set aside.

❸ Sauté onions and garlic in vegetable oil until softened, then add the meat and brown. Add reserved chillies, salt or bouillon cube, and lager; bring to a boil. Reduce heat, cover, and simmer over low heat until meat is tender, about 2 to 3 hours, adding water or broth occasionally if more liquid is needed.

❹ When meat is tender, make a paste of the masa harina and several tablespoons of the simmering liquid. Add this paste to the stew. Continue to simmer, stirring every so often, until stew thickens somewhat. (Note: If masa harina is unavailable, whirl several broken-up tostada or taco shells in a blender to the consistency of meal or coarse flour, and use that to thicken the chilli-stew.) Season to taste with salsa or cayenne. Serve right away, or reheat the next day. Like all long-simmered dishes, it's even better the next day. (You'll probably have to thin it with a little water or broth when you reheat it.) **Serves 4 to 6**

·························· **VARIATION** ··························

VEGETARIAN CHILI

Prepare the above recipe, but omit the meat. Add about 1 cup chopped tomatoes or tomato sauce, to taste, as well as a good sprinkling of oregano. A generous sprinkling of ancho or mulatto chilli powder and New Mexico/California chilli or paprika builds a lovely layer of flavor on top of the flesh of the mild chillies. Add cooked red kidney or pink pinto beans to taste and simmer for a half hour or so, to meld the flavors.

··

ROPA VIEJA
····························
SHREDDED BEEF

Ropa vieja translates as "old clothes." Perhaps it's because the meat is in shreds; more likely there is no reason at all, just another example of the Mexican way of giving whimsical names to dishes.

Though it is one of the simplest dishes to prepare, demanding little from the cook, it does demand a long simmering time. This makes it great for do-ahead meals.

Ropa Vieja is eaten with soft flour tortillas as do-it-yourself burritos; it also makes great fillings for *chimichangas*; or layer with corn tortillas, then top with a mild chilli or ranchera sauce and a fried egg or two. Try adding a handful of diced cooked potatoes when you cook the shredded meat, or seasoning the meat with a bit of oregano and/or cumin. Ropa Vieja makes a great basis for all sorts of flights of culinary fancy, yet it remains homey, unpretentious fare.

3 lbs. flank steak or beef chuck
1½ cups water or stock to cover
10 cloves garlic (leave 7 whole and unpeeled; the remaining 3 will be peeled and chopped to sauté with the onions once the meat is cooked)
Several grindings of coarse black pepper
Salt to taste (unless using salted broth for cooking)

4 jalapeños or 5 güeros, roasted, peeled, seeded, and coarsely chopped
1 Anaheim or poblano chilli, roasted, peeled, seeded, and coarsely chopped
About 2 tablespoons lard or vegetable oil
2 onions, sliced

....

❶ Place beef in heavy cast-iron or similar baking or simmering pan with water or broth, 7 whole, unpeeled cloves of garlic, and black pepper. Cover tightly and let meat simmer over low heat until tender and very well cooked through (about 3-4 hours). It is important that the cover fits tightly or the liquid will evaporate. If you have any doubts, check occasionally and add liquid if needed.

❷ When meat is tender, remove from heat and let it cool in its own liquid. When cool enough to handle, remove meat from its cooking liquid. Pull it apart into long shreds with your fingers or fork. Return meat to its cooking liquid.

❸ Heat lard or oil in large, heavy frying pan. Add remaining (peeled and chopped) garlic and quickly stir it through the hot oil, taking care not to let it burn. Add onion and sauté until softened, about 5 minutes, then add chillies. Add this mixture to the shredded meat in broth.

❹ Cook again, this time uncovered over medium-high heat, until flavors are blended and most of the liquid has evaporated, about 10 minutes. Serve immediately. ***Serves 4 with leftovers plus broth for other uses***

....

.... **VARIATION** ....

MOCHOMOS—CHIHUAHUA
Prepare the above dish using pork in place of beef. Serve the crisp shreds of meat topped with guacamole, shredded lettuce, and diced tomatoes.

....

TWO SALPICONS

Salpicón refers to a variety of dishes, the one thing in common being their hashlike texture and spicy vinaigrette. A *salpicón* can contain only vegetables, much like a relish; in the coastal areas it may be based on seafood or shredded fish. Or a *salpicón* may be made from shredded meats, combined with bits of crunchy and tangy vegetables, splashed with oil, vinegar, and citrus juices. A Cuban version combines mixed roasted meats such as pork, beef, and sausage with potatoes and a spicy, olive-filled dressing.

The following recipe uses the meat from Ropa Vieja and comes in two variations; they're both good, especially on a sweltering day when something hearty yet cool sounds enticing.

Meat from Ropa Vieja, simmered but not browned
2 tablespoons olive oil
2 teaspoons chopped cilantro
1 green onion, thinly sliced
Juice and grated rind of ½ medium-small orange

Juice of ½ lime
1 teaspoon vinegar such as sherry vinegar
Salt to taste

❶ Let meat cool in broth, then remove and chill both. The broth is your basis for this week's delicious soups. The meat will give you this salpicón—or fillings for any of a wealth of savory tacos, tostadas, or quesadillas.

❷ When beef is cool, shred with two forks. Dress in one of the two following mixtures. *Serves 4*

CHIPOTLE-AVOCADO-TOMATO

Combine 2 teaspoons chipotle marinade and 2 cloves garlic, chopped. Serve garnished with diced avocado and tomatoes.

YUCATAN

Combine 10 diced radishes, 1 chopped fresh green chilli (without seeds if hot), a bit of diced cucumber, and a small to medium tomato, diced. Season with salt and cayenne pepper to taste.

PUCHERO
ONE-POT SIMMER OF MEAT, CHORIZO, AND VEGETABLES

Like the *cocido* of Spain and *pot au feu* of France, this is a hearty one-pot meal. *Puchero* is enjoyed throughout the Republic, especially as a Sunday lunch, since it provides a potful of cooked meats and broth for meals throughout the coming week. Versions of the dish are eaten throughout Latin America, often less spicy, with the addition of fresh and dried fruit.

Long stewing of a selection of meats and vegetables gives the broth a complex range of flavors, and the meat should be spoon-tender. Besides the vegetables indicated in the recipe, other good additions are cabbage, green beans, spinach, and waxy, firm potatoes.

I like to accompany the meal with Guacamole, a spunky salsa, a platter of *adornos* for the meats, and crusty bread to sop up the juices.

1 lb. beef stewing meat
1 lb. lamb stewing meat
1 lb. pork stewing meat
2 chorizo sausages
3 heads garlic, halved crosswise
6 bay leaves
1 teaspoon marjoram
3 chicken bouillon cubes or 3 teaspoons powdered bouillon
3 tablespoons chopped cilantro

1 small chicken
3 carrots, sliced
4 zucchini, thickly sliced
1 chayote or 2 yellow crookneck squash, thickly sliced
1 turnip, cut into large dice
1 onion, thinly sliced
2 ears corn, each cut into 2- to 3-inch lengths

Garnishes and Accompaniments:

1 batch Guacamole
1 or 2 batches Salsa such as Salsa de
Chile Güero, Salsa Picante Verde,
and/or Salsa de Chiles y Ajo
3 cups cooked white rice
2 cups cooked chick-peas
3 or 4 poblanos chillies, chopped
Pan-browned potatoes and/or
plantains (optional)

Poached chunks of peaches, pears,
sweet potatoes, or winter squash
2 cups thinly sliced raw cabbage
¾ cup coarsely chopped cilantro
½ cup coarsely chopped fresh mint
6 green onions, thinly sliced
Lime wedges

••

❶ Place beef, lamb, pork, and chorizo into large pot, along with garlic, bay
leaves, marjoram, bouillon, cilantro, and plenty of water. Bring to boil, skim
off any surface scum, then reduce heat, cover, and simmer very slowly for 3
hours. Add chicken and continue simmering another hour.

❷ Add carrots, zucchini, chayote, turnip, onion, and corn, and cook another
30 to 45 minutes, or until the vegetables are very tender.

❸ Remove the meats to one platter and the vegetables to another. Slice or cut
up the meats, and arrange bowls of the garnishes and accompaniments.

❹ Serve shallow soup bowls filled with broth and let each person choose the
meats and additions he or she fancies. *Serves 4 to 6 with leftovers*

••

•••••••••••••••••••••••••••• **VARIATION** ••••••••••••••••••••••••••••

Mashed boiled pumpkin, seasoned well with sautéed onions and garlic, salsa,
and ancho chilli powder, makes a delicious sauce for Puchero.

••

ALBONDIGAS Y NOPALES
MEATBALLS AND NOPALES IN BROTH

This mysterious broth is strongly flavored with the smoky, elusive fire of
chipotle. Strands of tangy nopale cactus add a fresh counterpoint. For a soup
rather than stewy whole-meal course, increase broth accordingly.

Serve with fresh corn tortillas, or with homemade thick corn tortillas
fried into crispy crouton-like pieces to float in the rich broth.

½ lb. lean beef, minced
1 small to medium zucchini, finely chopped
2 teaspoons finely chopped cilantro
¼ to ½ chipotle chilli, finely chopped

About 3 tablespoons cooked rice or finely ground corn chips
2 cups beef broth
⅔ to 1 cup cooked nopales, cut into strips

● Mix beef, zucchini, cilantro, about half the chipotle chilli, and the rice or ground corn chips. Roll into meatballs and set aside.

❷ Heat broth with remaining chipotle chilli; when boiling, reduce to simmer and add meatballs. Cook, covered, over medium-low heat about 5 minutes, then add nopales and continue cooking until meatballs are cooked through, another 6 minutes or so, or until they are firm and no longer pink when cut into.

❸ Serve immediately, the meatballs and nopales in a bowl along with a bit of broth. Accompany with warm corn tortillas or top with strips of golden fried tortillas. *Serves 4*

LEFTOVERS

Tacos: Crumble and brown the meatballs in a hot frying pan along with an equal amount of the nopales, cut into bite-sized bits. Add a spoonful of rice. Heat together and roll up in a warm corn tortilla. Season with salsa to taste.

ESTOFADO
CHILLIED POT ROAST WITH VEGETABLES AND OLIVES

This is the sort of robust, informal dish that characterizes the warm hominess of southwestern Mexican food. It is unpretentious and delicious in the same way as a good French stew or a Sunday pot roast.

Serve with a stack of warm flour tortillas, a rice dish such as Arroz con Elote, and perhaps a salad of romaine leaves with slices of orange, avocado, and tart ruby-colored pomegranate seeds, dressed with olive oil and vinegar or lime juice.

1 large chuck steak roast, cut into several pieces
5 cloves garlic, coarsely chopped
½ cup tomato sauce
1 cup chopped tomatoes (canned are fine)
1 bay leaf
2 small to medium onions, chopped
1 teaspoon ground cumin
About 1 cup beef broth
1 green pepper, roasted, peeled, and cut into strips; or 1 poblano or Anaheim chilli, roasted, peeled, and cut into strips

1 to 2 serranos, chopped or thinly sliced
3 tablespoons chopped cilantro
½ teaspoon cinnamon
2 tablespoons ancho or pasilla chilli powder, or equal parts mild chilli powder and paprika
3 carrots, cut into bite-sized pieces
4 potatoes, peeled and cut into chunks
20 pimiento-stuffed olives
2 cups green beans
Salt and pepper to taste

❶ Place the meat, garlic, tomato sauce, tomatoes, bay leaf, onions, cumin, broth, pepper, chillies, cilantro, cinnamon, and chilli powder in a heavy oven-proof pan. Cover and place in oven.

❷ Bake in 350°F oven about 1½ hours, or until meat is almost tender. Add the carrots and potatoes, and more broth if needed. Cover, then return to oven for another hour or so or until meat is meltingly tender.

❸ Add olives, green beans, salt and pepper, and return to oven to heat through. Serve chunks of the meat and vegetables accompanied by flour tortillas and a hot salsa of choice. *Serves 6*

PICADILLO
SPICED BEEF HASH WITH RAISINS AND NUTS, OAXACA STYLE

Versions of *picadillo*, a sort of minced or shredded meat hash, are enjoyed throughout Mexico and the Caribbean. Its name comes from the Spanish *picar*, to mince. The nuts, sherry, and sweet spices also reflect the Spanish heritage.

It is a dish that is eaten all over Mexico, changing from region to region. In the north it is heavier on garlic and might have a handful of green olives stirred in. In the central areas diced potatoes are often added. Sometimes the *picadillo* is made with boiled and shredded meat rather than minced beef. Sadly, as with hash the world over, often *picadillo* is simply a way of stretching a few pathetic leftovers.

This particular *picadillo* is from Oaxaca, full of sweet spices, tomatoes, raisins, and nuts. It is especially enjoyed as a filling for roasted sweet red peppers or for crisp pastries called empanadas; good too in tamales or burritos.

2 onions, chopped
2 cloves garlic, chopped
1½ lb. ground beef
1 teaspoon cinnamon
¼ teaspoon ground cloves
Generous shake each: cumin, cayenne pepper, salt
⅓ cup raisins

⅓ cup coarsely chopped toasted almonds or peanuts
3 tablespoons tomato paste
½ to ⅔ cup dry sherry or red wine
1 tablespoon sugar or honey
1 tablespoons coarsely chopped cilantro (optional)
1 small ripe plantain or 2 medium-sized potatoes
Oil for frying

❶ Brown onions and garlic with the meat, then sprinkle with cinnamon, cloves, cumin, cayenne, and salt. Pour off any fat that accumulates.

❷ Add raisins, nuts, tomato paste, sherry or wine, and sugar or honey. Simmer until mixture is thickened and liquid has mostly evaporated. Taste for seasoning, then sprinkle in cilantro.

❸ Peel plantain or potato. Cut the plantain into large dice; if using potato, cut it into small dice. Brown, then add to the hash mixture. *Serves 4*

BIRRIA
PIT-COOKED LAMB OR GOAT WITH BROTH

Along with mole and pozole, *birria* is one of those comforting peasant soupy dishes that can be varied endlessly. Originally prepared by wrapping the meat in maguey leaves, then roasting in a pit, *birria* is usually prepared these days by steaming the chunks of marinated meat, then coating with a spice paste and roasting the already tender meat to form a browned glaze.

Because of its long cooking, *birria* is at its best with cuts of the fattier, stronger tasting (and usually the most economical) meats.

Serve *birria* as a Sunday supper pot roast type meal, starting with a vigorous broth such as Caldo Mexicana, Sopa de tortilla, or Caldo Tlapeño and accompanied by a crisp salad and crusty bread. Leftover *birria* makes delectable tacos, Guadalajara style.

2 batches Recado Rojo Enchilado, or
Salsa adobo, prepared to a thick,
paste-like consistency, or Recado
Negro
Juice of 2 limes or 2 tablespoons
vinegar
¹/₂ to 1 teaspoon chipotle marinade
5 lbs. bone-in meat: lamb shanks,
veal breast, pork shoulder, goat;
assorted cuts of meat give the richest
results
4 cups broth
2 cups water

Salt and pepper to taste
2 cups diced tomatillos (canned are
fine)
¹/₂ teaspoon oregano
3 cloves garlic, chopped
4 dried cascabel or New Mexico
chillies, seeded and broken into
small pieces, then lightly fried in a
little vegetable oil
1 onion, chopped
3 tablespoons chopped cilantro
2 limes, cut into wedges

....

❶ Mix spice paste with lime juice and chipotle marinade. Rub three-quarters of this mixture all over the meat. Save the rest for the baking. Let meat marinate in refrigerator at least 4 hours.

❷ Place marinated meat in steamer over broth and water. Cover well and steam over low heat about 3¹/₂ hours or until meat is fork-tender. (A large Dutch oven is excellent for this and can be placed in the oven, resulting in a baked steamed meat, much like pit-roasted meat). Skim as much fat from the broth as you can.

❸ Preheat oven to 400°F. Place steamed meat in baking pan and spread with reserved chilli paste and salt and pepper to taste. Bake for 20 minutes or until meat is crispy-browned.

❹ Meanwhile, make a sauce by combining 3 cups broth from meat's cooking with tomatillos, oregano, and garlic. Bring to boil and simmer while the meat bakes. Grind or crush the fried cascabel chillies, then add to the tomatillos. Taste for salt and pepper.

❺ Serve the meat with a spoonful of the sauce, a sprinkle of onions, cilantro, and wedges of lime, with a stack of soft corn tortillas and several bottles of cold *cerveza*. **Serves 4 to 6**

....

BARBACOA Y CARNE ASADA ❖ BARBECUED MEATS

Roasting meat over an open fire, that primitive and basic way of cooking, is a Mexican specialty. There are many methods and meats to choose from.

Mexican barbecues are apt to feature simply prepared meats with a wide assortment of accompanying goodies. *Frijoles refritos* and tortillas are, of course, perfect partners for barbecued meat, fish, or poultry. Vegetables are delicious added to the grill to roast along with the meats: especially corn, rubbed with melting butter and sprinkles of cayenne pepper before serving. Potatoes taste rustically delicious roasted on the open fire, good with dabs of salsa. Salads of leafy greens and herbs, a selection of salsas, and a platter of sweet, juicy fruits all provide colorful plate-mates for the roasting meats.

A Mexican *barbacoa*, however, can be a monumental fiesta, an all-day affair with much singing, dancing, and tequila drinking, as the beast roasts, whole, on top of the open fire, basted with some sort of savory, spicy marinade. (The English work *barbecue*, in fact, comes from this custom: the whole animal was laid on the grill, *barba* (beard, or head) to *coda* (tail). The expression *barba-coda* eventually became *barbacoa* in Mexico, *barbecue* in the English-speaking world.) The choice of meat usually depends on the region. In the north where cattle are plentiful, beef is the choice for the grill; while in most of Mexico pork is more widely available. In the central highlands, lamb might be chosen, or cabrito, baby kid.

There are many ways of preparing, seasoning, and serving the barbecued foods. In the Yucatán, pork is rubbed with a vermillion-colored paste of achiote seeds, then wrapped in banana leaves and placed in a *pib*, a pit with hot stones, to cook slowly to tenderness. In the central highlands, the pit is lined with maguey leaves, then stones, and a hot fire is built; on top of that are placed aromatic vegetables, a pot of stock with chick-peas and rice, and the meat—lamb, kid, or beef. The whole thing is enclosed in more maguey leaves, and a sheet of metal or wood and a layer of mud are added to keep the heat from escaping. It's somewhat like the *pib* and much like the Hawaiian luau pit. When, after six hours or so, the great feast is unwrapped, it is a celebration! The meat has dripped into the broth and the vegetables. Portions of everything are served, along with mountains of tortillas, lots of drink, and a *salsa borracho*, or a "drunken salsa" in which chillies, garlic, and onion have been mixed with a bit of pulque tequila, or beer.

Sometimes a simpler *barbacoa*, the meat roasted over an open fire, is accompanied by a smoky broth based on the drippings from the roasted meat, perhaps flavored with a bit of chipotle chillies. Lamb is delectable like this, and kid is always considered a treat, burnished with a paste of mild chillies and garlic, perhaps a dash of tequila or lime juice, and roasted until crispy on the outside and tender within.

··

CARNE ASADA
BARBECUED MEAT PLATTER

Barbecues of grilled meats—steaks, juicy chorizos, great deviled rib bones—are the basis for a full-meal *carne asada*, variations of which are eaten throughout Mexico. The meat is usually beef or pork or both, very simply seasoned: it might be marinated in a bit of oil and vinegar, but often it is simply rubbed with salt, pepper, a squeeze of lime (in Jalisco it would be orange) juice and a glistening of oil before being grilled, preferably over an open flame.

It is the accompaniments that make the meal: strips of sautéed sweet and hot peppers; a piece of cheese set out on the grill, melting into a deliciously stringy mess; plump, spicy chorizo or other sausages; guacamole; creamy re-fried beans or other beans simmered in broth; a *cazuela* of cheese-stuffed enchiladas; fried bananas; a selection of salsas and relishes; and, of course, the ever-present stack of tortillas. A platter of sweet tropical fruit is the perfect accompaniment, or a salad of sliced sweet oranges, red onions, and mixed greens, along with icy lager to drink, or tequila mixed with juice.

4 to 8 plump chorizo or other spicy cooking sausages
About 12 oz. each beef tenderloin and pork tenderloin

4 to 8 green onions, trimmed (optional)
Any of the accompaniments mentioned above
About 12 corn tortillas

● Place the sausages in a pan and cover with water. Bring to boil, reduce heat, and simmer until almost cooked through, about 20 minutes. Drain and let cool.

❷ Arrange the accompaniments: prepare or reheat enchiladas, make salsa, mash avocados for guacamole, warm tortillas, sauté chillies and peppers, fry bananas.

❸ Arrange the sausages and steaks over very hot coals, close enough to sear the meat, then move them further away so as not to overcook. The pork should just lose its pink color; the beef should not. Grill the onions, and place a piece of meltable cheese on the grill (see Queso Fundito). Keep any accompaniments warm that need to be kept warm; if your barbecue is large enough, this can be at the back of the grill, or any part of the grill where the heat is not too high.

❹ As soon as the meat is cooked through, serve slices of meat and sausage flanked by beans, peppers, an enchilada or two, a bit of cheese, and so on. *Serves 4*

CHULETAS A LA PARILLA
PORK OR LAMB CHOPS, POUNDED FLAT, COATED WITH CHILLI PASTE, AND GRILLED

The evening was sultry and humid the way only a night in the tropics can be—the sky an inky black spattered with a pattern of endless tiny stars. I walked along the narrow, palm-fringed path that wound around next to the beach following the spicy, smoky smells that wafted through the warm night. The restaurant I came to was little more than a shack, with nothing remotely related to a proper menu, just platters of savory, spicy grilled meats, tortillas, and fresh salsas.

This is the sort of simple Mexican fare that is so memorable. The meat is left attached to the bone, the flesh rubbed with a mild red chilli paste, then pounded to a thin cutlet. This not only tenderizes the meat and flattens it to a thickness good for quick grilling, it pushes the chilli paste into the meat so that the flavors permeate it. The grilled chops are then served with sliced avocado, a sprinkle of cilantro, and wedges of orange and/or lime to squeeze over the cooked meat. I often add a slice of papaya to the line-up. Salsa de Chiles Chipotles is a delicious accompaniment, the smoky flavor of the chilli echoing that of the grilled meat.

1 tablespoon mild pure chilli powder (ancho, New Mexico, guajillo, cascabel, or a combination)
2 teaspoons paprika
1 teaspoon ground cumin
3 cloves garlic, chopped
1 small onion, finely chopped
2 tablespoons olive or vegetable oil
4 pork, lamb, or veal chops, rib or loin cut

Salt to taste
1 ripe avocado, preferably one that is dark-skinned and rich-tasting
1 orange and/or 2 limes, cut into wedges
Cilantro leaves as a garnish, either chopped or whole
Salsa of choice

❶ Mix together chilli powder, paprika, cumin, garlic, onion, and oil.

❷ Slash fat around edges of chops every so often so that the meat will open up as it is pounded. Spread a spoonful or two of the chilli mixture onto each side of each chop.

❸ One by one, place each chop between 2 sheets of plastic wrap large enough to let the meat expand to about twice its size. Using the flat side of a meat mallet, pound meat evenly and firmly, taking care to reach the areas around the bone so that it does not remain too rare while the rest of the cutlets are overcooking. You want an even ¼-inch thickness.

❹ Grill chops over open coals about 3 minutes on each side. Meat should no longer be pink at the bone. Serve immediately. **Serves 4**

Serving Suggestions:

Beef or veal: Top each grilled chop with slices of avocado, finely chopped onions, thinly sliced serranos, and a scattering of cilantro. Accompany with wedges of lime.

Pork or lamb: Top each grilled chop with a sprinkle of oregano, thinly sliced red onions, jalapeños or serranos *en escabeche* including a bit of the vegetables in marinade, and sliced green olives. Serve with wedges of Seville oranges or a wedge each of orange and lime.

·············· **VARIATION** ··············

SABANA

Pound tender beefsteaks until ¼ inch thick and coat with the above chilli paste, adding a bit of olive or vegetable oil to protect the lean meat from the fire. Place a portion of mashed cooked black beans and a sprinkling of shredded Jack or mozzarella cheese down the center of each steak and roll up; secure with bamboo skewers. Grill over an open fire along with green onions and serve with Arroz Verde.

ARROZ, FRIJOLES, Y SOPAS SECAS DE MACARONI

··

RICE, BEANS, AND PASTA CASSEROLES

Those of us who grew up eating Mexican-American food became aficionados of "Spanish rice," a red concoction that tasted of tomato, mild red chilli, and cheese. I ate it every Tuesday for school lunch and remember it with an embarrassingly excessive fondness.

However, this vaguely spicy dish bore little resemblance to the wealth of well-prepared, pilaf-like rice dishes that I tasted when I first visited Mexico. There, rice is first sautéed, then simmered in stock with a variety of flavors: green herbs (Arroz Verde), black bean broth (Arroz Negro), tomatoes and bits of vegetables (Arroz Mexicana), lightly sautéed onion and garlic (Arroz Blanco), and so on. Rice is not usually served as a hearty main-course dish (except for paella, which is a popular Sunday afternoon lunch in areas with a strong colonial tradition). Rather, rice dishes are usually served at the beginning of a meal, after a light, clear, brothy soup. The peculiar name of this starchy course is *sopa seca*, or "dry soup."

Sopa seca refers not only to rice, but also to macaroni casseroles as well as tortilla casseroles baked with broth and zesty seasonings. (Such tortilla casseroles are found in the chapter on Tortillas, Platos de Tortillas, y Tamales. If you wish to begin your meal with any of those savory corn-based casseroles, refer to that chapter.)

Then there are frijoles, a wide variety of beans. Simmered to tenderness in an earthenware *cazuela*, they are a cornerstone of the Mexican table. They may be served ladled next to the rice, but not routinely; often they will be rolled into tortillas or spread onto tostadas, or pureed into soup. In traditional midday *comidas*, beans usually come to the table alongside the main course, or sometimes just a few spoonfuls are served at the end. Indeed, it is said that "a proper meal begins with rice and ends with beans."

ARROZ ❖ RICE

When cooking rice, the most important thing is to not overcook. Measure the amount of rice and liquid with care. Too much liquid and you might be tempted to continue cooking until it is absorbed; by that time the grains will be soft and mushy.

Choosing the rice is important—whole grains give fluffier, lighter results; too many broken grains will make a stodgy potful. Converted rice gives a rather foolproof result, having been treated with a steaming process that results in the grains keeping their integrity when cooked. The process also retains more vitamins from the outer layer than regular rice. Brown rice may be used in place of white, but take into consideration its nutty flavor when adding seasonings. Use long grain brown rice, double the amount of liquid, and increase cooking time to about 40 minutes.

When cooking Mexican rice dishes, a heavy cast-iron pot is best: it sautés the rice to golden nuttiness, conducts the heat most evenly, and keeps the rice from burning. These qualities result in firmer-textured, plumper grains.

ARROZ MEXICANA
MEXICAN "SPANISH RICE"

Arroz Mexicana is the rice you'll most often find at the *comida corrida*. It is ubiquitous throughout the Republic, with variations depending upon the region and the ingredients on hand. Arroz Mexicano can be wonderful or dismal; it all depends on the spirit—and pantry—of the cook. At its best, it is tinted with the brick-red hue of dried mild chillies and tomatoes, studded throughout with brightly colored bits of vegetables.

1 onion, chopped
1 tablespoon vegetable or olive oil
1 clove garlic, chopped
1 small to medium carrot, diced or coarsely chopped
2 cups raw rice
1 tablespoon ancho or New Mexico chilli powder
1 teaspoon cumin

½ cup chopped tomatoes (canned are fine)
1½ cups chicken, beef, or vegetable broth
¼ to ½ cup peas (precooked, or frozen are fine)
¼ cup corn kernels
¼ green pepper, diced
Generous pinch oregano leaves

❶ Sauté onion in oil until softened, then add garlic and carrot and cook a minute or two. Stir in rice and cook with other ingredients until light golden, then sprinkle in chilli powder and cumin and cook a few more minutes.

❷ Add tomatoes, broth, peas, corn, green pepper, and oregano.

❸ Bring to boil, then cover and reduce heat. Simmer over low heat until rice is just tender. This will take between 10 and 20 minutes, depending upon the type of rice. *Serves 4*

VARIATIONS

CON PLATANOS ❖ WITH BANANAS

In the Veracruz area especially, rice is frequently topped with bananas. You can slice regular sweet bananas, and add directly to the rice as a garnish; or use plantains (cooking bananas), sliced and browned in a little butter until tender. Bananas and plantains are served on all types of rice dishes as well as on plain, unadorned steamed rice.

CON MARISCOS
WITH SHELLFISH

Add a handful of shellfish of choice to Arroz Mexicana, and use fish broth for cooking.

CON CHORIZO
WITH CHORIZO

Add diced Mexican or Spanish chorizo to Arroz Mexicana for a meaty, hearty rice dish.

CON LEGUMBRES
WITH VEGETABLES

Add several halved cooked artichoke hearts or diced hearts of palm, along with 10 or so pimiento-stuffed green olives, and a teaspoon or two of capers. Serve the dish sprinkled with cilantro and thinly sliced medium to hot green chillies or with your favorite salsa.

ENSALADA DE ARROZ MEXICANA
MEXICAN RICE SALAD

Any of the rice dishes are delicious as a next-day salad. Splash the chilled rice with a zesty vinaigrette and enjoy. Good and colorful stuffed into roasted, peeled whole red peppers.

ARROZ BLANCO
WHITE RICE

Arroz Blanco is the most basic rice dish, one that appears most often as a prelude to a *comida*. It is, however, scarcely the unadorned boiled rice we think of when we hear "white rice." This is pilaf style, the grains sautéed first, often with a bit of onion or garlic.

Arroz Blanco can be varied endlessly. Add a bit of achiote paste for *arroz amarillo*, or cook it in chicken broth for a richer Arroz Blanco. Add a handful of prawns and cook the rice in seafood or fish broth and you have Arroz con Camarones, a traditional Lenten *sopa seca*.

1 small to medium onion, chopped	2½ cups raw rice
3 cloves garlic, chopped	2½ cups broth (chicken, beef, vegetable, or fish)
2 tablespoons lard, butter, or oil of choice	Salt and pepper

❶ Lightly sauté onion and garlic in fat, then add rice and cook over medium heat until rice is golden.

❷ Add broth. Reduce heat, cover, and simmer until cooked through, 10 to 20 minutes, depending on the type of rice. *Serves 4*

ARROZ CON CAMARONES ❖ RICE WITH SHRIMP

Prepare as above, using fish stock for the cooking liquid. Add a handful of diced prawns or shrimp when the rice is half-cooked. Serve sprinkled with chopped parsley.

ARROZ VERDE
GREEN RICE WITH PUREE OF CHILLIES, CILANTRO, ROASTED ONION, AND GARLIC

A well made Arroz Verde is one of those simple, classic dishes in which the finished result surpasses its humble ingredients. Arroz Verde gets its distinctive color and flavor from a paste of roasted, chopped poblano chillies and lots of fresh cilantro. Roasted onions and garlic, soft and fragrant, are added to the paste that cooks into the sautéed rice, and the whole is steamed together.

2 small to medium onions, halved and unpeeled
6 large cloves garlic, whole and unpeeled
1 large or 2 small to medium poblano chillies
2 fresh jalapeños (less if poblanos are quite picante; or more to taste)

1 cup fresh cilantro, coarsely chopped
1 cup chicken or vegetable broth
¹/₃ cup vegetable oil
1 ¹/₂ cups raw rice

❶ In an ungreased, heavy skillet over the stove top, roast the onions, garlic, poblano and jalapeño chillies until charred and blistered, turning so that they cook evenly. (This could also be done on a grill or over an open fire.)

❷ Let cool, then peel the onions, garlic, and chillies (discard seeds) and chop finely. Place in blender and puree; when smooth, add the cilantro and broth. Whirl until it forms a liquid puree.

❸ Heat vegetable oil and sauté rice until it is glistening and lightly browned.

❹ Add green puree to the rice. Cover, reduce heat, and cook over medium-low heat until rice is just tender. This will take 10 to 15 minutes, depending on the type of rice.

❺ Fork the rice to fluff it up, and let it stand for 5 minutes or so, covered with a clean towel. Serve immediately. ***Serves 4***

······························ **VARIATION** ·······························

ARROZ VERDE CON MARISCOS
GREEN RICE WITH SHELLFISH

Fragrant green rice takes exceedingly well to the addition of briny seafood; it looks especially beautiful topped with red langostino, or pink-fleshed prawns. Or try a handful of clams, their shells open to yield their juicy bodies; or mussels, black shells and orange flesh against the green rice.

Proceed as in the above recipe, substituting fish stock for the vegetable or chicken broth. You have quite a bit of leeway in the amount of seafood—several ounces of one type will keep the dish in the territory of side dish, whereas a large amount of varied fish and seafood will make a full meal, paella style. **Serves 4**

ARROZ CON ELOTE
RICE WITH CORN

Sweet corn and bits of green and chilli pepper stud this gentle, flavorful dish. It is distinctively Mexican yet adaptable enough to serve with a wide variety of hearty dishes. Preparing it with a vegetable broth gives a zesty vegetarian dish, good as accompaniment to cheese-stuffed chillies or perhaps a spicy roasted fish. I particularly like to serve it with the delicate Verduras con Crema.

Since the dish is so gentle, a splash of spicy fresh salsa is welcome.

1 small to medium onion, chopped
2 cloves garlic, chopped
1 green pepper, roasted, peeled, and diced or cut into strips
1 mild green chilli such as poblano, or jalapeño, roasted, peeled, seeded, and diced

3 tablespoons butter
2 cups raw rice
1 cup corn kernels (frozen are fine)
2 cups vegetarian or chicken broth

❶ Lightly sauté onion, garlic, green pepper, and chilli in butter until onion is softened. Stir in rice and raise heat a bit, cooking the rice in the onions and butter until the grains are light golden.

❷ Stir in the corn, then add broth. Raise heat and cook until mixture just begins to boil, then cover and reduce heat to a low simmer. Cook another 5 to 15 minutes (depending upon the type of rice), until rice is just cooked through. (Easy-cooking rice will hold its shape and integrity longer; regular long-grain rice tends to give itself up to mush early in the game.) Keep warm until ready to serve. *Serves 4*

ARROZ NEGRO
RICE COOKED IN BLACK BEAN STOCK, YUCATAN STYLE

This comes to the table with the same startling color as an inky black risotto, or the cuttlefish-tinted rice dishes of Spain, but in this case the color comes from the cooking liquid from black beans. They impart a haunting, mellow flavor to the rice, emphasized by the bay leaf that simmers with it. Though simple, this is a standout dish that makes a splendid accompaniment for hearty meat or seafood stews or braises.

2 tablespoons vegetable oil
3 cloves garlic, chopped
2 cups raw rice
2 cups cooking liquid from black beans
½ cup chopped tomatoes (canned, with their juice, are fine)

1 vegetable, chicken, or beef bouillon cube (optional; it gives extra flavor)
1 bay leaf
Generous pinch pure mild red chilli powder
¼ to ½ jalapeño or similar chilli seeded and chopped

❶ Heat oil and lightly sauté garlic. Add rice and cook until golden, stirring to cook evenly.

❷ Add black bean liquid, tomatoes, bouillon cube, bay leaf, and chilli powder. Bring to boil, then cover and reduce heat to a simmer. Cook over low heat until rice is just tender (10 to 20 minutes, depending on the type of rice).

❸ Fluff rice with a fork, adding chopped green chilli. *Serves 4*

Two Simple Rice Dishes

WHITE RICE TOPPED WITH CHILLI, GREEN ONIONS, CILANTRO, AND LIME

An invigorating dish to accompany complex, dark, spicy sauces and simmers. Top freshly steamed, lightly buttered rice with chopped green onion, fresh green chilli, cilantro, and diced lime.

ARROZ CON JACOQUI

Layer steamed white rice with a generous amount of the following ingredients: mild green chillies, roasted, peeled, and diced (canned are fine), shredded cheese, and sour cream. End with a layer of cheese. Bake in a medium-hot oven until the cheese melts. Serve with sour cream and more chopped chillies or green onions.

Garnishes and Serving Suggestions for Arroz Dishes

CAZUELA DE ARROZ Y CARNE
CASSEROLE OF SAVORY RICE TOPPED WITH MARINATED MEAT AND TANGY SALAD

Top rice dish of choice with lamb or pork chops marinated in *recado rojo* and lightly browned. Bake in hot oven until meat is savory and crispy around the edges. Serve with half an orange squeezed over it all, garnished with shredded lettuce dressed in oil, vinegar, and oregano, and diced cooked beets.

ARROZ MEXICANA CON CHORIZO Y PLATANOS

Surround a platter of Arroz Mexicana with grilled smoky meaty sausages and butter-browned banana or plantain slices.

"DIRTY RICE"

Embellish Arroz Blanco with a mixture of sautéed diced onion, garlic, chicken livers, gizzards, and chorizo or ground meat (beef, turkey, etc.), for a sort of Mexican "dirty rice."

ARROZ CON HUEVO

Serve rice of choice topped with a fried or poached egg and splash of tart, spicy green salsa.

ARROZ NEGRO CON CARNITAS Y SALSA

Accompany Arroz Negro or Arroz Verde with garlicky *carnitas*, a cilantro-lime salsa, and dollops of sour cream.

ARROZ CON ELOTE Y CHILLIES RELLENOS

Serve Arroz con Elote as a bed for Chiles Rellenos.

FRIJOLES ❖ BEANS AND LEGUMES

The ever-present pot of beans simmers slowly, a portrait of rustic tradition. No meal in Mexico would be complete without frijoles. Mexican beans come in a wide variety of sizes, shapes, and colors; the ancient Indians bred a rainbow-range of beans far wider than those we know today.

A large variety of beans eaten in Mexico are not too familiar north of the border (except in the Southwest, where a veritable bean renaissance is taking place). There are purple *flor de mayo* and beige-brown *bayo*, yellowish beans called *piruano*, and large mottled beans in a variety of colors. Generally, certain regions favor certain types of beans: pink *bayo gordo* and pinto beans are most popular in the north and central areas, black beans are favored south from Oaxaca and the Yucatán toward Guatemala.

Beans are simmered slowly in a pot until creamy and tender. They are then served in a variety of dishes. You'll find beans in soups, stews, with vegetables and so on, but the most popular way of serving them is *frijoles refritos*, or pureed fried beans. This rich puree may be eaten as is, with rice and salad or an entree, or spread onto all sorts of *antojitos*. It might be stuffed into a burrito or mild green chilli, or topped with cheese and melted into a rich, delicious mixture.

Rules for Making Good Beans

◆ Clean them and inspect for tiny pebbles.

◆ Soak in cold water overnight; or bring to boil, let sit one hour in the hot water to soften in lieu of soaking.

◆ For the most Mexican of flavors, cook them in an earthenware pot.

◆ Beans should simmer very slowly over a low flame.

◆ Always start with water to cover rather than drowning the beans; as liquid is absorbed, add more water (hot is best).

◆ Add salt only when beans are almost done; if they are not yet tender, the salt will toughen them.

◆ If available, add a sprig or two of the herb epazote to the simmering beans, especially black beans. It is said to cut the gaseous effect of the legumes; it also gives a wonderful, distinctive flavor.

FRIJOLES DE OLLA
BASIC BEANS

¾ lb. beans of choice, cleaned and soaked
About 2 quarts to 1 gallon water, as needed
1 onion, halved

2 tablespoons lard or other fat
1 large sprig epazote (for black beans; optional)
Salt to taste

❶ Put beans in pot with about half the water and the onion. Bring to boil.

❷ When the skins of the beans begin to wrinkle, add the fat. Continue to simmer, adding more water as needed.

❸ When beans are just about tender in 1-2 hours (black beans) to 2-3 hours or more (pinto beans), add salt.

❹ Use the beans in stews, soups, or refried beans; or simply enjoy them country style: spooned into bowls along with a bit of the cooking broth or other flavorful stock, seasoned with a little chopped raw onion, tomato, fresh cilantro, chillies, and oregano.
Note: Save bean cooking liquid for rice. Arroz Negro, cooked in the liquid of black beans, is startlingly good with it its ebony hue and rich, dark flavor. Pinto bean liquid gives a lighter flavor, more conducive to serving with chicken. *Makes about 6 cups*

VARIATIONS

FRIJOLES CON PUERCO
WELL-SIMMERED BEANS WITH TOMATOES AND BACON

Combine 3 cups cooked and drained beans with ¾ cup of chopped tomatoes, 1 chopped onion, ½ cup fresh cilantro, and 4-5 slices diced bacon. Simmer covered until beans are meltingly tender, adding bean liquid or broth as necessary. *Serves 4*

FRIJOLES BORRACHOS
"DRUNKEN" BEANS

Borracho means drunk; the name appears in dishes that contain alcoholic beverages such as beer, tequila, or pulque. Here a bit of rich Mexican beer emphasizes the earthy flavor of the beans.

Combine 4 cups cooked and drained beans with 1 cup chopped tomatoes, 2 serranos or jalapeños, several tablespoons cilantro, and 1 cup Mexican beer, as well as ½ to 1 cup of the bean liquid. Bring to boil, reduce heat, and let simmer until beans are very tender and liquid has evaporated to form a flavorful gravy. Season with salt; it may want quite a bit. *Serves 4 to 6*

FRIJOLES CON CHORIZO
BEANS MASHED WITH CRUMBLED SPICY SAUSAGE

Cook two chorizos in a pan, crumbling as the sausage browns, then add 3 cups cooked pinto or black beans with a little of their cooking liquid. Press and crush the beans with the back of a wooden spoon as they cook with the chorizo and the excess liquid evaporates. *Serves 4*

FRIJOLES REFRITOS
"REFRIED" BEANS

This rich paste of mashed beans is only fried once, despite its name. Any sort of bean may be used, with pink/pinto beans the most common in most areas and black beans favored in the south.

Canned versions are readily available. Using refried beans from a can (especially the vegetarian ones) is one of the few times I use canned foods. Their major drawback is that they can be rather salty. They are convenient, however, and lend themselves to a wide variety of dishes that would otherwise be impossible without the omnipresent pot of beans simmering on the back burner.

Why make your own? Homemade beans have more character, plus you are able to control the fat and salt content. When time is of the essence but I want my beans to have a more homemade quality, I use a combination of canned refried beans and plain ordinary canned pinto beans, well-drained.

2 to 3 cups cooked beans from
Frijoles de Olla, plus enough of the
cooking liquid to make a soupy puree
Salt to taste (beans take quite a bit)

3 oz. lard (preferably well-flavored,
lard; the traditional choice) or about
¼ cup vegetable oil in which you've
sautéed a chopped onion (reserve
onion for other use)
Cumin to taste (optional)
4 to 8 oz. grated cheese (optional)

❶ Mash the beans with a fork gradually as you add them to the pan; or puree
about half of them in a food processor or blender and leave the rest a bit
chunky.

❷ Heat about 2 tablespoons of the fat in a pan. Add a small amount of the
beans, cooking them down as their liquid evaporates, then adding more fat
and beans. Cook this way until mixture is a heavy, rather dry paste. Season
with salt. (and cumin, if using)

❸ If adding cheese, place the hot Frijoles Refritos in a casserole or shallow
baking dish. Top with the cheese and bake or broil until the cheese is melted
and bubbly. *Serves 4 to 6*

VARIATION

FRIJOLES MEXICANAS
ONION AND ROASTED TOMATO-SEASONED REFRIED BEANS

This rich and savory bean paste comes as a revelation even to those who
have doted on refried beans for years. The seasoning paste of roasted tomatoes
and raw onions, "fried" or cooked in a small amount of fat (I use oil; lard is the
traditional choice) until it forms a thick, highly seasoned paste, is what gives
the beans their layers of complex flavor.

8 small to medium tomatoes, whole
4 small to medium onions, peeled
and cut into small pieces

3 to 4 tablespoons vegetable oil or
lard
2 cups refried beans, either
homemade or canned

❶ Roast tomatoes over the open flame on a gas stove, or grill under the highest possible heat. Roast until skin chars and bursts into black bits. Remove from heat until cool enough to handle.

❷ Cut tomatoes into halves, leaving on the blackened skins (or what is left of them), and squeeze or cut out seeds. Cut into pieces.

❸ In a blender, puree the onions, then add tomato pieces and whirl into a puree.

❹ Heat the oil or lard in a heavy ungreased skillet. Add tomato mixture, letting it splatter and "fry" into a dry, well-concentrated puree. Add beans and cook together until well mixed and heated through. ***Serves 4 to 6 as a side dish***

·············· **VARIATION** ··············

FRIJOLES CON SARDINAS
REFRIED BEANS WITH MASHED SARDINES AND ASSORTED SAVORY GARNISHES

The strong savor of sardines balances brilliantly with the creamy beans.
Season approximately 2 to 3 cups Frijoles Mexicana with 1 small tin (about 3½ oz.) mashed sardines. Serve garnished with shredded cheese, shreds of chipotle chilli, diced avocado, shredded lettuce, sliced radishes, and crisp-fried tortilla wedges. Or spread the bean-sardine mixture onto crisp tostadas and garnish with the toppings.

FRIJOLES NEGROS ENCHILADOS
CHILLIED BLACK BEANS

Black beans seasoned with red chillies make an excellent filling for burritos, tacos, even pita bread sandwiches. Try them spread on crisp tortillas for the classic of the Yucatecan kitchen, eggs *Motul*, or topped with melted cheese and spread onto crusty bread along with a fresh salsa.
Cooked, pureed black beans are also an excellent addition to sauces; freeze small amounts so that you can always have them available.

2 onions, chopped
2 cloves garlic, chopped
1 tablespoon vegetable oil
1½ teaspoons cumin seeds or ground cumin
3 steeped and rehydrated New Mexico/California type chillies, scraped from their skin and pureed (or pure chilli powder to taste, about 1 to 2 tablespoons)

2 medium tomatoes, chopped
3 to 4 cups cooked black beans, with some of their cooking liquid, about half the beans mashed well
Salt to taste

❶ Sauté onions and garlic in vegetable oil until softened. Sprinkle in the cumin seeds and lightly toasted until they smell aromatic.

❷ Add chilli puree (or powder) and chopped tomatoes; cook until saucy in consistency, about 5 minutes.

❸ Add black beans and their cooking liquid. Raise the heat and cook down until it is the thickness you desire. Season with salt. ***Makes 6 to 8 cups***

Dishes to Make with Black Beans

Black beans are the basis for a wide variety of tostadas, tacos, and *antojitos*. They are a delicious accompaniment for grilled meats and salads, or the basis for rich and spicy soups. Refer to appropriate chapters for recipes.

BLACK BEAN CHILLI WITH HOMINY

Prepare Frijoles Negros Enchilados but leave the beans whole. Serve each bowlful topped with a spoonful or two of cooked hominy. Sprinkle with chopped cilantro, wedges of lime, and offer salsa on the side.

BLACK BEAN AND DUCK TOSTADA

Spread mashed Frijoles Negros Enchilados on tostadas; top with shreds of roasted duck, a spoonful of salsa, sour cream, sliced chillies, green onion, radishes and cilantro.

BLACK BEANS WITH SAUSAGES

Simmer thickly sliced spicy chorizo and/or longaniza sausages in black beans, along with a generous amount of coarsely chopped garlic and diced tomatoes, until the sausages are cooked through. Serve sprinkled with lots of chopped onion and cilantro, shredded lettuce (optional), and offer a fresh salsa on the side.

BLACK BEANS WITH PUMPKIN

With either Frijoles Negros Enchilados or Black Beans with Sausages, simmer bite-sized chunks of peeled pumpkin. Adjust the seasonings with cumin, cilantro, and mild chilli powder. Serve topped with a spoonful of sour cream.

YUCATECAN BLACK BEAN SAUCE

Puree cooked black beans with enough of their cooking liquid to form a rather thin, soupy mixture. Season with lime or Seville orange juice and any garlicky salsa such as Salsa de Chiles y Ajo. Use as sauce for barbecued or grilled meats.

LENTEJAS COSTEÑAS CON FRUTAS
BROWN LENTILS SIMMERED WITH FRUIT

It sounds alarming: lentils with fruit. The surprising thing is that the earthy, substantial bits of legumes are nearly transformed by cooking with the light sweetness of fruit.

This dish is particularly good paired with rich simmered or spice-roasted pork. A piquant vegetable dish or two on the side such as Palmitos en Vinegreta and *quelitas con chile* (just-cooked and squeezed dry greens, tossed in a small amount of Salsa de Chile Rojo that has been "fried" for several minutes to thicken it and intensify its flavors). Offer crusty bread to soak up the rich juices.

½ cup brown lentils
About 3 cups water
6 shallots or 2 small to medium-
sized onions, coarsely chopped
4 cloves garlic, coarsely chopped
2 tablespoons vegetable oil
1 large tart apple, diced

¾ cup diced unsweetened pineapple
(fresh or canned)
3 small or 2 medium tomatoes, diced
1 almost-ripe banana, cut into bite-
sized pieces
Salt and cayenne pepper to taste

❶ Place lentils in saucepan with water. Bring to boil, reduce heat, and simmer until lentils are tender and water is nearly evaporated.

❷ Meanwhile, sauté onions and garlic in vegetable oil until lightly browned and softened. Add apple and brown along with onion mixture. Then add pineapple, sauté a bit, and add tomatoes. Cook down until saucy.

❸ Add this mixture to the lentils and heat together about 5 minutes, just long enough to cook through and mingle the flavors.

❹ Add banana (either as is or gently sautéing first) to the lentils and fruit, and heat through a few minutes longer. Serve immediately, or store in refrigerator to heat and serve later. ***Serves 4 as a side dish***

SOPAS SECAS DE MACARONI
"DRY SOUPS" OF PASTA

Pasta, while it does take a backseat to the rice and tortilla dishes, is greatly enjoyed in Mexico. It is filling, an important consideration when there are many mouths to feed.

Of all the shapes, *fideos*, the very thin angel-hair strands, are probably the most popular: they seem to good-naturedly accept the vibrant Mexican seasonings and bake into savory, thick, and filling *sopa seca* casseroles. Other shapes are also enjoyed in hearty casseroles, or tossed into cooked broths for the soup course: macaroni added to a pork and spinach broth, flat ribbon noodles in garlicky tomato soup, and so forth.

SOPA SECA DE FIDEOS
CASSEROLE OF THIN NOODLES IN BROTH, WITH CHORIZO, TOMATOES, AND CHEESE

This satisfying dish is typical homefood. Its top should be crusty and cheesy, the pasta underneath soft and yielding, at one with the tomato-rich sauce.

First the vermicelli are simmered with a bay leaf, taking on the slightly piney aroma of the bay laurel. Then they are layered with a savory sauce, bits of spicy chorizo and cheese, then baked. Diced vegetables are often added in addition to or in place of the chorizo.

Serve the vermicelli as a first course, followed with charcoal-grilled chicken that you have first marinated in salsa, pineapple juice, chilli powder, and garlic; accompany by soft warm tortillas and a selection of salsas, relishes, and salads. For dessert, Helado de Praline y Espresso, combine 1 pint of pralines and cream ice cream with 1½ cups cooled super-strong espresso and 8 double amaretto or similar almond cookies soaked in rum and crumbled. Whirl together, then refreeze for 2 hours to firm up.

12 oz. thin *fideo*, vermicelli, or *cappelini*
2 to 3 bay leaves
About 8 oz. chorizo sausage
2 small to medium onions, chopped
1 poblano or Anaheim chilli, chopped
1 to 2 jalapeños, seeded and chopped (retain seeds if more heat is desired)

3 cloves garlic, chopped
1 cup tomato sauce
1 cup broth of choice
1 cup green beans, blanched and cut into 1-inch lengths (frozen are fine), or peas and diced carrots, both blanched
About 12 oz. shredded Jack, mozzarella, or similar cheese

❶ Boil noodles in water with bay leaves. When almost tender (it will take only a few minutes), drain pasta and discard bay leaves.

❷ Fry chorizo, crumbling as you go; when it begins to brown add onions and chillies and cook together until onion has softened. Add garlic, tomato sauce, and broth.

❸ Combine sauce with cooked pasta and place in baking dish. Cover with a layer of grated cheese.

❹ Bake in a 400°F oven until the top is bubbly and lightly browned and the dish is heated through. Serve immediately. ***Serves 4***

VEGETARIAN VERSION

Omit chorizo and increase onion. Add 1 teaspoon mild chilli powder, 1 teaspoon paprika, 1/2 teaspoon cumin, 1/2 teaspoon oregano, and a dash cinnamon to the onion as it sautés.

....

Two Simple Sopa Seca Dishes

BAY-SCENTED BUTTERED FIDEOS

Increase quantity of bay leaves to 4–6. When pasta is al dente, drain and remove the bay leaves. Butter generously, then serve with salt and pepper for a cozy supper bowlful. Dabs of a fresh salsa on the side make a punchy addition.

....

MACARONI CON QUESO, CHILLIES ROJOS, Y CILANTRO
MACARONI WITH CRISP-FRIED NEW MEXICO CHILLI BITS, SHARP CHEESE, AND HERBS

A quickly thrown together, comfortingly delicious bowl of pasta inspired by Mexican ingredients rather than a traditional dish.

Prepare fried chilli strips: Cut 1 mild smooth-skinned red chilli into strips, removing and discarding seeds and veins, then quickly fry in 2 tablespoons olive oil until they just change color and become crisp. Let cool.

Cook 12 oz. short elbow macaroni al dente. Drain, then toss with the oil from frying the chillies (use one-quarter to half of the chillies; reserve the rest for another use), 2 to 3 thinly sliced green onions or 1/4 cup chopped chives, 8 oz. shredded sharp Cheddar or similar cheese, and a dab of flavorful mustard such as Creole or a French Dijon type. Serve immediately, topped with lots of cilantro; salt and black pepper to taste. *Serves 4*

ENSALADAS Y VERDURAS

....

SALADS AND VEGETABLES

To appreciate Mexican vegetables and fruit, visit a marketplace in Mexico. Most are open-air, the vibrant center of community life.

I remember my first venture into Mercado Libertad, Guadalajara: the aroma of vegetables, the smells of fruit, sweet in its ripest stage as it settled into peak flavor, then slightly sickly as it slid into its rotten state too quickly in that hot, hot climate.

Fruits and vegetables were piled high, appearing more like the ancient Aztec and Mayan pyramids than produce displays that were destined to be sold and disappear within hours. Chillies lay in great heaps, this one a pile of black-green poblanos, here baskets of fiery habaneros, there fleshy red jalapeños: There were nopales (cactus paddles), fierce-looking but so delicious; and some sort of squash that had a distinctly prehistoric look. There were baby onions, strong green shoots ending with purple-white bulbs; bunches of delicate lettuce, still dewy but beginning to wilt in the heat of the day. And the fruit: papayas the size of watermelons, tiny yellow mangos and gigantic orange-red ones; sweet strawberries with a heady perfume. And the bananas! From thumb-sized red nuggets to unwieldy yellow-and-blackening monsters, firm green cooking ones and delicate yellow sweet ones; bananas for every eating and cooking use.

Visiting the market is the best way of learning about cooking, because it gives you a chance to ask the produce sellers' advice on their fruits and vegetables; inevitably a recipe or two comes along with the advice. Even without much in the way of Spanish language skills, you can learn a great deal using hand signs, smiles, and nods.

Because so many of the dishes in Mexico's restaurants are based on meats, added to the fact that most of us are frightened to eat raw vegetables and fruit south of the border, the visiting diner might think that there is little vegetable cuisine in Mexico. Not so. No soup or stew is complete without a garden basketful of vegetables simmering in it, and no hearty chilli-sauced dish is without its garnish of shredded greens and cabbage. Tossed green salads are not traditionally eaten to end the meal, as they frequently are in Europe, nor to begin a meal, north-of-the-border style, but most dishes are garnished with shredded greens, radishes, chopped herbs, sliced chillies, and other fresh vegetables. Tostadas come to the plate piled high with shredded raw vegetables; soups, stews, and chilli-spiced meat and fish dishes are scattered with a handful of what we would think of as salad.

Sometimes vegetables are pureed into complex sauces such as pipiáns or moles, other times prepared simply and served as a separate course before the main meat or fish dish, reflecting the Mediterranean influence of Spanish and French occupation. You'll find vegetables prepared in a wide variety of ways: diced, grilled, mashed, simmered, cosseted in cream and mild cheese, braised in chillies, simmered with tomatoes, hollowed out and stuffed, or breaded and fried. Large fresh mild chillies and chayotes might be stuffed with cheese, meat, fish, or beans, dipped in batter, then fried; diced zucchini might be lashed with oil and vinegar or tossed into a guacamole.

Vegetable relishes appear frequently on the table—picked cabbage, onions, carrots, and chillies. Then, too, there are the fresh salsas: chopped tomato, chillies, onions, combined with radishes, garlic, green onions, garlic, and so forth.

Sometimes vegetables are enjoyed as a snack in the same way fruit is: nibbled on raw, sprinkled with lime juice and cayenne pepper. Cucumber and jícama are especially good this way, often combined with oranges or pineapple.

ENSALADAS—SALADS

STREET VENDOR FRUIT PLATTER

In the streets of markets in cities, towns, and villages throughout the country you will find similar snacks of fruits and hot peppers. Along the road leading to many of the pyramids in the Yucatán, for instance, vendors sell sweet, juicy oranges that have been powdered (somewhat alarmingly) with hot red pepper. In the oppressive heat of that region, they refresh uncompromisingly. In Guadalajara you might find chunks of pineapple, jícama, and cucumber sold on sticks in the marketplace or park, sprinkled with enough chilli to brighten your outlook on life or at least wake up your taste buds.

This platter is a more citified and social version of the traditional, ancient fruit and chilli snack.

½ **lb. jícama**
1 small to medium-sized ripe
flavorful pineapple, or 3 flavorful
sweet oranges
1 cucumber (peeled if peel is bitter or
tough), sliced
Juice of 1 to 1½ limes

Pinch salt
Several pinches of either hot chilli
powder or a pure chilli powder made
from one type of chilli only (ancho,
pasilla, etc.), or a pinch of cayenne
pepper.

⬤ Peel and cut the jícama into bite-sized pieces and arrange on a platter.

❷ Peel the pineapple (or oranges) and do the same.

❸ Arrange the cucumber slices on the platter as well. Sprinkle the whole thing with lime juice, salt, and chilli powder. Enjoy immediately. *Serves 4 to 6*

ENSALADA DE NOPALES
CACTUS PAD SALAD

Nopales, or nopalitos, are the cactus pads of the same plant that produces the prickly pear. The pads are scraped to remove their extremely irritating prickles, then they may be simmered until tender. They are often cut into strips for more manageability.

Nopales have a flavor somewhat like green beans and a slight viscosity reminiscent of okra. They are delicious tucked into tacos along with spicy rich meat, since their own taste is so clean and fresh. Nopales are delicious with seafood, or chopped and added to various taco and tamale fillings, and are a classic scrambled with eggs, chillies, and tomatoes. Occasionally nopales are left whole and stuffed with cheese or meat, then simmered until tender and served with a mild, ancho chilli-based sauce.

Nopales are one of the few vegetables that I do not find objectionable when preserved in a bottle; in fact, the spiced brine often adds flavor. If using bottled nopales, simply drain (and rinse if needed).

For aficionados, the cooked strips of nopales make a delicious salad on their own. The combination of tangy nopales with either bland, hard-cooked egg or rich, nippy cheese is superb.

About 2 cups cooked nopales, drained
2 ripe tomatoes, cut into thick slices (optional)
1 small onion, chopped
¼ cup chopped cilantro
2 tablespoons vegetable oil
1 tablespoon mild vinegar or lime juice

½ jalapeño or serrano, thinly sliced (optional)
Salt to taste
Either: 1 hard-cooked egg, diced; or 2 to 3 oz. crumbled *queso fresco* (or fresh pecorino or not-too-salty feta); or 2 to 3 oz. cooked shrimp

....

❶ Arrange nopales on a platter. Garnish with tomatoes, sprinkle with onion and cilantro, then drizzle with oil and vinegar or lime juice.

❷ Sprinkle with chilli, a bit of salt, and either the hard-cooked egg, cheese, or shrimp. Enjoy immediately. *Serves 4*

....

ENSALADA DE CALABAZA Y JITOMATE
ZUCCHINI AND TOMATO VINAIGRETTE

A simple vinaigrette-splashed salad of zucchini and tomatoes. Almost Mediterranean in flavor and attitude, it makes a lovely dish for a languid summer's evening or afternoon. Good as an accompaniment for a barbecue of fish or meat, along with crusty bread.

1 lb. small to medium zucchini, cut into large dice or bite-sized pieces
3 medium to large ripe, sweet, and flavorful tomatoes, peeled, seeded, and diced
¼ cup olive oil
½ serrano or jalapeño, chopped

3 green onions, thinly sliced
1 tablespoon finely chopped cilantro
¼ cup wine vinegar
Salt and black pepper to taste
1 or 2 hard-cooked eggs, peeled and diced

....

❶ Cook zucchini in boiling water and cover for about 5 minutes or until just tender. Drain.

❷ Place zucchini in bowl and toss with tomatoes, then dress with olive oil, chilli, green onions, cilantro, wine vinegar, salt, and pepper.

❸ When ready to serve, garnish with diced egg. **Serves 4**

··

PALMITOS EN VINAGRETA
HEARTS OF PALM SALAD

While fresh is almost always best, hearts of palm are seldom available fresh. Canned ones are better than none, for they are unique among vegetables both in flavor and texture. In Mexico they are sometimes served in a *sopa seca* of rice, in soups, or as a tangy salad.

Drain hearts of palm, then serve garnished with strips of roasted red peppers, green olives, capers (optional), and lots of parsley. Dress with a garlicky, lightly chilli-seasoned vinaigrette. **Serves 2 to 4, as appetizer or first course**

··

COLIFLOR CON GUACAMOLE
CAULIFLOWER WITH GUACAMOLE

Steam one medium-sized whole cauliflower until just tender, then dress with a simple vinaigrette and let cool. Serve at room temperature or chilled, with your favorite guacamole spooned over. Diced lightly pickled beets and shredded lettuce are the traditional garnishes. **Serves 4**

··

ENSALADA DE PIÑA CON PIMIENTOS MORRONES
SALAD OF PINEAPPLE AND SWEET RED PEPPERS

Actually, I've had this salad more often with thinly sliced green pepper than with red, and it is good, but the red pepper is so very sweet and it becomes more of a fruit when paired with pineapple. The vibrant red and yellow of the platter are festive and enticing. You could dress it with your favorite vinaigrette, or serve as is. This is refreshingly good for brunch: follow with Huevos Oaxaquenos, crisp rolls, and Frijoles Refritos.

1 ripe, sweet pineapple, peeled and   2 ripe, sweet red peppers, seeded and
trimmed, cut into bite-sized pieces   thinly sliced

....

Arrange on a platter and serve chilled. *Serves 4 to 6*

....

LEGUMBRES Y VERDURAS—VEGETABLES AND GREENS

ENCHILADO DE COL
CHILLI-BRAISED CABBAGE

Mild chillies and tomatoes make a delicious braising mixture for cabbage. Richly flavored but not heavy, it is an agreeable partner to any savory braised or roasted meat mixture, accompanied by rice or soft flour tortillas.

Leftovers make the basis of a good free-wheeling vegetable soup: add diced cooked potatoes, broth, a squeeze of lime . . . and perhaps serve with a spoonful of sour cream.

2 small to medium onions, diced $^1\!/_2$ teaspoon mild chilli powder
$^1\!/_4$ to $^1\!/_2$ medium serrano, seeded and $^1\!/_2$ teaspoon paprika
chopped $^3\!/_4$ cup broth of choice
3 tablespoons vegetable oil   Juice of $^1\!/_2$ lime
$^1\!/_2$ head of cabbage, cut into large dice   Salt and pepper to taste
4 to 5 small to medium tomatoes,
diced (seed and peel if
desired)(canned are fine)

....

❶ Lightly sauté onions and chilli in oil until softened and onion begins to brown. Add cabbage and continue to sauté, then add tomatoes, chilli powder, and paprika and continue to cook. When tomatoes seem saucy, pour in broth.

❷ Cook over medium to medium-high heat until cabbage cooks through and liquid has almost evaporated.

❸ Season with squeeze of lime and salt and pepper if needed. *Serves 4*

....

LEGUMBRES ENCHILADOS
GARNISH OR SIDE DISH OF POTATOES, CARROTS, PEAS, AND GREEN BEANS WITH CHILLI SPICING

Informal mixtures of vegetables are quickly tossed in a little chilli and other spices, then served garnishing nearly anything: enchiladas, tostadas, grilled meats, *huevos*, and so on. The mixture varies with the ingredients on hand; sometimes the vegetables may be tossed in a little oil and vinegar with a pinch of oregano rather than served with chilli.

1 onion, diced	2 teaspoons mild chilli powder of choice
2 steamed but firm carrots, diced	
3 tablespoons vegetable oil	Generous pinch cumin seeds or ground cumin
4 cold boiled potatoes, diced (peeled or unpeeled)	
1 cup peas or green beans	Salt and pepper to taste
2 cloves garlic, chopped	2 teaspoons coarsely chopped cilantro

Sauté onion and carrots in oil until lightly browned, then add potatoes, peas or green beans, garlic, chilli powder, and cumin. Cook until heated through. Season with salt and pepper. Serve sprinkled with cilantro. *Serves 4*

VERDURAS CON CREMA
SPINACH WITH CREAM

A delicious version of creamed spinach, this has the elusive warmth of roasted and peeled green chillies. It is not really spicy-hot: the flavor comes gently wafting through.

Delicious paired with Arroz con Elote and a simple grilled meat or fish.

1 small to medium onion, chopped	⅔ to 1 cup sour cream
3 cloves garlic, chopped	2 cups cooked, squeezed-dry, chopped spinach (fresh or frozen)
2 jalapeños, roasted, peeled, seeded, and diced	
1 tablespoon unsalted butter	Salt and pepper to taste
	Chopped green onions (optional)

❶ Combine onion, garlic, and chillies in blender and whirl until it forms a fine mixture or a near paste. (Food processors for some mysterious reason can turn onions bitter, so use a blender.)

❷ Melt butter in a heavy skillet, then add the onion-garlic-chilli mixture. Cook until soft and golden, then add a spoonful or two of sour cream and cook down into a pastelike mixture.

❸ Stir in the spinach, cook a minute, then add remaining sour cream and continue to cook for a few minutes or until it thickens. Serve hot or tepid. Season with salt and pepper and sprinkle with chopped green onions if desired. **Serves 4**

LEGUMBRES EN PIPIAN
POTATOES, CORN, CARROTS, AND PEAS IN PUMPKIN-SEED SAUCE—YUCATAN

Pipián, or spice pastes of ground toasted pumpkin seeds, are enjoyed throughout much of Mexico, especially in the Yucatán Peninsula. It is a taste of ancient Mexican tradition, virtually the same sauce served by the pre-Columbian tribes. When Cortés' men were feted by Montezuma—before the latter's tragic downfall—pipián was on the menu (though the modern name is derived from the Spanish word for pumpkin seed: *pepita*).

Pale green, with a nutty spiciness that is mysteriously reminiscent of Southeast Asian *saté* sauces, pipián is traditionally served with duck, roast turkey, or thin steaks grilled over a fire. With a generous addition of lime juice it is transformed into a sassy dip for flour tortillas or crusty bread.

Though it is delicious in these traditional ways, I recently had a jar of leftover pipián and tossed it into a pan of mixed vegetables. It was sublime, the rice sauce balanced by the wisp of vinegar I had splashed the vegetables with and the sprinkle of mild red chilli they were browning with. Tomatillos add a tangy quality to the rich pureed seed sauce.

In preparing the sauce, it makes sense to prepare a double batch and freeze the leftovers. It reheats nicely and makes a splendid ingredient to keep on hand.

Serve Legumbres en Pipián with roast poultry: turkey, chicken, duck, or poussin; or as an accompaniment for thinly pounded fire-grilled steaks, duck breast fillets, or plump grilled duck sausage; flour tortillas and a fresh tomato sauce such as Salsa Ranchera alongside.

Pipián Sauce:

1 cup hulled, unsalted pumpkin
seeds
2 teaspoons whole cumin seeds
1 jalapeño, chopped
About 1 cup chicken or vegetable
broth
1 small onion, chopped

2 cloves garlic, chopped
10 cooked tomatillos or 1½ cups
canned, drained, and pureed
4 large-leaf lettuce leaves or 2
romaine leaves, cut into strips
2 tablespoons vegetable oil

Vegetables:

4 medium-sized potatoes, boiled,
cooled, and diced; 4 carrots, boiled
with the potatoes, cooked and diced;
both tossed with a teaspoon or so of
vinegar
2 or 3 zucchini, boiled, drained, and
diced

¾ cup each cooked peas and corn
(fresh or frozen)
2 tablespoons vegetable oil
2 teaspoons mild chilli powder
Salt and pepper to taste

❶ Make Pipián Sauce: Toast pumpkin seeds and cumin seeds in an ungreased frying pan until toasted and lightly brown, popping and sputtering and fragrant. Remove from heat, taking care to protect your eyes from the popping seeds.

❷ Grind seeds into a meal in a blender, then add chopped jalapeño and broth and whirl it all together. Pour out sauce and set aside.

❸ Whirl onion and garlic in blender to chop, then add tomatillos, lettuce, and vegetable oil and blend into a sauce consistency.

❹ In a heavy pan, combine both sauces and heat until bubbles form around the edge and sauce thickens and comes to the boil. Remove from heat and keep warm.

❺ Sauté vegetables in 2 tablespoons oil. When hot, sprinkle with chilli powder and continue to brown. Add half the pipián mixture and continue cooking until thickened.

❻ Serve immediately or tepid, seasoned with salt and pepper if needed. Offer hot salsa on the side. *Serves 4*

GORDITAS AZTECAS
PLUMP PEANUT-TOPPED PATTIES OF POTATOES, MASA, ZUCCHINI, AND CHEESE

These fetching patties are crisp on the outside, softly potatoey inside. With a splash of tangy green salsa and a scattering of crunchy peanuts, their simple potato taste is elevated to one of lively sophistication. They make a pleasing snack or substantial appetizer; partnered with a bowl of clear broth filled with bits of vegetables and/or meat, they're a memorable lunch.

4 large baking potatoes, peeled, boiled, and mashed	1 egg, lightly beaten
8 oz. crumbled *queso fresco*, fresh pecorino, or not-too-salty feta cheese	Salt, black pepper, and oregano to taste
2 cloves garlic, chopped	Vegetable oil for frying
2 tablespoons masa harina	Green salsa
1 or 2 zucchini, coarsely chopped	1 to 1½ oz. (about ¼ cup) roasted peanuts, coarsely chopped

❶ Combine mashed potatoes with crumbled cheese, garlic, masa harina, zucchini, and egg. Mix well, then season with salt, pepper, and oregano.

❷ Form patties about 4 inches long, 3 inches wide, and an inch or so thick.

❸ Heat enough oil to reach a depth of about 1 inch. When oil is hot, brown the patties until crisp and golden. Turn and brown on the other side.

❹ Serve the patties hot, drizzled with a spoonful or two of green salsa and a sprinkling of peanuts. ***Serves 4 as a snack or first course, 6 as an appetizer***

PAPAS CON COMINO Y SALSA DE CILANTRO Y LIMON
CUMIN-ROASTED POTATOES WITH CILANTRO-LIME SALSA

Cumin accentuates the flavor of the potatoes and their earthy skins, while tangy cilantro and lime salsa bring it all to life. The complex flavors of this savory dish belie the simplicity of its preparation and ingredients.

Enjoy as an accompaniment to a simple roasted meat or fish course, or as part of a selection of vegetable dishes for a robust meatless meal.

8 to 12 medium-sized waxy potatoes, preferably white or light brown
2 tablespoons olive oil
1 teaspoon cumin
Salt to taste
3 cloves garlic, chopped

1 or 2 serrano chillies, chopped (more if desired, but it shouldn't be too fiery)
2/3 cup cilantro leaves
1/3 cup lime juice
Cayenne (or mild chilli powder) and cumin to taste

❶ Boil potatoes in their skins until just tender. Drain and let cool.

❷ When potatoes are cool enough to handle, cut into halves or quarters and place in one layer in a 12-inch baking dish. Toss with olive oil, cumin, and salt.

❸ Roast in a 375-400°F oven for 30 to 40 minutes, or until golden brown.

❹ Meanwhile, prepare the salsa: In a blender, whirl garlic, chillies, cilantro, and lime juice. Season with salt, cayenne, and cumin. You want a thin, tangy salsa.

❺ When potatoes are ready, remove from oven. Serve immediately, tossed with several spoonfuls of salsa. Offer the remaining salsa at the table (with the addition of several chopped or thinly sliced serrano chillies if desired). *Serves 4 to 6*

VARIATION

CON CHORIZO

Follow the recipe above, but omit the olive oil and add 1 diced chorizo to the baking dish. Roast as above, tossing the potatoes with the sausage cooking fat every so often until the potatoes roast to a golden turn. Serve with cilantro-lime salsa (if chorizo is rather spicy, decrease or omit the serrano chillies in the salsa).

CHAYOTE
DELICATE SQUASH

Chayote is the most elegant member of the squash family, with a flavor that is reminiscent of zucchini but ever so delicate and sweet. Its elusive, mild taste lets it pair good-naturedly with a variety of other flavors; the seasonings may be gentle or strong, as long as they are fairly simple so as not to muddle up the delicacy of the squash.

In appearance, the chayote resembles a pale, shiny avocado. Botanically a fruit, it is generally eaten as a vegetable (the only exception I can think of is a chayote relleno in which the squash halves are stuffed with a concoction of its mashed flesh mixed with cake crumbs, eggs, and sherry). Dipped in flour, then battered and fried, chayote is delicious. It is good in soups, robust meat and vegetable stews, and shredded and made into croquettes and pancakes. Chayote is even good simply boiled, mashed, and buttered, with a dab of table salsa.

Following is a good, simple introduction to the chayote; it's delicious as part of a more elaborate meal, or to accompany Carne Asada.

4 chayotes, cut into quarters	**½ small hot chilli, chopped finely (optional)**
1½ tablespoons butter	
2 small to medium onions, chopped	**Salt and black pepper to taste**

....

❶ Place the chayotes in a saucepan with water to cover. Cover the pan and bring to a boil, cooking gently until the chayotes are just tender, 20 minutes or so.

❷ Drain and cool. Remove the seeds with a paring knife, then peel gently, taking care not to remove too much flesh, only the paper-thin skin. Cut chayote into large dice.

❸ Melt butter in a frying pan and sauté onions and chilli until softened and lightly browned in parts. Add chayote and toss. Season with salt and pepper. *Serves 4 to 6*

....

.... **VARIATION** ....

CHAYOTES CON QUESO

Prepare the above recipe and top with about 4 oz. shredded white cheese such as a white Cheddar or other tangy, meltable cheese. Cover the pan and cook about 5 minutes, or long enough to melt the cheese.

....

CHAYOTE RELLENO
TOMATO AND ONION-STUFFED CHAYOTE

Here the gentle chayote is stuffed with a savory mixture of its flesh along with tomatoes, garlic, onions, and parsley, then topped with cheese. The flavors and presentation are much like Middle Eastern stuffed eggplant dishes; no doubt it is a direct descendant, courtesy of the Spanish colonists.

Chayote rellenos are appealing to look at and delicious to eat. Serve as a separate course, following with Pollo a la Mérida or Ropa Vieja, or as a main vegetarian plate, accompanied by Arroz Mexicana and Frijoles Negros.

With just one half a chilli chopped and scattered into the filling, it is only a bit picante. Not enough to cause alarm: just a tiny thrill.

2 large chayotes, cut into halves lengthwise
1 tablespoon butter
2 small to medium onions, coarsely chopped
½ jalapeño, chopped (remove seeds for less heat)

2 medium tomatoes, seeded and diced
2 cloves garlic, finely chopped
3 to 4 tablespoons chopped parsley
Salt to taste
3 to 4 oz. shredded white Cheddar cheese

❶ Place chayotes in saucepan with water to cover. Bring to boil, then reduce heat and simmer, covered, until chayotes are tender when pierced with a fork, thin sharp knife, or cake tester, about 30 to 40 minutes. Drain and cool.

❷ Scoop out flesh with a sharp spoon and paring knife, taking care not to pierce the skin (or at least not too badly). Reserve shells and dice the flesh.

❸ In a large frying pan, melt the butter and sauté the onions until softened and golden. Add the chilli and tomatoes and cook until tomatoes are no longer raw. Stir in the garlic, reserved chayote flesh, and half the parsley. Salt to taste (you won't need much if the cheese is salty).

❹ Pile the reserved chayote shells high with the stuffing mixture, then mix the cheese with the remaining parsley and sprinkle it over the stuffed chayotes, patting it in to make it stick.

❺ Bake in a 350°F oven until cheese is melted and vegetables heated through, about 20 minutes. *Serves 4*

CHILES RELLENOS
STUFFED MILD GREEN CHILLIES

Like tacos, enchiladas, tamales, and other well-loved Mexican dishes, chillies rellenos tend to be lumped into the combination-plate syndrome. Often they arrive plopped next to the rice and beans, looking tired and soggy: a deflated lump.

But freshly made, tasting of fresh chilli pepper, a zesty filling of spiced meat or melted cheese, a crisp batter coating, and a fresh tomato sauce, they are delight, especially the cheese-stuffed ones—melted cheese deliciously oozing from each bite, the crisp batter coating contrasting with the simmered tomatoes and peppers in the salsa—a dish both cozy and lively.

Traditionally these are made with large mild poblano chillies, though restaurants frequently use canned Anaheim chillies that pale in flavor next to the fresh poblanos.

4 poblano chillies

Filling:

About 12 oz. mild meltable cheese such as Jack, cut into thick strips; or ½ recipe Picadillo Fiambre de Jaiba, shrimp filling from Flautas de Camarones con guacamole, Machacha de Camarón, or other Seafood filling

2 eggs, separated
2 tablespoons flour, plus extra for dusting the chillies
Salt to taste
Oil for frying
Salsa Ranchera

❶ Roast, peel, and seed the peppers, leaving the stems on; simply make a slit in each pepper and cut out the seeds and heart. (If poblanos are particularly hot, place them in the freezer overnight. When defrosted, their heat will be alleviated somewhat.)

❷ Fill the cavity of each pepper with the filling you have chosen. Set aside.

❸ Make the batter: Beat the egg whites until almost stiff. Lightly beat the yolks and add the flour to make a light paste. Combine both egg mixtures and season with salt to taste.

❹ Heat oil in frying pan. Dust the stuffed chillies with flour, shaking off excess flour. Prepare the chillies with the egg batter for frying. I find the best way of coating the chillies with batter is to spoon a bit of the batter into the pan, then top with the chilli, and spoon a bit more of the batter over it. It seems to work better this way than dipping the chilli.

❺ Fry each chilli until golden brown, then remove from pan and serve blanketed or resting in a puddle of Salsa Ranchera. I like a scattering of lightly vinegared shredded lettuce on top, as the heat of the chilli lightly wilts the lettuce. **Serves 4**

Four Unfried Stuffed Chilli Recipes

Stuffed chillies are also delicious without batter-frying. Roast and peel the chillies as in the basic instructions. Stuff as directed below. Instead of coating with batter and frying, place the stuffed chillies in a baking pan and proceed as instructed.

......

PIMIENTOS MORRONES RELLENOS CON PICADILLO
SWEET RED PEPPERS STUFFED WITH PICADILLO

Stuff Picadillo filling inside roasted, peeled, and seeded sweet red peppers. Place stuffed peppers in a baking dish, sprinkle with about ¼ cup warm broth, and bake in a medium-hot oven, covered, long enough to heat through. For 4 - 6 peppers you will need about ½ recipe picadillo. **Serves 4**

.... **VARIATION** ....

STUFFED PEPPERS IN CHEESE CUSTARD
Add 1 cup shredded Jack or Cheddar cheese to the egg batter in the basic Chiles Rellenos recipe. Pour this batter over the stuffed peppers in their pan. Bake in a 375°-400°F oven until the batter is browned and bubbly. Enjoy immediately. **Serves 4**

......

CHILES EN NOGADA
GREEN PICADILLO-STUFFED CHILLIES IN NUT SAUCE

Prepared in the red, green, and white colors of Mexico's flag, this dish is often served for Mexican Independence Day. Prepare the recipe for Pimientos Morrones Rellenos con Picadillo but use poblanos instead of red peppers. Prepare the traditional creamy nut sauce by grinding 1 cup finely chopped walnuts, then whirling them in a blender with 1 slice French bread soaked in milk, 8 oz. cream cheese, and ½ to 1 cup milk until mixture forms a smooth, creamy sauce. Season with salt, and cinnamon if desired. Serve the warm stuffed chillies masked with the room-temperature sauce, and garnish with ruby-red pomegranate seeds and leaves of green cilantro. **Serves 4**

CHILES RELLENOS CON FRIJOLES
BEAN-STUFFED CHILLIES

Stuff roasted and peeled poblano chillies with refried beans, then cover the slit in each pepper with lots of shredded mozzarella or Jack cheese, either by itself or mixed with fresh goat cheese such as Montrachet or California chèvre. Refried pinto beans are particularly good with the mild melty cheese, while refried black beans are *delicioso* with the addition of goat cheese. Broil or bake in a hot oven until cheese is melted and bubbly.

Leftovers make wonder next-day burritos: Warm stuffed chillies in oven or frying pan, then plop each whole stuffed chilli into a warmed flour tortilla. Season with salsa of choice, sprinkle with a handful of chopped onions, and roll up. **Serves 4**

CEBOLLITAS ASADAS
GRILLED GREEN ONIONS

Order *carne asada* (an assortment of charcoal-grilled meats, sausages, cheeses, and vegetables) nearly anyplace in Mexico, but especially in Mexico City, and they will come accompanied by grilled whole onions, somewhere between green onions and bulb onions, still attached to their strong green shoots. The open-fire roasting gives a sweet edge to their assertive flavor, and there is something so pleasing about their undisguised simplicity. (No doubt the custom was brought over from Spain, where tender grilled onions shoots are served with Romescu sauce for dipping.)

The best onions for this dish are ones that have grown beyond their infancy, with little knobs already formed.

8 to 12 large spring onions	**Sprinkle of salt**
A bit of vegetable oil	**Lime juice**

---

❶ Prepare a charcoal fire and let burn until medium-hot. Cut off the roots of the onions, as well as trimming the greens down to their nicest parts.

❷ Brush the onions with oil and lay them on the hot grill. You might place a piece of foil under the green parts, as they are more tender, cook more quickly, and are more apt to burn. Onions should take 5 to 10 minutes to cook, depending on size. Serve sprinkled with salt and lime. *Serves 4 to 6*

EJOTES CON PIMIENTOS MORRONES
GREEN BEANS WITH SWEET RED PEPPERS

Bits of sweet red peppers are often paired with green beans in Mexico. I think the combination appeals not only to the taste—the peppers bringing out the fresh sweetness of the beans—but to the eye, with the bright color contrast of red against green.

1 lb. green beans, cut into bite-sized lengths	2 sweet red peppers, stems and seeds removed, cut into strips or large dice
2 to 3 cloves garlic, chopped	Salt to taste
1 to 2 tablespoons olive oil	Dash lemon juice, balsamic vinegar, or sherry vinegar

❶ Cook green beans in boiling water about 3 minutes or until crisp-tender. Drain and either rinse with cold water or toss a few ice cubes around the hot beans to stop the cooking and chill them immediately. This helps retain their bright color and crisp texture.

❷ Heat garlic and olive oil for a minute in a frying pan, then toss in red peppers and quickly sauté.

❸ Add reserved green beans and toss together. Season with salt and a dash of lemon or vinegar. Serve either warm or at cool room temperature. *Serves 4 to 6*

HONGOS—MUSHROOMS AND OTHER FUNGI

During the rainy season, beginning around July, the Mexican marketplace abounds with a wide assortment of mushrooms and other fungi. All seem startlingly exotic; most are seldom seen outside the region they grow in. Pick your way through baskets of small, earthy brown nuggets; large, fleshy orange-yellow-toned near-leafy shapes; mushrooms brick-red or creamy white, the color of apricots or a brown shade, like whole wheat bread; fungi that are violet-hued, pale bluish lilac, or tinged with gray.

In general, the wide variety of mushrooms and fungi in Mexico are prepared rather simply—a quick jump through the sauté pan with a splash of chipotle chilli, or a spoonful of tomato sauce, and a dose of the requisite chopped onions and garlic. Prepared like this, you might find them adorning a grilled steak, or enchiladas, or simmered along with a chicken. In a cross-cultural vein, a whisper of mild chilli powder (such as New Mexico or California) gives a lovely warmth to any porcini and cream sauce for pasta.

One of the stranger fungi is *huitlacoche*. A pearly-blue-white fungus that grows on kernels of corn, it deforms them to monstrous lumpy proportions. When cooked, the *huitlacoche* exudes a black, inky liquid. I find it amazing not only that it is delicious, but that anyone was brave enough to taste it for the first time.

Huitlacoche is cooked like other mushrooms, simply, with chillies and seasonings. It might be combined with other vegetables such as zucchini and corn, or simmered into soup; *huitlacoche* is a prized quesadilla or taco filling, the mysterious flavor a perfect pairing for the soft dry-corn flavor of the tortilla.

POSTRES Y PANES

··

SWEETS AND BAKED GOODS

The ancient Mexican kitchens of the Aztec, Mayan, and other nations had no tradition of desserts. Without wheat flour, milk, cream, butter, or sugar, their sweets were limited to fresh tropical fruit, fruity tamales, honey-scented atoles, and fruit pastes known as *ates*.

The tradition of modern Mexico's sweets originated in the colonial convents. It reflects the Moorish-influenced Spanish penchant for sugary, egg yolk-rich sweets. The painters of that era used egg whites to "fix" the colors of their tempura paints in their frescos. The leftover yolks were sent to the convents for the sisters to put to good use.

The New World nuns lavished their creations with the Spanish-transplanted foods and introduced chicken eggs in place of the strong-flavored wild bird eggs. While the nuns favored cloves, cinnamon, and nutmeg, they ignored the native vanilla, pecan, allspice, and—strangely enough—chocolate. (Perhaps they were concerned with chocolate's dubious reputation as inciting other hungers, and the fact that in pre-conquest Mexico chocolate was forbidden to women.)

Other influences helped shape Mexico's sweet tooth: the brief French occupation left a penchant for rich patisserie fare and those crisp rolls, *bolillos*, that are as good as any you might find in France. While the German/Jewish immigration around World War II has left its imprint in the form of hearty European-style baked goods, the proximity and influence of the United States is reflected in the abundance of pies and cakes. You'll find fluffy mousselike pies based on citrus fruit as well as tarts filled with nuts in sweet syrup, a la pecan pie, and towering cakes with an esthetic excess that goes far beyond Betty Crocker.

With sweltering heat and weather that begs for refreshment, flavored ices and ice creams are enjoyed throughout Mexico. Montezuma is said to have been the first to enjoy ice cream, sending runners high into the mountains for ice, which was mixed with sweet flavorings for him. Modern refrigeration opened the way for a wealth of icy sweets, prepared with the same vivacity that other Mexican foods are: brilliantly colored and flavored ices of tropical fruits, sweet milk, spicy chocolate, and so on. There are *paletas*, intensely refreshing frozen ice bars made from chunky, lightly pureed sweet fruit in flavors such as watermelon, strawberry, cantaloupe, coconut, lime, mango, papaya, guava, cactus fruit, and almond. *Helado* is the Mexican equivalent of the Italian *gelato*, rich ice cream based on luscious tropical fruits.

Rice puddings, custards (flans), and other egg-based puddings are immensely popular throughout the Republic. The French *isle flotant* reappears in Mexico as fluffs of pink and green meringues cosseted with a creamy custard sauce. Jellied desserts, in shimmering garish hues, are doted on as well.

In the Yucatán, the traditional sweetener is honey, intensely fragrant with the aroma of the jungle. In the rest of the country piloncillo is favored. A fragrant, dark brown unrefined sugar that tastes of molasses, it is sold in semihard cones and makes delicious nibbling.

Many of the sweets found in Mexico are heavy or gaudy, sweeter than contemporary Euro-American tastes. There are sweet fruit pastes and concentrated goat's milk fudges, sweets made from sweet potato paste, sugary cakes of sweet corn or carrots, and nut pastes fashioned into gaily colored shapes. Cakes, candies, and sturdy puddings are based on pureed chick-peas or pinto beans, sweetened and formed into hefty treats. They can taste almost excruciatingly sweet.

Traditional Mexican baked goods are too wide and varied to do justice to in such a small space. Instead I've chosen a few of the most representative baked goods that seem to fit best within the scope of this book. There are many more: king's bread, studded with bits of sweet fruit, and "bread of the dead" with its sugar-coated crossbones topping are among the most outstanding.

The sweets in this chapter include traditional ones as well as contemporary ideas using regional ingredients. They were chosen for their appeal to our modern tastes rather than to offer an anthropological collection of "authentic" sweets.

Postres de Frutas—Fruit Desserts

NARANJAS Y FRESAS
ORANGES AND STRAWBERRIES, WITH LIME AND ORANGE-FLOWER WATER

The lush, verdant region of Michoacán grows the most fragrant, sweet strawberries in Mexico. Often they are made into aromatic, delectable preserves, spooned onto a butter *bolillo*, accompanied by a mug of *café con leche*, and enjoyed in the still-cool early morning.

Combining sweet strawberries with oranges, splashing them with lime and orange-flower water, is a contemporary idea with traditional ingredients. It makes a fresh beginning to a spicy weekend breakfast, or a refreshing finish for a lavish meal.

3 ripe, sweet, and juicy oranges, peeled and cut into bite-sized pieces
1 box strawberries, hulled and sliced
Grated rind and squeezed juice of ½ lime

1 tablespoon orange flower water
Sugar to taste

Combine oranges and strawberries, then toss with lime rind, orange flower water, juice and sugar. Chill to serve. ***Serves 4 to 6***

NARANJA NAHUATL
AZTEC ORANGES

Inspired by drinks such as the tequila sunrise and the margarita, this is a perky fruit compote to begin a robust *huevos rancheros* brunch.

6 ripe, juicy oranges, peeled and sliced
2 tablespoons each: tequila, lime juice, and orange-flavored liqueur or grenadine
1 tablespoon sugar, or to taste

Toss oranges with remaining ingredients. Chill until ready to eat. ***Serves 4 to 6***

TUNAS Y PIÑAS A LA MEXQUITIC ❖ PRICKLY PEARS AND PINEAPPLE COMPOTE, MORELIA STYLE

Prickly pear, with its neon pink-red color and distinctive flavor, is doted on in Mexico, much as it is in the Mediterranean regions where it also grows. You can find it sold on the street, looking fetching with its sharp prickles removed, the fruit peeled and ready for eating. As with all fruit desserts, take care that the fruit is ripe and full of tropical flavor.

Choose sliced ripe pineapple and prickly pear cactus fruit in place of the oranges. Omit grenadine or orange liqueur. *Serves 4 to 6*

MANGOS CON SALSA DE FRAMBUESA Y FRESCA
MANGOES WITH MIXED BERRIES AND BERRY SAUCE

A puree of berries, lightly sweetened and brightened with a dab of lime juice, makes a vibrantly colored and flavored sauce to puddle around other fruit, especially mangos and whole berries. For a Fauvist-inspired presentation, add slices of green kiwi to the mix, along with a handful of blueberries and perhaps a few leaves of mint.

1 box strawberries, cleaned and picked over
1 box blackberries or raspberries, cleaned and picked over
Dash balsamic vinegar or lime juice

Sugar to taste
2 medium-sized ripe, flavorful mangos
Fresh mint for garnish (optional)

❶ In a blender, puree about two-thirds of the berries with balsamic vinegar or lime juice and sugar to taste. Whirl until it forms a saucy consistency. Set aside.

❷ Peel and slice the mangos (save the stone for the cook to munch on secretly).

❸ Puddle the sauce on plates and arrange the mango slices and reserved berries on the sauce. Serve immediately, garnished with mint. *Serves 4 to 6*

GAZPACHO DE FRUTAS
FRUIT GAZPACHO

A whimsical variation of fruit salad: icy, fruity dishes make such splendid ending for spicy Mexican meals. Don't be a slave to the recipe—choose whatever looks best in the market. Like its vegetable counterpart, a fruit gazpacho can take nearly any amount of interpretation.

Enough orange or other fruit juice to fill 2 ice cube trays
2 cups white grape juice
½ large sweet pineapple
1 papaya, peeled, seeded, and diced; or 2 sweet peaches; or 4 sweet apricots
1 ripe banana, diced

¼ cup tequila (optional)
1 tablespoon lime juice
2 tablespoons sugar, or to taste
1 kiwi, peeled and diced
Strawberries, cut into quarters (optional)
Mint leaves as garnish

❶ Freeze orange juice in ice cube trays.

❷ In a blender, combine 1 tray of the orange ice cubes with the grape juice. Add half the pineapple, half the papaya (or peaches or apricots), the banana, tequila, lime juice, and sugar. Whirl until it is a chunky puree.

❸ Ladle into bowls and serve garnished with remaining pineapple, papaya, diced kiwi, strawberries, and remaining orange juice ice cubes. Garnish with mint and serve immediately. **Serves 4**

VARIATION

In place of the grape juice choose any tropical juice: guava or a combination juice drink would be good.

BANANAS AL HORNO A LA LEAH
BAKED BANANAS WITH MELTED CHOCOLATE

This little decadent combination of two ingredients (not counting any whipped cream or coffee ice cream you might want to dollop on top and let melt in) is here not because it is an authentic Mexican dish, but because both of the ingredients are Mexican and because it tastes awfully good following a spicy, robust meal. Also, it is simple to put together, so you can still serve it rich and gooey sweet even if the rest of the meal leaves you too exhausted to pick up a whisk for any mousse-whipping.

This is a contribution from my daughter, Leah. (It is one of the few dishes known to lure her into the act of food preparation.) The bananas bake to a soft sweetness as the chocolate melts into a warm sauce.

4 bananas, unpeeled
About 24 bite-sized squares of milk or dark chocolate

Whipped cream or coffee ice cream (optional)

••

❶ Preheat oven to 400°F. Make a slash lengthwise in each banana, cutting through the skin into the flesh.

❷ Tuck as many chocolate squares as will fit into the slash-cavity of each banana. Wrap each stuffed banana in foil.

❸ Bake about 10 minutes, or long enough to melt the chocolate. Serve immediately, with a drift of whipped cream or coffee ice cream on top, the banana somewhat pulled open to accommodate it. *Serves 4*

••

BANANAS AL HORNO CON NARANJA
BANANAS BAKED WITH ORANGE JUICE AND CINNAMON

Baked bananas, drenched with a bit of orange juice, sprinkled with cinnamon, butter, and a bit of sugar, then baked to caramelize the sugar, is a dish that seems too simple to be as good as it is.

Baked bananas are fiesta food, sold at holiday times from street vendors, buttery and sweet, often scented, as this one is, with orange juice. Amounts need not be specific—adjust them to suit your taste.

4 bananas, peeled and left whole
Several tablespoons dark brown sugar
About 2 teaspoons ground cinnamon

Unsalted butter to dot bananas with
⅓ to ½ cup orange juice
Whipped cream

••

❶ Arrange bananas in a baking dish and sprinkle with sugar and cinnamon, then dot with butter and pour orange juice all around.

❷ Bake in a 350°F oven 30 minutes, or until bananas are soft and sugar somewhat caramelized, the orange juice having turned into a sauce. Serve immediately, topped with a drift of lightly whipped cream. *Serves 4*

···································· **VARIATION** ····································

Use rum in place of orange juice. Heat the rum first over the stove to cook off the alcohol (keep your face and any curtains or potholders away from the pan, as it might ignite) so that the rum will not catch fire in the oven.

CALABAZA ENMIELADA
WINTER SQUASH WITH DARK DEMERARA SUGAR

This is a simple sweet, probably prepared since ancient times when honey was used for sweetening rather than the Spanish-imported sugar. For the most spectacular presentation, use a whole pumpkin, the jack-o'-lantern Halloween type. Bake the sugar-stuffed pumpkin in a baking dish with a little water at the bottom until the flesh is tender.

In Mexico, this soft, sweet pumpkin is eaten scooped out into a deep bowl, then doused with milk and enjoyed for breakfast.

2¼ lbs. winter squash such as pumpkin or other orange-fleshed squash, with seeds removed, cut into large pieces; or a large jack-o-lantern type, seeded and left whole with a lid cut off the top

Dark brown Demerara or raw sugar to taste
About ⅓ cup water
Cinnamon (optional)

❶ Pack the pumpkin or each piece of squash with sugar, then place in a baking dish or large kettle with a tight-fitting lid.

❷ Pour water around, cover tightly, and cook on the stove top until tender, about an hour, or bake in a 350°F oven for an hour or so. Add water occasionally if necessary. Sprinkle with cinnamon before serving. *Serves 4*

CHIMICHANGAS DE FRUTAS
FRUIT-FILLED *CHIMICHANGAS* WITH FRESH FRUIT SALSA

This whimsical dessert makes no pretensions for authenticity, rather it is inspired by the savory *chimichangas* of the Southwest. They make a delectable sweet stuffed with fruit and blanketed with sugar and cream. The filling can vary according to whatever fruit is in season. If you're feeling particularly energetic, serve the *chimichangas* garnished with a puddle of pureed fruit "salsa."

4 flour tortillas
Oil for frying
***Fruit filling*: 1 diced banana; 1 diced kiwi; 1 diced nectarine, peach, or mango; 1 small diced apple; a handful of berries; or whatever fruit is in season**

Sugar for sprinkling
Ice cream or whipped cream for topping
Mango or strawberry "Salsa"

❶ Soften flour tortillas one at a time in a very lightly oiled frying pan.

❷ Spoon several spoonfuls of the fruit filling down the middle of the tortilla, then roll up to enclose the filling, parcel style.

❸ When all four parcels have been assembled, heat oil to a depth of ½ to 1 inch. Fry parcels to a golden crisp.

❹ Drain on absorbent paper and serve immediately, sprinkled generously with sugar, topped with ice cream or whipped cream. (For the ambitious: Arrange the *chimichangas* in a puddle of pureed fruit "salsa." Whirl fruit of choice in a blender; season with sugar and lime juice, and add a sprinkling of chopped fresh mint. ***Serves 4***

Puddings and Frozen Desserts

ARROZ CHOCOLATL
CHOCOLATE RICE PUDDING

After the conquest, Mexico took readily to rice: sweet and creamy puddings have been well-loved since then. The following rice pudding is particularly nice since it is chocolate. A delicious topping is *crema Mexicana*, a thickened ripe cream similar to the French *crème fraîche*.

¹/₄ cup raw rice
1 cup milk
2 tablespoons sugar
Tiny pinch salt
¹/₄ cup cocoa powder

¹/₄ teaspoon cinnamon
¹/₂ teaspoon vanilla extract
Crema Mexicana, or half sweet cream and half sour cream, stirred together

❶ In a clean coffee grinder or blender, grind the rice into a fine meal.

❷ Combine ground rice with milk, sugar, and salt. Bring to boil, reduce heat, and simmer over very low heat until thickened.

❸ Add cocoa, cinnamon, and vanilla. Serve cool, topped with a spoonful or two of *crema Mexicana*. **Serves 4**

FLAN DE CAFE
COFFEE CUSTARD

Flan, or *crème caramel*, is as ubiquitous in Mexico as it is in Spain, where it originated. Often in Mexico you'll find the creamy, delicate egg custard combined with the strong flavor of New World seasonings such as coffee.

Syrup:

¹/₄ cup strong brewed coffee
¹/₄ cup sugar

Custard:

¹/₃ **cup sugar**	**2 cups milk**
6 eggs, lightly beaten	**1 teaspoon vanilla extract**

....

❶ Preheat oven to 350°F.

❷ Heat coffee with sugar and bring to boil. Cook 5 minutes, until syrupy.

❸ Pour into large baking dish or smaller custard cups, swirling around to coat bottom and sides. Set aside.

❹ Make a hot-water bath for the custard by setting a large baking dish filled with hot water in the oven.

❺ Beat together the ¹/₃ cup sugar, eggs, milk, and vanilla. Pour into prepared coffee caramel–lined dish bowls, then place dish or bowls in the hot-water bath.

❻ Bake about 25 minutes. Test for doneness by pressing the back of a spoon onto the custard. It should make a crevice about ¹/₂ inch deep.

❼ Remove from oven and from hot-water bath to cool. Then refrigerate.

❽ To serve, loosen custard edge with a knife, then invert onto a plate. The coffee caramel on the bottom will form a thin sauce. *Serves 4 to 6*

....

DULCE DE COCO
....
COCONUT FUDGE OR JAM

Somewhere between a pudding and a candy, this is an intensely sweet concoction of caramelized coconut and coconut milk, light brown in color. Its flavor conjures up Mexican sweet shops, with their sugary smells woven into the languid air. It is delicious in tiny spoonfuls with a cup of black unsweetened Café de Olla. (Note: In Mexico this is prepared more in a fondant style, and the resulting macaroon-like sweets are tinted bright green and pink.)

2 cups dried coconut	**1 cup sugar**
1 can (14 fl. oz.) coconut milk	**Pinch salt**
(unsweetened)	**Juice from ¹/₄ lime or lemon**

....

❶ Combine coconut, coconut milk, sugar, and salt in a saucepan. Slowly bring to a boil, then reduce heat and simmer, letting it bubble away, stirring every so often, until very thick (about 15 to 20 minutes). It should turn somewhat golden brown and caramelized in color. Stir often, as the coconut will settle and burn if you are not careful. Use a long spoon: the bubbling-hot sugar mixture stings when a drop inevitably sputters onto your hand.

❷ Add lemon or lime juice and spread coconut mixture over the bottom of a large baking dish or onto a large plate to cool. Chill.

❸ Roll the chilled mixture into balls. Serve as a sweetmeat, with strong unsweetened coffee or a glass of brandy. ***Makes about 2 cups***

HELADOS Y PALETAS
ICE CREAMS AND FROZEN FRUIT ICES

Frozen confections are adored in Mexico, especially in the Yucatán. Custards and creams, combined with fruit, chocolate, or other sweet flavorings, are whirled into a frozen frenzy and sold on a stick to be licked at as they quickly melt under the relentless sun.

Following are but a few examples.

HELADO DE CHOCOLATL
CHOCOLATE-CINNAMON ICE CREAM

Deep and dark, with the exotic aroma of cinnamon, this is an extraordinary frozen dessert. Like an Italian *gelato*, this is so richly chocolatey, it is nearly chewy. Since it is so rich, serve only small portions. Follow, perhaps, with a strong espresso-style coffee, no milk or sugar.

3 cups whipping cream
1½ cups milk
¾ cup sugar
4 cinnamon sticks plus 1 teaspoon ground cinnamon

8 oz. semisweet chocolate
4 egg yolks
⅓ cup unsweetened cocoa

❶ In a heavy saucepan, combine whipping cream, milk, sugar, and cinnamon. Cook over medium heat until sugar is dissolved and cream mixture is quite hot, stirring every so often. Remove from heat.

❷ Break chocolate into bits and add to hot cream. Let sit about 5 minutes, or until the chocolate softens and melts.

❸ Meanwhile, beat egg yolks.

❹ When chocolate has softened, stir or beat well to mix and dissolve it. (There will be tiny bits of chocolate that refuse to melt and mix with the rest— ignore them; they will give themselves up later.) Gradually add a cup of this hot chocolate mixture to the eggs, beating as you go, then stir the egg mixture into the hot chocolate.

❺ Make a thin paste of the cocoa using several ounces of the hot chocolate mixture, then add this to the hot chocolate. Your hot chocolate mixture will now contain the beaten egg yolks and the cocoa paste, all stirred into smoothness.

❻ Cook gently over low heat, stirring occasionally. When mixture is hot and slightly thickened—enough to coat the back of a spoon like a custard— remove from heat.

❼ Let cool, then remove cinnamon sticks. Place in freezer, either in an ice cream freezer or in an ice tray. While still slushy, stir with a fork every so often to form a granita-like consistency. *Serves 4 to 6*

HELADO DE YERBABUENA CON TOSTADOS DE CHOCOLATL
FRESH MINT ICE CREAM WITH CHOCOLATE TOSTADOS OR *TOSTADITOS*

Fresh mint ice cream is a revelation to those who have only tasted the garishly green stuff made from overly strong mint essences. Fresh mint is mildly bracing, its cooling sweetness tasting of the particular type of mint. If you have a garden, now is the time to forage for a nice collection of mint leaves. I like to use a combination of peppery peppermint, fragrant tiny leaves of Corsican mint, pungent bits of ginger mint, as well as a bit of sweet spearmint. (By the way, *yerbabuena* means good herb, the name once given by the Native American Indians to what is now San Francisco, likely because of the wild mint that grew on its hillsides.)

1 cup whipping cream
1 cup milk
$^1/_3$ to $^3/_8$ cup sugar
About 3 tablespoons finely chopped fresh mint(s) of choice

4 flour tortillas, whole or cut into wedges
Bland vegetable oil for frying
8-oz. semisweet chocolate bar, broken, chopped, or coarsely grated

••

❶ Place whipping cream, milk, and sugar in saucepan. Heat over medium heat until sugar melts and dissolves.

❷ Remove from heat and add mint leaves. Let cool.

❸ Freeze in ice cream freezer or in ice cube tray or any other shallow freezable pan.

❹ When ready to serve, fry the tortillas or tortilla wedges in hot oil until golden. Drain on absorbent paper and quickly sprinkle generously with the chocolate. The heat from the tortillas should melt the chocolate nearly immediately. If not, they may be placed briefly in a warm oven.

❺ Serve the mint ice cream garnished with chocolate-topped tostadas or *tostaditos*. **Serves 4**

••

HELADO DE PRALINES Y ESPRESSO
PRALINE, AMARETTO, AND ESPRESSO ICE CREAM

Sweet pralines and amaretti soaked in rum flavor this deliciously simple frozen dessert. The jolt of strong espresso is invigorating.

8 double amaretti
Several tablespoons dark rum, for sprinkling

1 pint pralines and cream ice cream
1 $^1/_2$ cups cooled super strong espresso

••

❶ Place amaretti in bowl and sprinkle with rum. Let sit for about 15 minutes, then crumble.

❷ Combine crumbled cookies with ice cream and espresso, then return to freezer.

❸ Freeze only until firm, stirring once or twice with fork. Serve within several hours for maximum fresh flavor. **Serves 4**

••

FRUIT BLIZZARD
NIEVE DE FRUTAS

Fresh fruit, frozen, then whirled into a sweet and tangy froth, makes a refreshing end to a meal, especially if the meal is spicy and the weather outside as hot as the food.

Freeze sliced ripe fruit or use commercially prepared unsweetened fruit: strawberries, pineapple, mango, nectarines, watermelon, cactus fruit, papaya, cantaloupe, blackberries—anything juicy.

Whirl 2 to 3 cups frozen fruit in a food processor with sugar to taste and enough fruit juice or tequila to form an icy sorbet-like consistency. Add a dash of lime or lemon juice for balance if needed. *Serves 4*

VARIATION

For a near-instant ice cream, whirl cream along with frozen fruit such as peaches or strawberries, and season with vanilla, almond, or other extract as desired.

NIEVE DE MANGO CON FRESAS BORRACHAS
MANGO ICE WITH STRAWBERRIES IN LIQUEUR

A suggestion rather than a rigid recipe, this is refreshing and enticing after a chilli-laden meal.

Freeze 1 quart sweetened mango juice (or tropical juice combination) in cubes; when ready to serve, whirl the frozen cubes to a froth in a blender or food processor with enough citrus or pineapple juice to form a granita-like slushy ice. Top with strawberries splashed with a dash of liqueur (or lime juice) and sugar to taste. Enjoy immediately.

PASTRIES AND BAKED GOODS

Many visitors to Mexico find it a surprise that the bread there is so good and so much a part of the diet. Rather than overtake the tortilla, Mexico has created a separate tradition of baking. *Bolillos* and *virotes*, crusty rolls not unlike those found in France, are a legacy from the brief reign of Maximilian and Carlotta. There are a wide variety of sweet breads and rolls, often iced with sugary frostings that attract the attention not only of patrons, but of handful of flies and the odd bee or two.

Mexican bakeries entice with the same excitement as does a French patisserie: the wide range of colors, shapes, textures, and beckoning aromas. Often, the goods lie in large display cases behind a sliding glass window. You take a tray, slide open the glass, and with a pair of tongs pick out your pastries. There might be *gaznates* (fried cakes made with rum), empanadas filled with candied sweet potatoes or pineapple, *polvorones*, *merengues* (meringues), pecan-filled tartlets, coconut-iced cakes, lime custard pies, and on and on and on. Many sweets are local, particular to each region, town, village. In Zacatecas they favor syrup-dipped cinnamon doughnuts. Fiestas demand their own breads: my favorite is the *cocodrilo*, the slightly sweet dough fashioned into tiny spikes and the finished bread decorated with sugar icing features. I have celebrated even the most ordinary days with loaves of this bread.

Mexican candies are very sweet and often gaudily colored in pastel-brights of pink, green, blue, and yellow. Confections may be made from simmering milk (usually goat's) into a thick fudge, or by grinding and shaping coconut, squash seeds, nuts, and candied fruits, often sweetened with brown-black piloncillo sugar.

CHURROS
LONG, CRISP, FLUTED FRITTERS

Freshly fried in huge cauldrons of viciously hot oil, *churros* are crispy golden on the outside, airily tender and nearly hollow on the inside, served blanketed with a flurry of sugar.

As in their original home, Spain, a *churria* is a common scene of daily life, especially in Mexico City. Peer in a window and watch the constant motion of squeezing the curls of dough into oil, fishing out the golden snakelike fritters, shaking on the sugar. Order a plate with a cup of dark rich chocolate or *café con leche*, then find a stool and sit back to savor the sweet treat as you observe the drama of life in Mexico unfold around you.

Churros are easy to make at home, but to get the characteristic fluted shape you'll need a pastry bag fitted with a star tip. An unusual aspect of these fritters is that the oil used for the frying is flavored by adding half a lemon or lime; by the time the moisture from the citrus pulp has evaporated, the oil is lightly perfumed. Adding lemon extract to the batter instead makes a handy shortcut.

Churros make a memorable breakfast, accompanied by a mug of hot chocolate or *Café con Leche*, or offer a basketful for Sunday brunch. They're good, too, as a late-night snack, accompanied by a glass of brandy or rum.

2 teaspoons aniseed or cinnamon
1 cup sugar
1 cup water
$^1/_8$ teaspoon salt
1 teaspoon sugar
6 tablespoons butter or margarine

1 cup flour
4 eggs
$^1/_4$ teaspoon lemon extract or half a
lemon or lime
Oil for frying

....

❶ Whirl aniseed and sugar in a blender or food processor. Set aside.

❷ In a saucepan, combine water, salt, 1 teaspoon sugar, and butter. Heat until butter melts, then bring to a boil.

❸ Add the flour all at once, remove from heat, and beat mixture with a wooden or other heavy spoon until it becomes a thick paste reminiscent of mashed potatoes.

❹ Add eggs one at a time, beating well after each addition until paste is smooth and shiny. Add lemon extract unless you are using a lemon or lime half in the oil.

❺ Fill pastry bag fitted with a star tip with batter. Set aside.

❻ Heat enough oil to reach a depth of 2 to 3 inches, or enough for deep frying. If not using lemon extract in the batter, add a lemon or lime half to the oil and heat. It will sputter a bit as the moisture in the fruit evaporates. (Lemon halves are the traditional Spanish method of freshening stale, reused oil, especially olive oil.)

❼ Discard lemon or lime half. Start squeezing batter into oil until you have a ribbon of paste about 7 to 9 inches long. You can fry several lengths at a time.

❽ Cook until they are browned and crisp, then drain on absorbent paper. Sprinkle with the reserved anise-scented sugar and serve immediately. ***Makes about 15 churros***

....

BUÑUELOS
CRISP FRIED DOUGH PUFFS

These crisp rounds of dough coated with cinnamon and sugar are especially doted on at Christmastime, when they are cherished by children, the sugary sweets clenched in little hands.

In Oaxaca a Christmas Eve tradition is a buñuelo feast accompanied by a smashing of the plates the fritters were served on. The plate-smashing is meant to bring good luck; next morning the town is nearly ankle deep in broken crockery.

Cinnamon Sugar:

1 cup sugar
1 tablespoon cinnamon

Dough:

4 eggs
1 cup sugar
2 cups flour

1 teaspoon baking powder
1 teaspoon salt
Vegetable oil for frying

··

❶ Combine 1 cup sugar and cinnamon. Set aside.

❷ Beat eggs together with 1 cup sugar until thick and golden. Stir together the flour, baking powder, and salt and slowly add to the egg mixture.

❸ Turn out onto a floured board and knead until dough is smooth and no longer sticky, about 5 minutes.

❹ Divide dough into 16 pieces. With floured hands, shape each piece into a ball and place in bowl or on board. Cover with a towel or waxed paper and let rest for about 30 minutes.

❺ On a floured board, roll each ball out to make as flat and thin a circle as you can.

❻ Heat about 2 inches of oil in a heavy pan. Fry the dough circles, one or two at a time, until golden brown.

❼ Remove from hot oil and drain on absorbent paper, then toss in the cinnamon-sugar mixture to coat lavishly. Serve immediately. Cooled pastries may be stored in an airtight container for up to 3 days, or frozen for several months. To recrisp, heat on a baking sheet in a 400°F oven for about 5 minutes.
Makes 16 fried pastries

··

CINNAMON BUÑUELO STARS WITH ICE CREAM, CARAMEL SAUCE, AND BANANAS
······································

This rather nouvelle dish makes no claims of authenticity, rather it is inspired by traditional south-of-the-border ingredients. Cutting the tortillas into star shapes may seem a mere whimsy, but in fact the crisp and browned points make a particularly delicious contrast to the rich sauce and ice cream.

Buñuelo Stars:

2 tablespoons cinnamon
¾ cup sugar
4 flour tortillas

Enough bland vegetable oil for deep frying

Caramel Sauce:

1 cup sugar
About ½ cup water
3 cups whipping cream
Pinch baking soda
1½ teaspoons good vanilla extract

About 1 pint ice cream, either dark-dark chocolate, strong espresso-like coffee, banana, walnut, pecan, caramel swirl, or pralines and cream
2 bananas

··

❶ Make the buñuelo stars: Mix the cinnamon and sugar and set aside. Cut the tortillas into pleasing star shapes. (Save the scraps to fry and nibble on powdered with sugar and cinnamon.) Heat the oil until hot enough to lightly brown almost immediately. Add the tortilla stars, one or several at a time, pressing down to cook until golden, about 1 minute. Drain on absorbent paper and sprinkle with the cinnamon-sugar mixture. Set aside.

❷ Make the caramel sauce: Place the sugar in a large, heavy saucepan and heat over medium-high heat until it turns golden, 5 to 8 minutes. Remove from heat and add water, taking care that it does not splatter you. Return to the heat, stirring to dissolve the caramel as it heats. Add the cream and baking soda and simmer, stirring every so often, until the sauce thickens and turns a golden caramel color; this should take about 30 minutes. Remove from heat and add vanilla. Set aside, stirring every so often as it cools.

❸ To assemble: Spoon the warm caramel sauce onto dessert plates. Top with a scoop of ice cream and decorate informally with slices of banana and buñuelo stars. Serve immediately. *Serves 4*

················· **VARIATION** ·································

The crisp-fried and sugar-sprinkled tortilla stars make lovely cookies or accompaniments for fruit puddings.

SUSPIROS
CHOCOLATE MERINGUES

These are richly chocolate and delicately textured, with a crisp-edged exterior and a soft chocolatey center. The name *suspiros* means sighs, and that may be more descriptive than any amount of prose. As with much of Mexico's baking and sweet-making heritage, *suspiros* are said to have been developed by the nuns.

Though the recipe calls for leaving the meringues in the shut-off oven for 3 hours, I find that sometimes they are still a bit soft at that stage: more fudgey or puddinglike than cookielike. This is because they are filled with chocolate rather than the dry sugar/cocoa ingredients other, crispier meringues are made with. It also has to do with humidity in the air and the heat of your oven. To be honest, they are rather good this way, topped with a dollop of whipped cream. To reach a crisper texture, simply reheat the oven and crisp the meringues for 10 minutes or so, then turn the oven off and let them sit to dry a bit.

4 egg whites, at room temperature
Pinch salt
1 teaspoon vanilla extract

3/4 to 7/8 cup sugar
2 teaspoons ground cinnamon
4 oz. semisweet chocolate, grated

❶ Preheat the oven to 350°F.

❷ Whip egg whites until foamy. Add salt and beat until very stiff, then beat in the vanilla.

❸ Whisk in the sugar, a small amount at a time, whipping as you add it until the meringue is shiny and stiff. It should take about 3 minutes by hand.

❹ Whisk in the cinnamon and grated chocolate, then spoon the meringues onto an ungreased baking sheet. Each suspiro will take about 1½-2 tablespoons meringue.

❺ Place in oven and immediately turn off the heat. Leave meringues in oven for 3 hours. *Do not open the oven door during this time.* (I often prepare the sweets the night before and leave them in the cooling oven overnight.)

❻ Remove from baking sheets. If they are too moist and soft, reheat and leave in oven to dry. ***Makes 2 to 3 dozen meringues, depending on size***

....

TORTA DE CIELO
FLAT ALMOND SPONGE

The sweet scent of almond in this cake is enticing. Flat, dense, and slightly chewy, it sits on the bakery shelf, looking plain next to the tarted-up beauty-contestant gaudiness of the more extravagant offerings. But do not be misled, for what this cake lacks in appearance it makes up in flavor. Serve as an accompaniment for tea, coffee, or a glass of brandy or as a sweet course at the end of a meal. If it still seems too plain, serve it in a pool of pureed and lightly sweetened berries or tropical fruit; for a more energetic presentation, plop each slice of almond cake onto a plate and surround with several puddles of pureed and lightly sweetened fruit: pale green kiwi, orange mango or apricots, scarlet strawberries. Scatter sweet raspberries and fresh mint leaves atop it all.

6 oz. raw almonds, preferably with skins on	3 medium eggs, lightly beaten
1 stick unsalted butter, at room temperature	1 teaspoon pure almond essence
1 cup sugar	¼ cup flour
	Pinch salt

....

❶ Butter an 8-inch square or round baking pan.

❷ In food processor or grinder, grind almonds into a mealy consistency. (If your blender can do this, use it.) Set almond meal aside.

❸ Cream butter and sugar together until smooth. Add eggs, almond meal, and almond essence. Mix until smooth.

❹ Stir in flour and pinch of salt and mix only until the flour is incorporated.

❺ Pour or spoon into the buttered baking pan and bake in a 350°F oven for 40 to 50 minutes, or until somewhat firm. Remove from oven and cool. ***Makes 1 cake, about 8 by 8 inches***

....

TERESA'S CHOCOLATE CAKE

This cinnamon-scented chocolate cake is from another of my books, *Sun-Drenched Cuisine* (J. P. Tarcher). It originated with my literary agent, whose palate for chocolate knows no international boundaries. It conjures up the image of sun-slaked Mexico with its fragrant whiff of cinnamon and its slightly caramelized sugar icing. Serve accompanied by mugs of hot, strong coffee.

1 stick unsalted butter
½ cup vegetable oil
½ cup unsweetened cocoa
1 cup water
1½ teaspoons white vinegar
½ cup milk
2 cups sifted flour

1 teaspoon baking soda
Pinch salt
2 cups sugar
2 eggs, beaten
1 teaspoon cinnamon
1 teaspoon vanilla extract

Fudge Icing:

1 stick unsalted butter
4 cups confectioners sugar
⅓ cup cocoa powder
⅓ cup milk

1 teaspoon vanilla extract
1 cup coarsely chopped pecans or walnuts

❶ Preheat oven to 350°F. Butter an 8-by-14-inch cake pan.

❷ Combine butter, oil, cocoa, and water in a saucepan and heat until cocoa has melted in.

❸ Mix vinegar and milk and set aside to sour.

❹ Combine flour, baking soda, salt, sugar, eggs, soured milk, cinnamon, and vanilla in a large bowl. Then combine with the cocoa mixture. (It will be soupy.) Pour into the buttered cake pan and bake for 20 to 25 minutes. The cake will pull away from the sides of the pan when ready. Cool for 5 minutes in pan, then cool on rack.

❺ When cool, prepare fudge icing: Heat butter until it melts, then continue heating over medium heat until it comes to a boil and gets foamy. Remove from heat and immediately add confectioners sugar all at once. This gives a slightly burnt, caramelized flavor. Then beat together until creamy and thick. Add cocoa, milk, and vanilla.

❻ Add pecans or walnuts and quickly spread icing on top and sides of cake. Work quickly, as it hardens very fast as it cools. Dip knife in hot water to facilitate spreading. ***Makes 1 cake approximately 8 by 14 inches***

BEBIDAS Y REFRESCOS

....

DRINKS

In a land that simmers in unrelenting heat, refreshing cool drinks form as important a part of the cuisine as do the savory and spicy foods. Walk down any street and along with the stalls selling all manner of enticing tacos and skewers, fruits and spicy nibbles, you will find stalls selling a wide variety of cooling, invigorating, gaily colored drinks.

In the street, vendors whip up cold *licuados de frutas* (fruit milkshakes) on the spot—a splash of milk or rice-milk in a fresh puree of fruit, then the whole thing is poured into your glass and drunk eagerly. The first time I tasted these drinks I returned home and tried to duplicate them, but of course I never could. Supermarket strawberries are not as sweet as those puny but strongly perfumed ones from the Mexican streets. And I could never be so parched from the sun as I was in those hot city streets, which made the drinks even more refreshing.

Huge glass crocks of rainbow-tinted fruit ades known as *aquas de frutas* line street stalls, ready to be ladled into glasses. Made from water and sugared fruit—melon, strawberries, limes, guavas, papayas, almonds, mangos, pineapple; indeed any fruit, or even ground nuts, rice, or seeds—they refresh utterly. With the typical Mexican sweet tooth they are often too cloying for my tastes; however, when homemade you can adjust the sugar to suit your own preferences. Ground rice is also used to make such drinks, lightly milky with a chalky edge.

There are warm drinks, too. Corn, the foundation of the Mexican kitchen, is thinned with water or milk and heated into a thick gruel-like drink called atole, often flavored with vanilla, strawberries, pineapple, or chocolate. Mexican coffee is strong, frequently seasoned with cinnamon or stirred with a cinnamon stick; hot chocolate also is fragrant with cinnamon and almond. Both drinks are invigorating, dating back to pre-Hispanic times when they were served as royal potions to the Aztec rulers. Tea in Mexico is usually herb, and often drunk as a medicinal or curative brew, with specific healing powers attributed to each herb.

But the liquid refreshment almost synonymous with Mexico is tequila and the wide variety of drinks made from that zesty firewater, especially margaritas. Mexico also brews excellent beers; indeed, even for those who seldom drink these brews, the combination of sultry weather and bracingly refreshing beer is difficult to beat. There is also mescal, distilled from the maguey, with its little worm curled up at the bottom of the bottle; and pulque, the slightly sour, foamy alcoholic drink of the Aztecs. Neither is easily found outside Mexico, even in American cities with large Hispanic communities. There is a small but thriving wine industry in Baja California. Some of the local wine is rather rough, but some is good. There are also a number of Mexican specialty drinks: liqueurs, rum, brandies.

AQUAS FRESCAS
....
FRUIT "WATERS"

A hot day on the plaza, the air thick and sultry. Is there a more appealing sight—much like an oasis in the desert—than the *aquas frutas* vendors with their huge jars of clear, fruit-flavored drinks? They offer a few moments' delicious respite from the heat.

Almost any fruit can be used to make the *aguas*—from the familiar strawberry or mango, to the exotic guava, or sour tamarind, or scarlet hibiscus flowers. They make a perfect accompaniment to a summer lunch, a children's party, or spicy brunch, or for a fiesta or Mexican celebration when a non-alcoholic drink is desired in addition to the tequila-spirited libations.

Most of the Agua Fresca recipes are generous indeed. I find them as simple to prepare in large batches as in small, and they are deliciously refreshing for crowds, or to keep in a bottle in the refrigerator for up to 2 days.

3 mangos, peeled and sliced; or 1 quart fresh strawberries, hulled; or 1 to 1½ lbs. guavas; or 2 lbs. ripe sweet cantaloupe, red or yellow watermelon, or honeydew melon	**2 quarts water** **Sugar to taste** **Juice of half a lemon or lime (with either the mango or melon)**

....

❶ Whirl fruit of choice with about 2 cups of the water in blender. Let stand an hour, then strain.

❷ Combine with remaining water, sugar to taste (and lemon or lime juice if using mango or melon). Serve over ice. Garnish with matching fruit: strawberries for strawberry *agua*, mango slices for mango, and so forth—or plop a sprig of fresh mint into each glass. *Makes 2¹/₂-3¹/₂ quarts, depending on the fruit chosen*

·· **VARIATION** ··

AGUA DE GRANADA ❖ POMEGRANATE ADE
Whirl the seeds of 10 pomegranates in a blender, then strain to obtain the juice. Add to 2 quarts of water and sweeten to taste. Chill and serve with ice. *Makes about 2¹/₂ quarts*

TAMARINDO
TAMARIND ADE

Tamarinds originated in Asia, where they are still used a great deal as a tart but earthy flavor in curries, sauces, and sweets. Tamarind pods are intimidating to deal with, filled with rock-hard beanlike seeds and a sticky pulp, but they are not as difficult as they appear. They yield their sour flavor readily. Tamarind can also be found in liquid form or in blocks of pressed tamarind flesh. Either form delivers fine flavor and is easier to work with than the pods. Latin American and Asian stores usually sell them.

Tamarindo is less cloying than the other Mexican fruit-based drinks. It makes a good nonalcoholic alternative to beers, its refreshing lightness well-suited to spicy and smoky foods.

¹/₂ lb. tamarinds (either the pods, lightly crushed, or the already crushed and pressed chunk, or the syrup)

2 cups boiling water
2 quarts cold water
Sugar to taste (start at ³/₄ cups and add more to taste)

Mix tamarinds with boiling water. Let stand overnight. Strain and mix with the cold water and sugar to taste. Serve over ice. *Makes 2¹/₂ quarts*

AGUA DE NARANJA
ORANGEADE

Combine 4 cups orange juice and 2 cups water with sugar to taste. Add 1 orange, thinly sliced, to the pitcher of orangeade. (It gives more than a decorative touch—the aromatic oils in the orange skin flavor the drink.) *Makes 1½ quarts*

······· VARIATION ·······

NARANJA DE SANGRE
Use the juice of blood (Seville) oranges, either on its own or combined with regular orange juice. Float slices of blood orange in the drink.

······· VARIATION ·······

AGUA DE PIÑA
Use pineapple instead of orange juice. Float bits of chopped pineapple in the drink, along with a little chopped fresh mint leaves.

LIMONADA
LIMEADE

Often in Mexico this sprightly refreshment will be tinted with an artificial-looking green food color to denote its lime flavor. I find it much more esthetic (as well as more flavorful) to add slices of lime, rind and all, to the pitcher. If you are serving it in individual glasses, make a cut in each lime slice and stick onto the glass rims.

10 large, juicy limes   **Sugar to taste**
2 quarts water

❶ Squeeze 8 of the limes into the water, adding one or two of the squeezed-out lime halves as well (or grate the rind from one or two of the discarded halves).

❷ Slice the remaining limes, discard seeds, and add to pitcher, or save some to decorate the glasses with.

❸ Sweeten with sugar to taste. Limes are very tart; this will take more sugar than other ades.

Note: Mexican limeade welcomes a jolt of vodka or tequila. **Makes 3 quarts**

···································· **VARIATION** ····································

Use sparkling or soda water in place of still water in the basic limeade.

···································· **VARIATION** ····································

LIMONADA DE OAXACA

In Oaxaca the rinds of very green and fragrant limes are finely grated to add color and fragrance to this drink. In the Oaxacan central marketplace, Indian women grind the lime peel with *molcajetes* to extract the fragrant green oils. Often the juice is not added at all, since it bleaches out the color the peel imparts. However, the tangy citrus juice makes a much more refreshing drink to my taste.

AGUA DE JAMAICA
HIBISCUS DRINK

Hibiscus has a startlingly tart, almost puckery flavor and a bright, tropical scarlet color. Its taste quenches with vigor and its color is so vivid that a glassful lends an air of festivity. Agua de Jamaica is sometimes combined with dry, fruity light red wine and a bit of fresh lime juice for a lively sangria.

Accentuate its exotic appearance, if you like, by garnishing the glasses or punch bowl with gaily colored edible (unsprayed) blossoms and/or chunks of tropical fruits.

½ lb. dried hibiscus flowers (sold as herb tea)
2 cups boiling water

3 quarts cool water
Sugar to taste

Steep the hibiscus blossoms for 30 minutes in the boiling water. Strain and combine with the cool water and sugar to taste. Serve over ice. **Makes 3½ quarts**

····················· **VARIATION** ·····················

SORBETE DE JAMAICA

Freeze well-sweetened Agua de Jamaica, scraping it as if it were an Italian granita, or freezing it in ice cubes, then whirling it in a blender to an icy consistency. If you have an ice cream maker, prepare it in that.

····················· **VARIATION** ·····················

Mix equal parts Agua de Jamaica, soda water, and well-chilled rosé wine or a shot of vodka. Serve garnished with thinly sliced citrus fruit.

CHICHA DE FRUTAS
MIXED FRUIT PUNCH

½ cup fresh mint leaves
½ cup very finely ground sugar
1 quart pineapple juice
2 cups orange juice
Juice of 2 lemons, plus 1 lemon cut into thin slices

Juice of 2 limes, plus 1 lime cut into thin slices
¼ cucumber, unpeeled, cut into thin slices
Crushed ice or large block ice

Mix mint with sugar and muddle the leaves a bit in the sugar. Add remaining ingredients and let the ice chill the drink as you serve it. If you are not serving it in a large punch bowl with ice, thin the punch (the lime and lemon will be quite strong and tart) with plain or soda water.

Note: Though one of the delights of this punch is its virgin (nonalcoholic) nature, it is also good with a shot of vodka or tequila. ***Makes about 2 quarts***

LECHE CON FRESAS
STRAWBERRY MILK

Every marketplace and bus station throughout Mexico has at least one stall devoted to this drink, with several blenders lined up, whirling away and serving up various concoctions of frothy fruit and milk.

This makes a delicious brunch or breakfast drink. As with other simple foods, the quality of the raw ingredients makes all the difference. Highly perfumed sweet fruit will make a memorable drink, indifferent fruit will not.

3 cups cold milk
1 cup sliced, hulled strawberries
1 teaspoon cinnamon

Sugar to taste
Several ice cubes, crushed

Place all ingredients in blender and whirl until frothy. ***Makes about 2 quarts***

VARIATION

CON HUEVO

In the streets of Mexico the vendors keep an egg basket next to the blender and toss a raw egg into the whirly sweet milk.

VARIATION

LECHE CON PLATANOS ❖ FROTHY BANANA MILKSHAKE

Use 2 ripe bananas in place of the strawberries; sweeten with honey in place of the sugar.

VARIATION

LICUADO DE FRUTA ❖ FRUIT-ICE DRINK

Frothy whirled drinks are often based on water instead of milk when made with acidic, juicy fruits that wouldn't work with milk; pineapple, cantaloupe, watermelon, or mango. Strain and serve with chunks of fruit floating in it; pour over crushed ice if desired.

VARIATION

LECHE CON MANGO ❖ MANGO MILKSHAKE

While mango is often whirled with milk, I like a mixture of half milk and half fruit-flavored yogurt for this drink. A combination of mango, banana, and strawberry is delicious whirled with milk, strawberry yogurt, and crushed ice.

COCONUT-LIME-FRUIT DRINKS
BEBIDAS DE COCO, LIMÓN, Y FRUTAS

Creamy coconut milk pairs beautifully with tart, fresh lime juice; add any of a range of tropical fruit juices to this mixture and you have a taste of Mexico. For a lazy-afternoon cocktail, add a dose of rum to the concoction.

2 cups coconut milk
½ cup fresh lime juice
About 1 quart tropical fruit juice
(mango, papaya, guava, passion fruit,
or any mixture)

Sugar to taste
Crushed ice
Rum (optional)

Combine coconut milk, lime juice, fruit juice, and sugar to taste. Serve over ice, with or without rum. ***Makes about 1½ quarts***

AGUA DE ARROZ
RICE COOLER

It seems curious—a drink based on steeping rice overnight, then sweetening and straining. It is, however, extremely refreshing with an edge of pleasing chalkiness that slakes the fierce thirst the scorching climate creates.

It's also known as *horchata* in the Yucatán and in regions that lie close to Guatemala. Variations of this drink are popular throughout Central America, the Caribbean, Spain, and other areas of the Mediterranean as well as Mexico. Commercial *horchata* is often based on rice powder and condensed milk and is very rich and sweet, on the order of Thai tea. This recipe, however, is light and refreshing. It separates a bit upon standing, so stir it up before drinking.

2 cups raw white rice
¾ cup almonds
3 tablespoons cinnamon
2 quarts hot water, or half water and
half milk

½ to ¾ cup sugar, or to taste
1 teaspoon almond extract or vanilla
extract
Ice cubes

❶ Rinse rice to rid it of any powdery residue. In a large bowl, combine rice, almonds, and cinnamon with warm water and let soak for at least 6 hours or overnight in the refrigerator. Drain, reserving both the liquid and the solids.

❷ Puree the solids in a blender, adding 1 to 2 cups of the liquid. Whirl until it is as smooth as possible.

❸ Strain this combination of solids and liquid through several layers of dampened cheesecloth, squeezing well to extract all of the milky liquid. Discard the solids.

❹ Sweeten with sugar and season with almond or vanilla extract. Chill and serve over ice cubes. Refrigerated, this lasts up to a week. ***Makes about 2 quarts***

·········· **VARIATION** ··········

CHOCOLATL

Add ¼ to ½ cup cocoa powder, or to taste, to the rice and almond mixture.

·········· **VARIATION** ··········

FRESA ❖ STRAWBERRY

Combine the prepared drink with crushed strawberries.

·········· **VARIATION** ··········

CON KAHLUA

Add a splash of Kahlua, brandy, or other favorite firewater.

·········· **VARIATION** ··········

HORCHATA

Substitute ground melon seeds for the rice and add the grated rind o'

·········· **VARIATION** ··········

PRICKLY PEAR

For a bright, nearly neon color and exotic fruitiness, add s prickly pears to the rice drink; strain before serving.

CAFE DE OLLA
MEXICAN COFFEE

The air is warm though the hour is early; soon the sun will be high and hot. Now it is still pleasant, with sunbeams gently falling into the room through the shutters.

The first taste of the day in Mexico is a cup of steaming-hot, strong coffee. Coffee is indigenous to the Americas and was drunk by the ancient Aztecs to give strength and vigor. The best Mexican coffee is grown in Uruapan in the state of Michoacán, the highlands of Chiapas, Córdoba, Veracruz, and Oaxaca. A darkish roast, though not quite as black and oily as Italian or French roast, is preferred; lighter roasts are reserved for the better quality beans, so as not to overwhelm the flavor nuances.

Traditional Mexican coffee is brewed without aid of a coffee pot, simply by boiling it with a bit of sugar and spices, then letting it steep. Sometimes it is strained through a cheesecloth (or a clean sock), other times an eggshell or lump of coal is added to the pot to help settle the grounds. Since the grounds are heavy and sink to the bottom anyway, I find that just letting it sit for a few minutes eliminates most of them. If that is not acceptable, you could use a small strainer.

Throughout the country, especially in the cities, European-style drip coffee is often served instead of the traditional boiled version, *con leche*, with hot milk poured in, *café au lait* style. In Mérida in the Yucatán Peninsula with its large Lebanese population, Greek-style coffee is served in tiny cups as it is throughout the Middle East.

rt water
 cup dark brown sugar
namon sticks

4 cloves
6 to 7 tablespoons ground dark-roasted coffee beans

fo cinnamon, and cloves over medium heat until sugar has dis-
nd bring to a boil. Remove from heat, cover, and let stand
(if desired) and serve. *Serves 4 to 6*

CAFE CON LECHE
COFFEE WITH MILK

This is the equivalent of *café au lait*.

2 cups milk or more, as desired   **Extra sugar to taste**
Café de Olla

Bring milk to boil as coffee is steeping. Pour hot milk into cups at the same time as coffee. **Serves 6**

VARIATION

ICED CAFE DE OLLA OR CON LECHE

With or without milk, strong spiced Mexican coffee makes a refreshing drink served over ice.

CHOCOLATL MEXICANO
MEXICAN HOT CHOCOLATE

Chocolate is yet another culinary richness bequeathed to the world from Mexico. It was said to impart virility, strength, and power. During pre-Hispanic times it was reserved for royalty, the wealthy, and people of high position. Bernal diaz Castillo, one of Cortés' men who chronicled the conquest, tells of the gold filigreed gourds filled with the strong, bitter drink that Montezuma downed as an aphrodisiac before visiting his wives.

Chocolatl was prepared then much the same way it is now, with a *molinillo* in a jug over an open fire. The *molinillo* is a strange-looking carved wooden beater-like utensil that is rolled between the hands to whip the chocolate to a froth. While a whisk or blender in theory does as good a job, often nothing makes hot chocolate as distinctively Mexican and delectable as the *molinillo*.

The name *chocolate* is said to come from the Indian Nahuatl word (bitter) and *atl* (water), though some say it is derived from a Maya word for hot water.

While many Mexicans buy chocolate in bars or squares as we do, many still prepare their own chocolate much as we might do coffee, selecting, roasting, and grinding the beans. Watch a *chocoltera* at work: smelling bitter scent of the beans as they roast, listen to the crackling as they are ground into an oily brown paste. Chocolate beans come in a wide variety of colors and qualities. It is said that the best light-colored Mexican cacao comes from the state of Tabasco and the best dark beans from Soconusco in the state of Chiapas. (Venezuela grows excellent beans as well.) A combination of light and dark beans yields the most pleasing results.

Mexican chocolate is dark and deep, seasoned with cinnamon and often cloves and almond. To approximate it, use semisweetened chocolate and add a heady dose of cinnamon; include a dash of cloves and almond if you like.

4 to 6 oz. bittersweet dark chocolate, broken into small pieces
1 teaspoon ground cinnamon
Dash of cloves (optional)

Dash of almond extract (optional)
1 quart milk
Extra sugar to taste, if needed (this will depend on the chocolate)

Gently heat the chocolate with the cinnamon and milk (and cloves and almond extract if desired). Stir constantly until the chocolate is melted. Whirl in blender or whip into a froth with either a whisk or *molinillo*. Serve immediately.

Note: Cocoa powder may be used in place of chocolate; add sugar and vanilla extract to taste. *Serves 4*

•••••••••••••••••••• **VARIATION** ••••••••••••••••••••

LEAH'S CAFE MOCHA CON CREMA

invigorating, this near-dessert drink of cream and chocolate-topped is my daughter's favorite concoction, inspired by Aztec flavors. to two-thirds full with Mexican hot chocolate, then fill mug coffee. Top with whipped cream, a sprinkling of cinnamon, ng of milk chocolate.

••••••••••• **VARIATION** ••••••••••••••••••••

YAN HONEY HOT CHOCOLATE

xico, Mayan tradition still dictates pre-colonial honey rather than sugar.

························· **VARIATION** ·····························

HOT CHOCOLATE PREPARED WITH WATER

Prepare Chocolatl Mexicano using water instead of milk. Serve hot and frothy, or let cool and serve over crushed ice. This is a modern preparation of an ancient Aztec drink. When iced, it is good with a splash of Kahlua or brandy.

Te—Tea

Mexican teas are not the cups of bracing milk-laced black tea the British love, or the lemon-scented Russian beverage, or the iced drink Americans favor. Rather they are herbal teas, or tisanes in the French manner. Many people take them as curatives, and the seller will help you pair what ails you with the appropriate tea.

Prepare as you would any herbal tea, by pouring boiling water over the leaves and letting steep. Following are a few of the supposed healing powers:

◆ *Anís* (anise)—to soothe the stomach; often given, cooled, to help settle colicky babies

◆ *Asafétida*—for bad tempers

◆ *Azahar* (orange blossoms)—tranquilizer for both stomach and nervous system

◆ Boldo—for gall bladder trouble

◆ Borage—for fever

◆ *Canela* (cinnamon)—for coughs

◆ *Cedro* (cedar)—for the stomach

◆ *Clavo* (cloves)—for toothaches

◆ *Jamaica* (hibiscus)—for bad temper

◆ *Jazmín* (jasmine)—to sooth the nerves

◆ *Limón* (lemon)—to ease pain

◆ *Maíz* (cornsilk)—for the kidneys

◆ *Manzanilla* (camomile)—for nausea

◆ *Naranja* (orange leaf)—for the nerves

◆ *Yerbabuena* (mint)—a cure-all that helps stomach upsets

CHIA
COLD CHIA-SEED TEA DRINK

Chia seeds produce a strange and gelatinous liquid, a traditional Mexican beverage. The seeds are very high in fiber with an unusual, jellylike consistency; you can find them in Latin American or natural food shops. Despite the curious consistency, chia seeds make a remarkably thirst-quenching drink.

| 8 oz. chia seeds | Sugar (or diluted honey) and lemon |
| 3 quarts water | or lime juice to taste |

....

❶ Combine chia seeds and water in a large jug and let sit while the seeds swell and become somewhat gelatinous; this will only take a few minutes.

❷ Sweeten with sugar or honey and season with lemon or lime juice. Do not strain the seeds; their consistency is part of the drink's charm. *Makes about 3 quarts*

....

Atoles—Sweet, Thick, Warm Corn Drinks

Atoles are sweet, gruel-like drinks based on masa harina, the same corn flour that forms the base of tortillas and tamales. In fact, atoles are traditionally drunk as an accompaniment to sweet tamales. They may be one of those foods that you can't fully appreciate unless you grew up on it. I confess that they are too substantial and sweet for my tastes. Yet each time I am faced with a mug of this nourishing brew, I grow to like it a bit more.

Passed down from generation to generation through the millennia, atoles probably date back to the beginnings of civilization, predating the great ancient cultures. Father Sahagun, who chronicled Cortés' conquest of the Aztec nation, mentions that at a great banquet the women were given atoles to drink when the men were drinking the more provocative chocolate.

Atole can be made with water and/or milk; it can be flavored with vanilla and cinnamon, with almonds, with fresh or dried and soaked fruit, or with fruit preserves. Chocolate-flavored atole is called *champurrado*. Atole is classically quite thick, like an American milkshake, but I like it thinned with water.

ATOLE DE LECHE
....
MILK ATOLE

2 tablespoons masa harina	2 cups water
3 to 4 tablespoons sugar, or to taste	1 teaspoon cinnamon
1 cup milk	1 teaspoon vanilla extract

....

❶ Mix masa harina with sugar, milk, half the water, and the cinnamon. Use a whisk to dissolve the masa well.

❷ Bring to a boil over gentle heat, stirring as it cooks and adding remaining water to thin the mixture. When hot and thickened, season with vanilla and add more sugar if needed. Serve in small cups. *Serves 3 to 4*

·············· **VARIATION** ··············

ATOLE DE ALMENDRA ❖ ALMOND-SCENTED ATOLE
Add almond extract instead of vanilla. Atole de Almendra is traditionally thickened with beaten egg yolk and crushed almonds, but this makes a very rich, puddinglike drink.

·············· **VARIATION** ··············

ATOLE DE FRESA, FRAMBUESA, ZARZAMORA, OR PIÑA ❖ FRESH OR DRIED FRUIT ATOLES
Add crushed fruit such as strawberries, raspberries, blackberries, guava, or pineapple when you add the second batch of water to thin it out. Prunes, apples, apricots—or any dried fruit—soaked, pitted, and pureed, are sometimes added to atoles. Sometimes a spoonful of fruit preserves is stirred in to the basic atole; decrease sugar accordingly.

·············· **VARIATION** ··············

ATOLE DE COCO ❖ COCONUT ATOLE
Prepare the atole using coconut milk in place of milk.

·············· **VARIATION** ··············

CHAMPURRADO
Chocolate atole is always referred to as *champurrado*, not atole. It is traditionally eaten for fiestas, such as Christmas Eve, accompanied by tamales and/ or buñuelos.

Prepare basic atole, but replace sugar with dark brown sugar, and whisk in several tablespoons of cocoa or bittersweet chocolate.

·············· **VARIATION** ··············

POZOL DE CACAO
In the southern Pacific coastal area of Chiapas, where the weather can be oppressingly hot, *champurrado* is often served thinned down and ladled over ice. *Taxcalate*, a similar corn and chocolate beverage, is an ancient Aztec drink based on toasted hominy and tortillas ground and seasoned with chocolate, cinnamon, and achiote seed.

·· **VARIATION** ···

BLUE CORN ATOLE

This is popular in Sonora and across the border into New Mexico. Prepare basic atole with the blue-gray, steely-flavored blue corn masa.

··

Alcoholic Drinks

Salud, dinero, y amor . . . y tiempo para gustarlos. "Health, money, and love, with the time to enjoy them all"—a Mexican drinking toast.

Tequila is probably the best known of Mexican drinks; indeed, many consider eating tacos and salsa an excuse to bring out the tequila bottle. Walk through the swinging doors of any cantina, whether in a city, small town, or village, and you're in tequila country where life's cares are exchanged for a shrug of the shoulders and a full glass.

To foreigners there is something indefinably special about this potent brew—no doubt enhanced by its drinking ritual: a wedge of lime, a tiny pile of salt on the hand, and the bottle. Take a tiny taste of the salt, a swallow of the fiery tequila, then sink your teeth into the lime wedge. Suddenly your conversation seems livelier, your companions ever so much more pleasant, your meal (no matter how humble) more delicious, and the world in general more tolerable.

Most tequila is produced in the town of Tequila, a dusty place with unpaved streets and mud-brick houses not far from Guadalajara. (There are tours for visitors.) The nearby hillsides are covered with meticulous rows of hundreds of millions of blue agave plants, their profusion of spiny leaves looking almost prehistoric. Each plant takes 8 to 12 years to reach maturity, then the plants are harvested and the *cabezas*, the pineapple-like bases, are split, steamed, and juiced. The resulting liquid is fermented, then distilled to 80 to 100 proof. It's mighty harsh at this stage, but some tequilas are aged in wood and smoothed to as suave a spirit as good brandy or whisky.

Yet tequila—and mescal—are not all the agave is good for. The large, pointed leaves may be used to line barbecue pits, the membranelike skin used to wrap spiced bits of meat, in the manner of parchment. The thick maggots that feed on the plant, maguey worms, are fried into a crispy appetizer or tucked into tacos; some find their way into a bottle of mescal, curled up for the long, long sleep.

In addition to the salt-lime ritual, tequila is sometimes drunk with a chilli-tomato chaser, *sangrita*. In the cantina the chaser might be beer—a jigger of tequila, glass and all, placed at the bottom of a stein and a bottle of beer poured over it.

Drunk down neatly, tequila's tart yet smooth jolt seems as close to perfection as a drink can be. However, tequila's ability to mix sociably with a wide variety of other ingredients helped transport its popularity north of the border to the U.S.A. and eastward to Europe. Most notable of these drinks is the margarita—but there are also the tequila sunset, sangrita, tequila sour, or even the Martinez, with tequila replacing the gin in a Martini. Grapefruit juice is wonderful mixed with tequila—so refreshing, so vivacious. Orange juice is not bad either.

Despite its current popularity, tequila did not exist before the conquest. Pulque was the Aztec alcoholic drink prepared from the fermented sap of the spiky maguey plant. Ancient murals at the site of the Great Pyramid of Cholula show pulque drinkers carousing in A.D. 200; pulque cups are common pre-Columbian archaeological finds. Milky in color and slightly foamy, pulque is sold in small bars, *pulquerias*, where the drink is cured with various fruits and flavors to disguise its sourness.

It was after the conquest that Spain introduced distilling to Mexico, or New Spain as it was then called. Soon tequila was being distilled from the blue agave, a succulent that grows primarily in the state of Jalisco. Tequila can either be clear-colored or a golden hue that comes from being aged (*anejo*) in charred casks. A similar, though stronger-flavored drink is mescal, distilled from a different species of agave. Mescal is notable for its fire as well as the well-pickled maguey worm lying at the bottom of every bottle.

Mexico produces some excellent rums, though not nearly as well known as the Caribbean rums. Its coffee-flavored liqueur, Kahlua, is the definitive coffee liqueur enjoyed throughout the world. A luscious liqueur not terribly well known outside the country is *rompope*, a rich concoction based on raw egg yolks, sugar, and brandy, much like the Dutch *advocaat*. *Aguardiente* (literally, "firewater") is an often homemade brandy; in Veracruz it is made from sugar cane and used to macerate fresh fruit. Then there is *Xtabentun*, the Yucatecan firewater traditionally brewed from fermented honey and flavored with aniseed to make a Pernod-like drink, available in *seco* (dry) or *crema* (sweet).

TO DRINK TEQUILA

Salt
Tequila (white, unaged tequila is best
for mixed drinks; to drink straight
like this, aged [*anejo*] is lovely, but
white is fine also)
Lime wedges

··

❶ Have several wedges of lime ready and tequila poured in small glasses.

❷ Make an L shape with your hand, then lightly lick the spot between your index finger and thumb where your hand makes a well and put a pinch of salt on it. (Licking the spot makes the salt stick instead of falling off).

❸ Take a lick of the salt, swallow the tequila, and sink your teeth into the lime, sucking enough of the tart juice to take the edge off the firewater.

·························· **VARIATIONS** ··························

While lime is classic, other fruits and vegetables may be used: pieces of white jícama, limed and salted; lime-rubbed cucumber; or wedges of orange are all authentic tequila accompaniments.

FRUITY TEQUILA DRINKS

Following is a selection of fruity tequila drinks. Think tropical: warm breezes and few clothes, palm fronds shading you from the blazing sun, lush jungle-like gardens and emerald-colored streams, and an endless horizon of deep blue sea.

TEQUILA CURADO DE MELON
TEQUILA-MELON PUNCH

1 quart tequila	Sugar to taste
1½ lbs. melon (such as cantaloupe) flesh	Ice
	Lime wedges

In a blender, whirl the tequila with the melon and sugar. Let sit 2 hours. Strain if desired. Serve chilled over ice with wedges of lime. ***Makes about 1½ quarts***

PIÑA BORRACHA
TEQUILA-PINEAPPLE PUNCH

Literally "drunken pineapple," Piña Borracha is made by combining very ripe sweet pineapple, well crushed, with equal parts tequila.

1 large ripe and strongly perfumed pineapple, peeled and crushed	**1 fifth tequila** **¹/₂ cup sugar**

· ·

Combine pineapple, tequila, and sugar. Whirl in blender, then cover tightly and let sit in refrigerator several hours or overnight. Strain and serve well chilled. *Makes about 1¹/₂ quarts*

· **VARIATION** ·

TEQUILA CON FRESAS O FRUTAS ❖ TEQUILA WITH STRAWBERRIES:

Prepare as above, but choose strawberries in place of the pineapple. Peaches, apricots, guavas, raspberries, blackberries—any soft, sweet fruit—can be treated like this. Prickly pears are particularly good; season with a dash each of cinnamon, cloves, and black pepper.

· ·

PONCHE DE GRANADA
POMEGRANATE STEEPED WITH TEQUILA

Tart pomegranate juice combines particularly well with the rich strong flavor of golden (aged) tequila. It is delicious sipped as is or used in any margarita or other mixed drink that calls for tequila.

4 large pomegranates **2 cups golden (aged) tequila** **¹/₄ to ¹/₂ cup sugar**	**¹/₄ cup water** **1 cinnamon stick, about 2 to 3 inches long**

· ·

❶ Cut pomegranates into halves and remove seeds. Whirl the seeds in a blender to form a puree. Put this through a strainer, a fine cheesecloth, or a coffee filter to separate the juice from the hard, gritty bits. Combine juice with tequila and set aside.

❷ Make a simple syrup by combining the sugar, water, and cinnamon stick in a saucepan. Heat until sugar is dissolved, then let cool. Add to tequila and pomegranate mixture and pour into a 1-liter sterilized jar. Seal and let stand in a dark place for a month.

❸ Strain before serving. Keep in refrigerator. *Makes 2 to 3 cups*

· ·

CLASSIC MARGARITA
·······································

Margaritas are probably the first time one encounters tequila. It combines the salty, tangy, and sweet flavors of the classic tequila presentation (with salt, tart fruit, etc.) in a frothy, icy, almost addictively delicious way. For those who object, salt may be omitted from the rim.

Lime or lemon peel
Coarse salt for rim of glass
1½ fl. oz. tequila
1½ fl. oz. orange liqueur such as
Triple Sec, curaçao, etc.

3 tablespoons fresh lime or lemon juice
Cracked ice

···

❶ Moisten rim of cocktail glass with lime or lemon peel, then salt the rim by pouring a small amount of salt into a saucer and twirling the moistened glass rim in it.

❷ Combine tequila, orange liqueur, and lime juice with cracked ice in cocktail shaker or blender. Shake or whirl until well mixed and icy.

❸ Strain if desired (if you used a blender you won't need to). Pour into salt-rimmed glasses and serve immediately. ***Makes 1 serving***
···

SOPRESA DE DURAZNO
·······································
FROZEN PEACH MARGARITA

Somewhere between a Margarita and a frozen Daiquiri, this is a particularly enticing drink. Lovely to enjoy on a late Sunday morning for a summertime brunch.

½ peach, sliced and frozen; or ½ to ⅔ cup frozen unsugared peaches
1 fl. oz. tequila

½ fl. oz. Triple Sec
½ fl. oz. fresh lime juice

···

In a blender, whirl all ingredients until smooth and slushy. If too icy, add a bit of peach juice or tropical fruit juice. Serve immediately, garnished with a wedge of lime or peach. ***Makes 1 drink***

Mango: Replace peach with mango or frozen mango juice.

TEQUILA DEL SOL
TEQUILA SUNRISE

The layers of orange juice and crimson grenadine run into each other, resembling a vivid tropical sunrise, presumably after a night of debauchery and tequila drinking.

2 teaspoons grenadine
Crushed ice
2 fl. oz. white tequila

¼ cup orange juice
2 teaspoons lime juice

Pour grenadine over crushed ice in tall glass. Mix tequila with orange juice and lime juice, then pour over the grenadine. *Makes 1 drink*

Pour several fluid ounces of club soda or fizzy mineral water over the tequila-orange mixture. Don't stir.

TEQUILA SUNSET

Heady tequila is sparked with lime juice and grenadine, then whirled into snowy bliss with crushed ice. It is cold and refreshing and evocative of sunsets over the Pacific.

1½ fl. oz. tequila
½ fl. oz. fresh lime juice
½ fl. oz. grenadine

½ cup crushed ice
Lime slices

Combine tequila, lime juice, grenadine, and crushed ice in blender. Whirl until mixed. Serve immediately, poured over extra ice cubes if desired, and garnish with lime slices. **Makes 1 drink**

SANGRE DE MARIA
TEQUILA BLOODY MARY

The distinctive flavor of tequila combines with spicy tomato juice even better than vodka. (In the same way, try adding a shot of tequila to your favorite, quite spicy, gazpacho).

Recipe for a city summer afternoon: a sunny rooftop, interesting neighbors, pitchers of Sangre de Maria.

1 ½ cups tomato juice	Large pinch salt
Juice of half a lime	4 fl. oz. tequila
Dash Worcestershire sauce	Cracked ice
Generous dash hot red pepper sauce	Finely chopped cilantro as garnish
½ teaspoon finely minced or grated onion	

Combine tomato juice, lime juice, Worcestershire sauce, hot red pepper sauce, onion, salt, and tequila. Serve over cracked ice, sprinkled with a little chopped cilantro. For a ferocious, slightly mischievous garnish, cut a slice into a fresh chilli and fit it over the side of the glass, much as you would a slice of lemon or lime. **Makes 2 drinks**

VARIATION

Several fluid ounces of the tomato juice may be replaced with orange juice.

SANGRITA
JALISCO

Sangrita (literally, "little blood") is a spicy sip drunk as a chaser to quell the fires of tequila. It's only fitting that this invigorating drink comes from Jalisco, the home of tequila. Serve chilled tequila in one glass, the *Sangrita* in another and alternate mouthfuls as desired.

⅓ cup tomato juice
Dash grenadine syrup to taste
Juice of 1 lime or ½ lemon
Juice of ½ orange
Pinch salt

Chopped ice to taste
Chopped fresh chillies or hot red
pepper sauce to taste
Cilantro leaves
2 fl. oz. tequila

Combine everything except the tequila. Serve a small glass of Sangrita with one of tequila and sit back and enjoy.

VARIATION

SANGRE DE VIUDA

Literally, "blood of the widow." Serve the above drink combined with the tequila rather than separate.

VARIATION

Sangrita Guadalajara

½ cup orange juice
1 fl. oz. lime juice
1 tablespoon grenadine

Pinch each salt and pepper
Dash hot pepper sauce, to taste
2 fl. oz. chilled tequila

Combine all ingredients except tequila, serve as for Sangrita.

COCO LOCO

The sands on the beach at Acapulco are hot, the air sultry and thick. You lie in a beach chair under the strong sun. It is exquisitely hot, balancing the fine line between delicious and unpleasant; somehow, just when you feel closer to the latter than the former, a young white-jacketed waiter brings you a huge coconut filled with a bit of its cooling liquid and the rest tequila. You sip and feel blissfully revived, as you run your toes through the hot sand contemplating cooling off in the gentle sea.

This drink is said to have originated on those Acapulco beaches; it is delicious during a heat wave anywhere.

1 whole coconut   **Crushed ice as desired**
1 jigger tequila

❶ Punch two holes in the top of the coconut at the location of its "eyes" using an ice pick and hammer or similar sort of tool. Pour off the liquid.

❷ With a hacksaw (this is serious business), saw off the top of the coconut, making a cuplike shell (save for future servings).

❸ Combine coconut liquid and tequila (with crushed ice if desired) and pour into coconut shell. Sip with a straw.

······························· **VARIATION** ·······························

Much more complicated Coco Loco drinks are often prepared containing dark and light rums, pineapple juice, coconut milk, and Kahlua in addition to the tequila and coconut liquid.

SANGRIA BLANCA
WHITE SANGRIA

White sangria always seems so much more refreshing and lyrical than the more usual red. A particularly festive presentation, and one that alludes to the Aztecs' fondness for eating fresh flowers and blossoms, is to freeze edible flowers suspended in ice cubes.

3 oranges, thinly sliced   **Large piece of ice**
4 lemons or limes, thinly sliced **1 bottle dry to medium-dry, fruity**
1 cup sugar   **white wine**
1 apple or pear, peeled and thinly **1 bottle champagne, sparkling white**
sliced   **wine, or club soda**
4 fl. oz. tequila

Place oranges and lemons in large punch bowl or pitcher; combine with sugar, apple or pear, and tequila. Let sit at least 2 hours, preferably overnight. Just before serving, add the ice and pour in the wine and champagne or club soda.
Makes 10 to 12 servings

···················· **VARIATION** ····················

The addition of a sliced peach and/or apricots make a fragrant summery refreshment.

···················· **VARIATION** ····················

SANGRIA ROJA

Red sangria is the classic; use a dry, fruity red wine such as Beaujolais in place of white and brandy in place of tequila, with only enough champagne or club soda as desired. Two cups of orange juice, along with several fluid ounces of orange liqueur, make delicious additions, as do thinly sliced fresh peaches.

SANGRIA DE GUADALAJARA
LIME-RED WINE FLOAT

Though it sounds unlikely, this makes an exquisitely refreshing drink—fragrant, tangy lime perfectly balanced with the dry, slightly tannic quality of the red wine. If you pour the wine carefully into the limeade, letting it glide over the back of a spoon, it forms two layers. You can then stir it, let it combine naturally, or sip it through a straw to drink the concoction in layers.

2 tablespoons lime juice cordial such as Rose's
¹/₃ cup (3 fl. oz.) chilled water or club soda

Several ice cubes
¹/₂ to ³/₄ cup (4 to 6 fl. oz.) dry, fruity red wine such as Beaujolais or simple table wine, chilled

❶ Combine lime cordial with water; pour over ice cubes.

❷ Over the back of an overturned spoon, carefully pour the red wine into the glass. It will more or less layer with the limeade. If it does not, it will not look as intriguing but will still be delicious. *Makes 1 drink*

MANGO DAIQUIRI

Enjoy on a sultry evening during summer's first dog days, when life seems too hot to be worth living.

Combining mango juice with fresh mangos gives this frothy drink a concentrated flavor.

About 1 cup canned mango juice
3 fresh mangos, peeled and diced
Extra–fine sugar to
taste (optional)

2 to 4 cups lightly crushed or broken-
up ice
8 fl. oz. rum, dark or light
Juice of 1 lime or to taste

Whirl mango juice with fresh mango in blender, adding enough of the liquid (or extra-fine sugar to taste) to sweeten and produce a smooth consistency. Add ice and whirl to mix well, then add rum and lime juice and continue whirling until slushy and icy-frothy. Serve immediately. **Makes 4 drinks**

VARIATION

Ripe papaya is delicious in place of mango.

TORO VALIENTE
"BRAVE BULL"

Kahlua, sweet and redolent of coffee, makes a delicious mixer with tequila. For a sweeter after-dinner drink, prepare it with equal amounts of Kahlua and tequila.

2 parts tequila
1 part Kahlua

Cracked ice

Combine tequila and Kahlua and pour over ice. Serve immediately. **Makes 1 drink**

BESITO
"LITTLE KISS"

This drink is also know as *beso de angel*, or "kiss of an angel." Is the cream that floats dreamily atop the liqueur the gentle kiss of a the drink's namesake? Don't let cute names scare you off; the drink is a good, sweet way to end a meal or to sip as you warm yourself next to a fire.

Fill a liqueur glass half full with Kahlua, then spoon a little whipping cream, either plain or lightly whipped, over the top. Serve immediately. *1 dessert-drink serving*

CERVEZA
MEXICAN BEERS

Mexico is one of the world's major brewing nations, a result of Emperor Maximilian's introduction of Viennese brewing techniques to a nation that had been brewing beer since 1544. The waves of Swiss, Bavarian, and Alsatian immigrants in the 1860's got the industry going in earnest.

Mexican beer, or *cerveza*, makes a superb accompaniment to the vivacious, spicy, and often filling Mexican food. It has a high alcoholic content with a wide range of flavors and degrees of heaviness and lightness.

Superior is amber-colored and refreshing. Dos XX's is mellow and somewhat dark, Tres XXX's a bock-type beer available in both dark and light. Corona from Mexico City is light and refreshing, though one could also say it lacks a bit of character. Nonetheless, it is a crisp partner to spicy food and best appreciated in sultry weather. Negro Modelo is its darker, fuller-bodied counterpart. In the Yucatán, Carta Clara is a pilsner-type brew, Montejo much like beer in Munich. Carta Blanca is light and clear, its toasty, malty flavors finish cleanly. The Southwest border-town fad of squeezing a wedge of lime into a crisp, cold beer is deliciously refreshing in the right situation, when the weather simmers and so do you.

At Christmastime, rich, dark Guinness-like brews appear in the market, known as *noche buena*, or Christmas Eve ("Good Night") beer.

SOURCES

··

La Palma Mexicatessen
2884 24th Street
San Francisco, CA 94110
(415) 647-1500

G. B. Ratto and Co. International Grocery
821 Washington Street
Oakland, CA 94607

To order toll-free: In California, 800-228-3515; in the rest of the continental U.S., 800-325-3483.

Every town with a Hispanic community has shops that cater to the cuisine. Seek them out. Also, large European or Latin American marketplaces are often to be found in areas that have a large Hispanic population; they are a joy and inspiration to visit. It's almost like a trip to Mexico. I particularly enjoy:

The Grand Central Market   El Mercado
317 S. Broadway   1st Avenue and Lorena
Los Angeles, CA 90013   East Los Angeles, CA 90063

Pecos Valley Spice Co.
186 Fifth Avenue
New York, NY 10010

Nichol's Garden Nursery
1190 North Pacific Highway
Albany, OR 97321
Seeds for chillies and other
Mexican plants and herbs.

Casa Moneo
210 W. 14th Street
New York, NY 10011
(212) 929-1644

La Casa del Pueblo
1810 South Blue Island
Chicago, IL 60608
(312) 421-4640

The Chile Shop
109 East Water Street
Santa Fe, NM 87501
(505) 983-6080

Mexican Grocery
1914 Pike Place
Seattle, WA 98104
(206) 682-2822

MIXTEC
1792 Columbia Road, N.W.
Washington, DC 20009
(202) 332-1011

Armando's Finer Foods
2627-2639 South Kedzie Street
Chicago, IL 60623
(312) 927-6688

M & S Produce
P.O. Box 220
Alcolde, NM 87511
(505) 852-4368
Posole, New Mexico Chile, Blue
corn, etc.

El Mercado de Los Angeles
3425 East 5th Street
East Los Angeles, CA 90063
(213) 269-2953

Fiesta Mart
numerous stores in Houston, Texas
area
(713) 869-5060

MAIL ORDER
Albuquerque Traders
P.O. Box 10171
Albuquerque, NM 87114

El Molina
117 S. 22nd Street
Phoenix, AZ 85034

Casado Farms
P.O. Box 1269
San Juan Pueblo, NM 87566

Tropicana Market
5001 Lindenwood Street
St. Louis, MO 63109
(314) 353-7328

Morgan's Mexican Lebanese Foods
736 South Robert Street
St. Paul, MN 55107
(612) 291-2955

INDEX

....